Contents

Mic...ine
an...

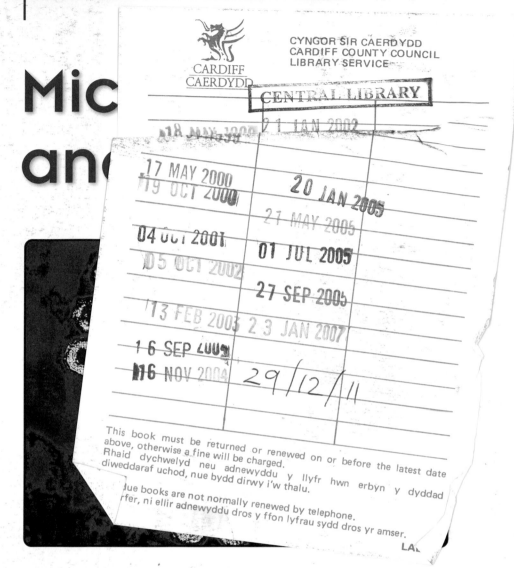

Peter Freeland

Hodder & Stoughton
A MEMBER OF THE HODDER HEADLINE GROUP

Acknowledgements

The author would like to thank all those who contributed to the
production of this book. Michael Carter and Michael Thain, who
read the text at various stages of its writing, made many positive and
helpful comments. The skills of Julia Morris and Charlotte Litt,
editors at Hodder & Stoughton Educational, ensured that the text
was presented with clarity and could be used by students as a work of
reference. Finally, to all those students who provided the motivation
and the rewards of this undertaking, go thanks beyond telling.

Cover photo of herpes simplex virus from Science Photo Library.

Chapter openers: Science Photo Library.

The publishers would like to thank the following individuals,
institutions and companies for permission to reproduce photographs
in this book. Every effort has been made to trace ownership of
copyright. The publishers would be happy to make arrangements
with any copyright holder whom it has not been possible to contact:

Biophoto Associates (8, 14 both, 40, 81, 103 top, 129, 130); Camera
Talks (24 both); Holt Studios International (41, 58 bottom, 69, 79,
80, 134, 139, 142); Life File/Emma Lee (84); National Medical Slide
Bank (39); Noro Nordisk Pharmaceuticals Ltd (60); Ruth Nossek
(122); Science Photo Library (37), /Andrew McClenaghan (22), /BSIP
VEM (82), /Charlotte Raymond (103 bottom), /CNRI (42), /David
Parker (109), /David Guyan (138), /Dr Jeremy Burgess (58 top, 117),
/Dr Kari Lounatmaa (11, 92), /Eye of Science (9, 38, 105), /Jane
Shemilt (43), /Omikron (52), /Peter Menzel (106), /Robert Isear (68),
/Rosenfeld Images Ltd (133), /Simon Fraser (143); Youngs & Co.'s
Brewery (78)

Orders: please contact Bookpoint Ltd, 39 Milton Park, Abingdon,
Oxon OX14 4TD. Telephone: (44) 01235 400414,
Fax: (44) 01235 400454. Lines are open from 9.00–6.00,
Monday to Saturday, with a 24-hour message answering service.
Email address: orders@bookpoint.co.uk

British Library Cataloguing in Publication Data
A catalogue record for this title is available from The British Library

ISBN 0 340 73103 6

First published 1999
Impression number   10 9 8 7 6 5 4 3 2 1
Year   2004 2003 2002 2001 2000 1999

Copyright © 1999 Peter Freeland

Cover photo from Science Photo Library.
Typeset by Wearset, Boldon, Tyne and Wear.
Printed in Hong Kong for Hodder & Stoughton Educational, a
division of Hodder Headline Plc, 338 Euston Road, London
NW1 3BH by Colorcraft Limited.

Preface

This book is about microbes and their importance in causing disease, producing ethical products such as antibiotics and vaccines, and the central part they play in many industrial processes.

Throughout the book the five-kingdom system of classification, recommended by both the Institute of Biology and the Association for Science Education, has been followed. Micro-organisms belong to three of these kingdoms: Prokaryotae, Protoctista and Fungi. Their relative simplicity, rapid growth rates and varied roles in nature make them of particular interest to biologists. After years of neglect, possibly on account of their small size, they have moved centre-stage, taken the spotlight and stimulated much new research.

Many infectious diseases are caused by viruses, bacteria, protoctistans and fungi. The body's immune system is the first line of defence against these intruders, although on occasions the immune system becomes damaged or malfunctions. The efficiency of the immune system in resisting specific pathogenic micro-organisms can be boosted by the administration of vaccines. Antibiotics assist recovery from infections caused by bacteria and some fungi.

Biotechnology is a term used to describe the commercial exploitation of a living organism or any of its metabolic products. Along with plants and animals, micro-organisms are currently being used to manufacture goods or provide services. In biotechnology, biologists and technologists work side by side. The biologists select organisms for commercial enterprises and enhance their usefulness through genetic manipulation. Chemical engineers, along with other technologists, provide the means by which useful organisms can be cultivated on a large scale, and their products harvested, purified and marketed.

The broad aim of this book is to provide A-level biologists with a modern classification of micro-organisms and a clear, logical account of the different branches of modern biotechnology, their potential benefits and possible shortcomings. Chapters 1 and 2 deal mainly with the structure and physiology of micro-organisms. Technological advances, such as genetic engineering and the design of fermenters on which the modern revolution in biotechnology is based, are covered in Chapters 3 and 4. The remaining chapters illustrate the applications of biotechnology in the food industry, in medicine, in agriculture and in environmental control.

Those terms which appear in red within the text are explained more fully in the Glossary on pages 146–148.

Finally, there is a colour section on the inside cover of the book which repeats some of the photos from the text which need to be seen in colour to be fully appreciated. These photos are highlighted by the symbol C1 and a page reference given.

CHAPTER

Micro-organisms: an introduction

Biologists have divided living organisms into major groups called **kingdoms**. In 1959 the American biologist R H Whittaker proposed a five-kingdom system of classification. Later, in 1988, L Margulis and K V Schwartz built upon this classificatory framework and suggested that the following five kingdoms should be recognised:

Prokaryotae
Protoctista
Fungi
Plantae
Animalia

A diagrammatic representation, or **cladogram**, of the evolutionary relationships between these kingdoms is shown in Figure 1.1. Although each kingdom is represented by many contemporary species, the Prokaryotae is the most primitive, first appearing at a relatively early stage in evolutionary development. Conversely, the Plantae, Fungi and Animalia are the most advanced. They first appeared at a much later stage in evolution. Furthermore, they all arose from a common group of organisms, the Protoctista, but have subsequently evolved over many millions of years into distinct groups.

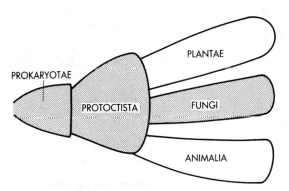

Figure 1.1 An outline of the five-kingdom system of classification. Shading indicates the kingdoms that contain micro-organisms

Although the organisation of this book is based on the five-kingdom classification, an alternative grouping, devised by Carl Woese in 1977, is currently gaining popularity. This classification, which is derived primarily from an analysis of base sequences in ribosomal (r) RNA molecules, recognises three primary groups, or **domains**: **Eucarya** (formerly called Eukaryotes), **Bacteria** (formerly called Eubacteria) and **Archaea** (formerly called Archaebacteria).

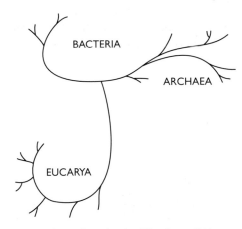

Figure 1.2 The three-domain classification of Woese (1977) based on rRNA analysis

1.1 'Micro-organisms'

The term **'micro-organism'**, originally applied to any small organism that could not be seen clearly without the aid of a microscope, now means different things to different people. At best, only a descriptive and never a scientific term, there is current confusion over its application to the viruses. This important group, traditionally known as 'micro-organisms' because of their small size, chemical composition and reactions with other organisms, does not feature in the five-kingdom classification. Strict adherents to that scheme do not regard them as living organisms, and so do not use the term 'micro-organism' when referring to them. Fortunately, no-one doubts that the term micro-organism applies to all the Prokaryotae, or bacteria, both photosynthetic and non-photosynthetic types. Elsewhere, among the more evolutionarily-advanced kingdoms, the term is applied more loosely and less specifically. For instance, in the Protoctista it is applied to all unicellular, heterotrophic organisms, collectively known as **protozoans,** and to many unicellular and filamentous **algae.** Larger algae such as 'seaweeds', however, are often excluded, even though they belong to the same taxonomic group. Among the fungi, the zygomycetes (e.g. moulds) and ascomycetes (e.g. yeasts) are clearly 'micro-organisms', but no-one is absolutely certain about the status of basidiomycetes (e.g. mushrooms), which have microscopic hyphae, yet produce large, conspicuous fruiting bodies. Biologists therefore find themselves in something of a dilemma. Should the term 'micro-organism' be dropped, because it is imprecise; or should it be retained, because it has been used for many years and has become part of the vocabulary of non-specialists? There is no obvious solution. Suffice to say that throughout this book the term 'micro-organism' is applied to **viruses,** Prokaryotae, and all organisms that are classified within the kingdoms Protoctista and Fungi,

regardless of their size. **Microbiology,** a term originally coined to describe the scientific study of micro-organisms, is also used in its broadest sense, to describe the biology of these four groups.

1.2 Viruses

Virology, the study of viruses, is the youngest branch of microbiology. It was not until the 1940s that microbiologists first saw viruses, when technical advances improved the resolution of electron microscopes. All viruses are intracellular **parasites,** ranging in diameter from 20–300 nm. Once inside their host cells they possess the ability to reproduce (replicate), but they cannot carry out any of the other activities that are characteristic of living organisms, namely growth, respiration, excretion, locomotion, feeding and response to stimuli. Although viruses do not have a cellular structure, they nevertheless consist mainly of nucleoproteins. This appears to give them some affinity to living organisms, because nucleoproteins are a major component of chromosomes in all the kingdoms that have evolved from the Prokaryotae. More specifically, all viruses have the following features:

(i)   a central core of nucleic acid, either **deoxyribonucleic acid (DNA)** – in DNA viruses – or **ribonucleic acid (RNA)** – in RNA viruses;

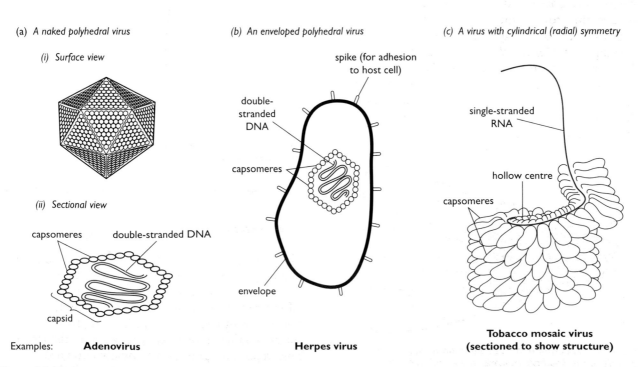

(a) A naked polyhedral virus

(i) Surface view

(ii) Sectional view

capsomeres   double-stranded DNA

capsid

Examples: **Adenovirus**

(b) An enveloped polyhedral virus

spike (for adhesion to host cell)

double-stranded DNA

capsomeres

envelope

Herpes virus

(c) A virus with cylindrical (radial) symmetry

single-stranded RNA

hollow centre

capsomeres

Tobacco mosaic virus (sectioned to show structure)

Figure 1.3 Viruses

(ii) a protein coat, or **capsid**, composed of individual protein elements called **capsomeres**;
(iii) genes for transferring viral nucleic acid to the chromosome(s) of its host;
(iv) the ability to multiply in its host, by taking over the host cell's machinery for synthesising nucleic acids and proteins.

In addition, (v) some viruses, after entering their host cells, produce one or two enzymes and (vi) others are surrounded by an **envelope** formed from carbohydrate or lipoprotein. The fact that viruses can multiply inside their host cells, yet are inert outside them has led to two views about their biological status. A few biologists still regard them as exceptionally simple living organisms, representing an intermediate stage in the evolution of the animate from the inanimate. Most, however, believe they have originated in some way from the genetic material of living organisms, possibly by detachment of a small piece of nucleic acid that became surrounded by a protective coat of protein.

Viruses can be subdivided according to their host range, and possible origins, into three main classes: **animal viruses**, **plant viruses** and **bacterial viruses (bacteriophages)**. Another classification distinguishes between **DNA** and **RNA viruses**. The DNA viruses are of two types, single-stranded and double-stranded. DNA viruses of both types attack plants, animals and bacteria.

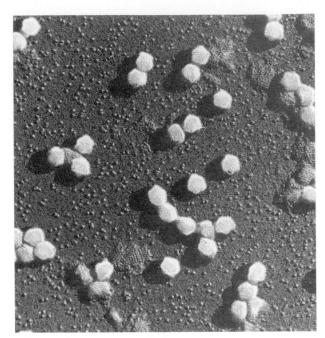

Adenovirus

The RNA viruses are also of two types: single- and double-stranded. Interestingly, the RNA viruses that attack plants are all single-stranded, whereas those that attack animals and bacteria may be single- or double-stranded. Several of the RNA viruses that attack animals, including those that cause influenza and AIDS, are surrounded by a membranous **envelope**.

A third type of classification is based on polyhedral, cylindrical and complex symmetry. Adenovirus, for example, a naked polyhedral type that infects the adenoids and tonsils, is an icosahedron. This means it has 20 faces, each face being a equilateral triangle. Herpes simplex virus, the cause of cold sores, is similar, but is surrounded by a spiked envelope. Tobacco mosaic virus, a single-stranded RNA type, has cylindrical (radial) symmetry. This virus, which affects plants, causing mottled mosaic-like areas on leaves, has a hollow centre surrounded by elliptical capsomeres. The single strand of RNA assumes a helical configuration, surrounding the central hole, and is partly embedded in the capsomeres. Bacteriophages, represented by both DNA and RNA types, are the most complex of all the viruses. They are discussed in the next section.

Bacteriophages

The bacteriophage T2 (Figure 1.5) infects the bacterium *Escherichia coli*. It is a complex virus, containing double-stranded DNA, with a **head**, forming an icosahedron, and a narrow hollow **tail**.

(a) *Based on host range*

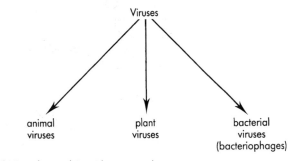

(b) *Based on nucleic acid content and symmetry*

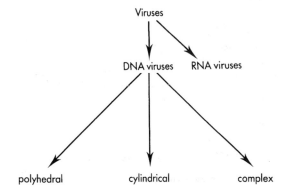

Figure 1.4 Schemes for classifying viruses

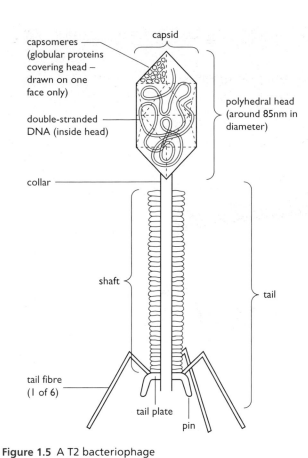

capsomeres (globular proteins covering head – drawn on one face only)

capsid

double-stranded DNA (inside head)

polyhedral head (around 85nm in diameter)

collar

shaft

tail

tail fibre (1 of 6)

tail plate

pin

Figure 1.5 A T2 bacteriophage

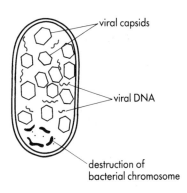

C1 Transmission electron micrograph (TEM) of a bacteriophage T4 virus of *E. coli* (see *Colour Section on inside cover*)

(a) *Adsorption to cell surface*

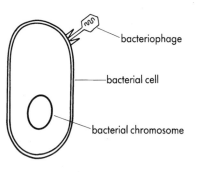

bacteriophage

bacterial cell

bacterial chromosome

(b) *Penetration of viral DNA by injection*

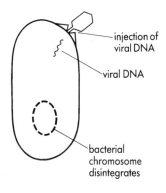

injection of viral DNA

viral DNA

bacterial chromosome disintegrates

(c) *Biosynthesis of viral DNA and capsids*

viral capsids

viral DNA

destruction of bacterial chromosome

(d) *Assembly of viral nucleic acid within each capsid*

(e) *Lysis of host cell; release of new phages*

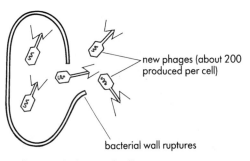

new phages (about 200 produced per cell)

bacterial wall ruptures

Lysis destroys the bacterial cell

Figure 1.6 Lysis – the lytic cycle of a T-even bacteriophage. Completion takes about 20 minutes

Micro-organisms: an introduction

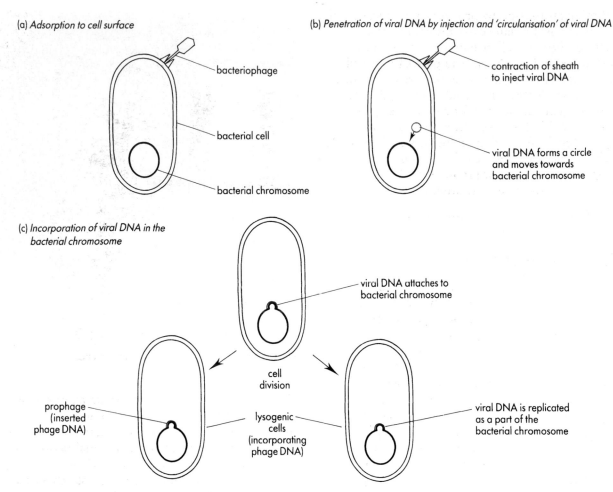

(a) *Adsorption to cell surface*

bacteriophage

bacterial cell

bacterial chromosome

(b) *Penetration of viral DNA by injection and 'circularisation' of viral DNA*

contraction of sheath
to inject viral DNA

viral DNA forms a circle
and moves towards
bacterial chromosome

(c) *Incorporation of viral DNA in the
bacterial chromosome*

viral DNA attaches to
bacterial chromosome

cell
division

prophage
(inserted
phage DNA)

lysogenic
cells
(incorporating
phage DNA)

viral DNA is replicated
as a part of the
bacterial chromosome

Figure 1.7 Lysogeny – phage DNA inserts and replicates as part of a bacterial chromosome (this process does not occur in the T-even phage)

At the end of the tail are six **tail fibres**, which attach the phage to the cell wall of its host. Each of the tail fibres is attached to a **tail plate**. When the tail plate makes contact with the bacterium, a lysozyme-like enzyme is released to punch a small hole in the cell wall. The **tail sheath** then contracts, injecting viral DNA into the host cell.

When a bacteriophage attacks a cell, one of two outcomes is possible. Firstly, the virus may multiply rapidly within the cell and destroy it. This is called **lysis** (Figure 1.6) because the host cell wall breaks down to release the new viruses. Alternatively, the virus may incorporate its DNA into the host cell's DNA and replicate, generation after generation, as part of the host cell's genome. Such a state is called **lysogeny** (Figure 1.7). Eventually, however, this incorporated phage DNA may initiate a **lytic cycle**, or viral life cycle.

The best understood viral life cycles, are those of the DNA-containing bacteriophages (phages) such as the so-called T-even phages (T2, T4, T6), parasitic in the cells of *E. coli*. Stages in the lytic cycle of a T-even phage are shown in Figure 1.6. An attack, or parasitisation, begins when a phage attaches to the bacterial cell wall, perforates it, and proceeds to inject its DNA. This injected DNA contains all the genetic information needed to take over the bacterial cell and convert it into a factory for the manufacture of more phages. The phage DNA inactivates the bacterial DNA, and may eventually cause the bacterial chromosome to break down. Before this happens, however, phage DNA is replicated many hundreds of times, by causing the host cell to make the enzymes necessary for its own replication. At the same time, the virus takes over cell protein synthesis, causing the host cell to make the proteins for the viral coat. Finally, in the cytoplasm of the host cell, the two components of a phage – its DNA and protein coat – come together and are assembled by enzymes to produce phages of the next generation. When this stage is complete, the bacterial cell dies. Its wall is lysed (or broken down) to release the newly-formed phages.

Viral parasitisation by phages is not typical of all viral infections. In many cases the entire virus penetrates the host cell membrane, before its coat disintegrates and its nucleic acid passes to the cell nucleus. **Retroviruses**, including the virus that causes AIDS, contain RNA. Once inside its host, this RNA serves as a template for the formation of single-stranded DNA. This molecule, in turn, acts as a template for the formation of double-stranded DNA, which attaches to a host cell chromosome. Here, among other functions, it produces viral RNA for retroviruses of the next generation.

1.3 Prokaryotae

The Prokaryotae, or **bacteria**, are very small (0.2–2.0 μm in diameter), relatively simple, single-celled micro-organisms. The kingdom includes both autotrophic and heterotrophic forms. All the bacteria lack nuclei organised within membranes. They also have no membrane-bound organelles or functional cytoplasmic units, such as centrioles. A gelatinous **capsule**, or **glycocalyx**, formed from polysaccharides, polypeptides, or both, surrounds a **cell wall**. The capsule helps the cell to adhere to surfaces, protects it from attack in parasitic forms, and probably conserves water. Motile bacteria have a **flagellum** (or several flagella) at one end, supported by a single central rod of the protein **flagellin**. Additional thread-like projections, looking like short flagella, are called **pili**. These serve to assist adhesion and join two bacteria together prior to the exchange of genetic material. Bacterial DNA is present in two locations. Firstly, in the **circular chromosome**, believed to be anchored to a folded part of the cell membrane called the **mesosome**, and in much smaller, unattached circular units, the **plasmids**

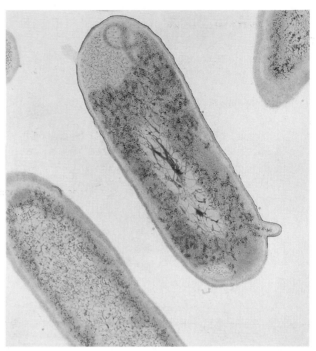

Electron micrograph of a longitudinal section through a bacterium

These carry genes that the bacterium may need on special occasions, such as those for antibiotic resistance (R-factors) or for conjugation (F-factors). Proteins are synthesised at the bacterial **ribosomes**, in the cytoplasm. Storage products, such as polyphosphate granules, glycogen or starch, occur throughout the cytoplasm in **inclusion granules**.

The classification of bacteria presents particular difficulties, because species that are totally unrelated bear a close physical resemblance to one another. Hans Christian Gram, a Danish biologist, made the first taxonomically-valid classification in 1884, on the basis of cell wall reactions to dyes. After spreading the bacteria on a microscope slide, a mixture of crystal violet and iodine solution was added. The bacteria were then washed in 95% alcohol (ethanol), then stained a second time with safranin. **Gram-positive bacteria** stained purple, whereas **gram-negative bacteria** stained red (Figure 1.10).

An alternative classification uses shape as the principal criterion. Bacteria may be spherical **(cocci)**, rod-shaped **(bacilli)**, shaped like a cork-screw **(spirilla)**, comma-like **(vibrio)**, or filamentous. Further differentiation is often possible according to the way in which bacteria tend to be grouped, especially after cell division. For instance, *Diplococci* occur in pairs, *Streptococci* form chains and *Staphylococci* are grouped into clusters, like bunches of grapes. The filamentous bacteria are of particular interest because most are photosynthetic. This group, formerly called blue-green algae because of their superficial resemblance to filamentous green algae, are now known as **Cyanobacteria** (see page 34).

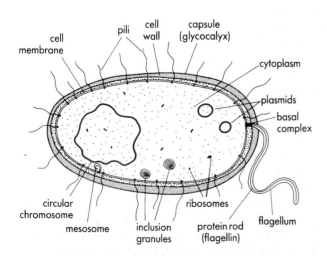

Figure 1.8 The generalised structure of a bacterium

Micro-organisms: an introduction

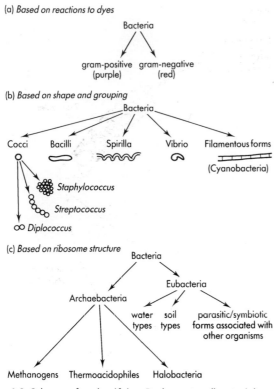

(a) *Based on reactions to dyes*

Bacteria

gram-positive (purple) gram-negative (red)

(b) *Based on shape and grouping*

Bacteria

Cocci Bacilli Spirilla Vibrio Filamentous forms (Cyanobacteria)

Staphylococcus

Streptococcus

Diplococcus

(c) *Based on ribosome structure*

Bacteria

Archaebacteria Eubacteria

water types soil types parasitic/symbiotic forms associated with other organisms

Methanogens Thermoacidophiles Halobacteria

Figure 1.9 Schemes for classifying Prokaryotae (bacteria)

Table 1.1 Some features of gram-positive and gram-negative bacteria

Feature	Gram-positive bacteria	Gram-negative bacteria
Response of Grams's stain	stain purple	stain red
Cell wall components	mostly polysaccharides, with a little lipid and protein	polysaccharides with more lipid (20%) and protein
Flagella		may be inserted at one or both ends of bacilli
Endospores	produced during unfavourable conditions by some species	not produced
Response to lysozyme	dissolves cell wall, causing bacteria to swell by osmosis and burst	
Examples	*Staphylococcus aureus* *Bacillus subtilis* *Lactobacillus bulgaricus*	*Escherichia coli* *Acetobacter aceti* *Agrobacterium tumefaciens*

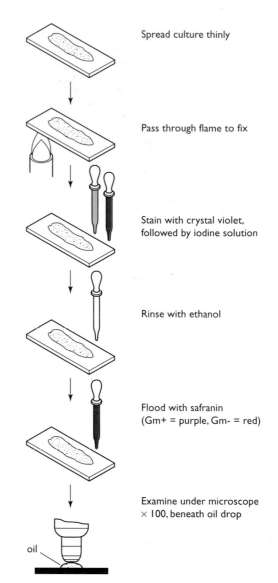

Spread culture thinly

Pass through flame to fix

Stain with crystal violet, followed by iodine solution

Rinse with ethanol

Flood with safranin (Gm+ = purple, Gm- = red)

Examine under microscope × 100, beneath oil drop

oil

Figure 1.10 Gram staining technique

A third system of classification, devised by Woese in 1977, recognises two domains:

(i) **Bacteria**, the most primitive group, with peptidoglycan as their principal wall component,

(ii) **Archaea**, more recently evolved, with histone- and tubulin-like genes, which have mostly proteins and no peptidoglycans in their walls.

The true Bacteria are widespread and common, and live in water, soil or in association with other organisms. The Archaea are a more exotic and relatively unknown group. Archaea comprise methanogens, which give off methane, thermoacidophiles, which can live in hot springs, and halobacteria, the occupants of very salty environments. To many biotechnologists, however, organisms from both groups are still referred to as 'bacteria'.

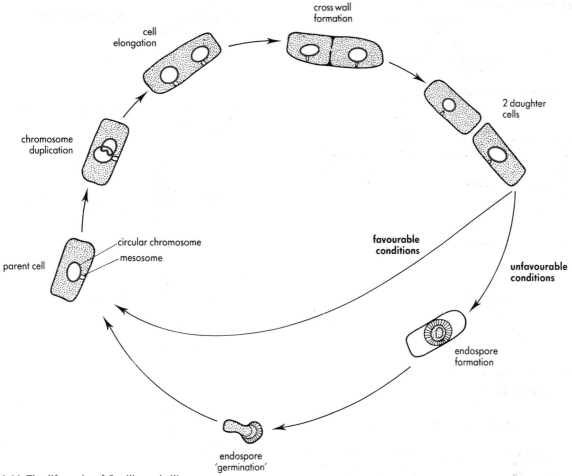

Figure 1.11 The life cycle of *Bacillus subtilis*

The life cycle of a bacterium often involves nothing more than vegetative growth and cell division. Typically, after growing to its maximum size, the rod-shaped *Bacillus subtilis*, a **saprophytic** fresh-water species, divides longitudinally into two daughter cells. This cell division begins with replication of the circular chromosome. The cell then elongates to separate the two chromosomes, before a cross wall forms to divide this elongated cell into two. Under unfavourable conditions, notably high temperatures or the presence of toxins, this bacterium may enter a state of suspended animation. It does this by forming an **endospore**, a thick-walled protective resting stage, which bursts open to resume growth as soon as favourable conditions return.

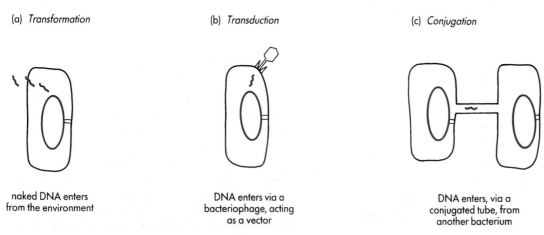

Figure 1.12 Transformation, transduction and conjugation in *E. coli*

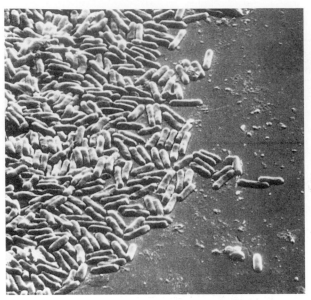

E. coli bacteria

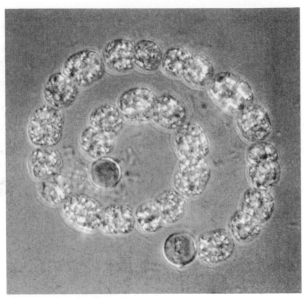

Anabaena circinalis

Studies of the bacillus *Escherichia coli*, a species found in the human intestine, have shown that during its life cycle it may receive additional DNA from three different sources, by processes known as transformation, transduction and conjugation.

(i) **Transformation** involves the uptake of naked DNA and its incorporation into the bacterial chromosome. The naked DNA, generally released into the environment when a neighbouring bacterium dies and decomposes, is taken up as a single strand (Figure 1.12). The incorporation of this additional DNA into the bacterial chromosome may result in the displacement of some other genes.

(ii) **Transduction** occurs when a bacteriophage transfers DNA from one bacterium to another. The bacteriophage acts as a DNA vector, often transferring DNA from a bacterium on which its attack was lethal to one that was resistant.

(iii) **Conjugation** takes place between two different strains of a bacterium known as F$^+$ and F$^-$. The F$^+$ strain has genes for the F (fertility) factor; the F$^-$ strain has none. This F factor may be present in a cell, either as part of the bacterial chromosome, or, more likely, a part of a plasmid. F factor-carrying plasmids can replicate within the cells that contain them. Conjugation begins when a F$^+$ bacterium produces a conjugation tube formed from a large pilus called a sex pilus. The F$^+$ factor, either in the form of an uncoiled plasmid or part of the chromosomal DNA, passes through the tube and into the F$^-$ bacterium. Here, as a plasmid or part of a chromosome, it transforms the F$^-$ bacterium into F$^+$.

The filamentous cyanobacterium *Anabaena* grows abundantly wherever there is warmth, light and moisture. For instance, in the rice fields of the tropical and sub-tropical regions it often forms a blue-green surface mat. In the UK, its common name is 'moon spit', because of the gelatinous bubbly nature of colonies that suddenly appear at the surface of ponds in summer. *Anabaena* is a colonial species consisting of straight or curved chains of dark green **vegetative cells**, in which photosynthesis takes place. Between these cells, spaced irregularly, are larger, thick-walled, colourless cells, the **'heterocysts'**, where nitrogen fixation occurs (see section 2.5). The heavy walls of the 'heterocysts' prevent oxygen from entering and inactivating the nitrogen-fixing enzymes, notably **nitrogenase**.

At both ends of 'heterocysts', where they border vegetative cells, are thickened regions called **peg projections**. These are effective in keeping out oxygen and in passing on the products of nitrogen fixation to vegetative cells. Each vegetative cell is bounded by a wall of mucoprotein (polysaccharides + protein), covered by a thick, slimy mucilaginous sheath. Attached to the cell membrane are many folded photosynthetic membranes, called **thylakoids**. They contain the photosynthetic pigments chlorophyll and carotenoids. Scattered between them are spherical sacs, or **phycobilisomes**, which contain accessory photosynthetic pigments. Elsewhere throughout the

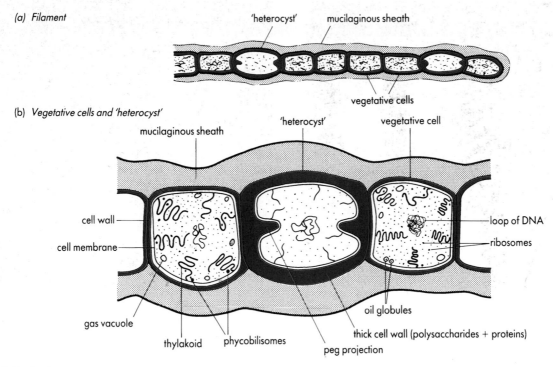

(a) Filament

'heterocyst'   mucilaginous sheath

vegetative cells

(b) Vegetative cells and 'heterocyst'

'heterocyst'   vegetative cell

mucilaginous sheath

cell wall

cell membrane

loop of DNA

ribosomes

gas vacuole

thylakoid   phycobilisomes

peg projection

oil globules

thick cell wall (polysaccharides + proteins)

Figure 1.13 *Anabaena*

peripheral cytoplasm there are some **ribosomes**, for protein synthesis, droplets of stored **lipids**, and **gas vacuoles** giving buoyancy. At the centre of the cell is a loop of DNA. Reproduction takes place by fragmentation of the filament or by 'spore' formation. The 'spores' are thick-walled vegetative cells (also called 'heterocysts'), with little, if any, photosynthetic activity. At the end of the growing season the 'spores' may break away, survive unfavourable conditions, and 'germinate' when favourable conditions return.

Crown gall disease

One bacterium of particular interest to biotechnologists is *Agrobacterium tumefaciens*. This bacterium, which genetic engineers use to introduce novel genes into crop plants, is capable of producing tumours in more than 100 different plant species, providing it is carrying a Ti (tumour-inducing) plasmid. The infection is transmitted by biting insects; tumours subsequently develop close to the site of a bite, which is often near the crown. The plasmids enter the host cell, where some of their genes become incorporated into the host cell's DNA. A number of these genes cause the host cell to produce **opines**, modified amino acids which serve as food for the bacterium. Other plasmid genes cause cells of the host to undergo rapid mitosis, forming a tumour.

1.4 Eukaryotae

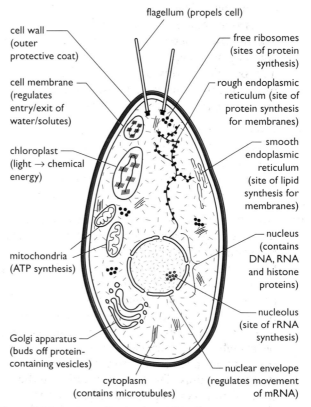

cell wall (outer protective coat)

flagellum (propels cell)

free ribosomes (sites of protein synthesis)

cell membrane (regulates entry/exit of water/solutes)

rough endoplasmic reticulum (site of protein synthesis for membranes)

chloroplast (light → chemical energy)

smooth endoplasmic reticulum (site of lipid synthesis for membranes)

mitochondria (ATP synthesis)

nucleus (contains DNA, RNA and histone proteins)

nucleolus (site of rRNA synthesis)

Golgi apparatus (buds off protein-containing vesicles)

cytoplasm (contains microtubules)

nuclear envelope (regulates movement of mRNA)

Figure 1.14 A generalised eukaryotic cell

Micro-organisms: an introduction

Table 1.2 Some differences between prokaryotic and eukaryotic cells

Feature	Prokaryotes	Eukaryotes
Size	approximately 1 µm diameter	approximately 50 µm diameter
Genetic material	not organised within a nucleus	organised within a nucleus
Chromosome(s)	one, circular	several, rod-shaped
DNA	not combined with histone proteins	combined with histone proteins, forming chromatin
Plasmids	occur in most species	confined to some species of fungi, notably yeasts
Membrane-bound organelles	none	several different types (e.g. mitochondria, chloroplasts, Golgi apparatus, endoplasmic reticulum (ER), lysosomes)
Microtubules/ tubulin (a protein)	absent	present
Ribosomes	70S type only, scattered in cytoplasm	80S type (some attached to ER) (70S type in mitochondria and chloroplasts)
Cell membranes	lack cholesterol	contain cholesterol
Flagella	if present, lack microtubules	if present, contain 9 + 2 microtubule structure
Asexual reproduction	binary fission	mitosis
Stored food	glycogen/lipids/ volutin (phosphate)	starch in algae glycogen in fungi
Cell wall	polymerised amino sugars, cross-linked by amino acids	polysaccharides (e.g. cellulose), formed from linked monosaccharides

The prokaryotes, or bacteria, have a distinctive structure which distinguishes them from all other types of cell, known collectively as **eukaryotes**. Eukaryotic micro-organisms belong to two kingdoms: Protoctista and Fungi.

QUESTIONS

1 Why are viruses not placed in a kingdom?

2 In each of the following classificatory systems, to which groups are the 'bacteria' assigned?

 a) 5-kingdom, b) 3-domain.

3 List five distinctive features of bacterial (prokaryotic) cells.

4 Thousands of different species of bacteria are known. How do biotechnologists distinguish between them?

5 List five distinctive features of a eukaryotic cell.

6 Define each of the following terms: transformation; transduction; conjugation.

In both of these groups, cellular structure and function is much more complex than it is in prokaryotes. Typically, eukaryotic cells are large, with a membrane-bound nucleus containing genetic material. In the cytoplasm, there are membrane-bound organelles – mitochondria, chloroplasts, Golgi apparatus, endoplasmic reticulum and lysosomes – each with a specific function. Furthermore, they differ from prokaryotic cells in relation to membrane, cell wall, chromosome and other cell structures, as listed in Table 1.2.

1.4.1 Protoctista

Protoctists are unicellular organisms or assemblages of relatively unspecialised similar cells. The kingdom includes organisms that were formerly classified as **protozoa**, algae and slime moulds. All consist of one or more nucleated cells, with a nuclear envelope surrounding each nucleus. They also have membrane-bound organelles and a 9 + 2 array of microfilaments in their cilia and flagella. For these reasons, they are grouped with plants, fungi and animals as **eukaryotes** to distinguish them from the bacteria **(prokaryotes)**.

Table 1.2 summarises the differences between prokaryotes and eukaryotes. Protoctists are neither plants, fungi nor animals. The Margulis and Schwartz classification places each of the four groups that were traditionally classes of the phylum protozoa into the 'phylum' taxon. It also places *Phytophthora*, the late blight of potatoes, in this kingdom rather than among the fungi.

The following classification scheme of protoctista, selected to include species that have been studied in schools, has been compiled by a joint working party of the Association for Science Education and the Institute of Biology.

Phylum – **Rhizopoda** (rhizopods)
  Organisms equipped with pseudopodia for locomotion.
  Example: *Amoeba*

Phylum – **Zoomastigina** (flagellates)
  Heterotrophic organisms equipped with at least one flagellum for locomotion.
  Example: *Trypanosoma*

Phylum – **Apicomplexa** (sporozoans)
  Organisms, mainly parasitic, with multiple fission stages in their life history.
  Example: *Plasmodium*

Phylum – **Ciliophora** (ciliates)
  Organisms, attached or motile, with surface cilia.
  Example: *Paramecium*

Phylum – **Euglenophyta** (euglenoid flagellates)
  A group with photosynthetic and non-photosynthetic members. Flagellate, with their own distinctive biochemistry.
  Example: *Euglena*

Phylum – **Oomycota** (oomycetes)
  A group which reproduces sexually by fertilisation of male and female gametangia; asexual sporangia produce biflagellate spores; hyphae non-septate (no cross walls).
  Example: *Phytophthora*

Phylum – **Chlorophyta** (green algae)
  Photosynthetic, with essentially the same pigments as plants, unicellular, colonial and filamentous.
  Example: *Chlamydomonas*

Phylum – **Rhodophyta** (red algae)
  Photosynthetic, with plastids containing red pigments as well as chlorophyll.
  Example: *Chondrus*

Phylum – **Phaeophyta** (brown algae)
  Photosynthetic, with plastids containing brown pigments as well as chlorophyll.
  Example: *Fucus*

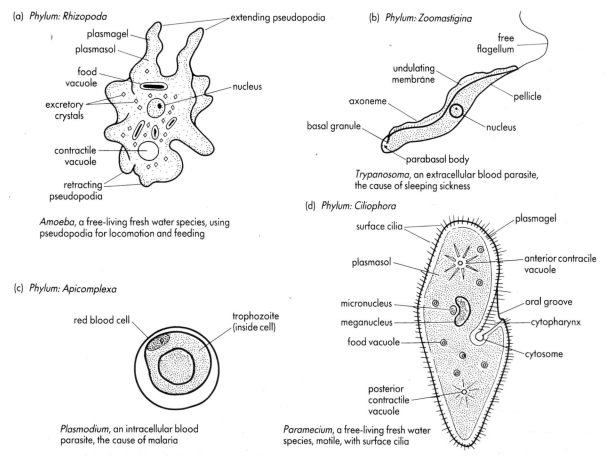

(a) *Phylum: Rhizopoda*

plasmagel
plasmasol
food vacuole
excretory crystals
contractile vacuole
retracting pseudopodia
extending pseudopodia
nucleus

Amoeba, a free-living fresh water species, using pseudopodia for locomotion and feeding

(b) *Phylum: Zoomastigina*

free flagellum
undulating membrane
axoneme
basal granule
pellicle
nucleus
parabasal body

Trypanosoma, an extracellular blood parasite, the cause of sleeping sickness

(c) *Phylum: Apicomplexa*

red blood cell
trophozoite (inside cell)

Plasmodium, an intracellular blood parasite, the cause of malaria

(d) *Phylum: Ciliophora*

surface cilia
plasmasol
micronucleus
meganucleus
food vacuole
posterior contractile vacuole
plasmagel
anterior contractile vacuole
oral groove
cytopharynx
cytosome

Paramecium, a free-living fresh water species, motile, with surface cilia

Figure 1.15 Heterotrophic members of the Protoctista kingdom

Figure 1.15 illustrates one species from each of the first four phyla listed above. Most of the species classified in these groups are unicellular and heterotrophic. Free-living representatives occur in fresh water, the sea and damp places on land. Parasitic types occur mostly in the body fluids of invertebrates and vertebrates. *Plasmodium*, the cause of malaria, and *Trypanosoma*, the cause of sleeping sickness, have considerable economic importance.

The phylum Chlorophyta includes all the green algae. Those that belong to the genus *Chlorella* occur in several different habitats, namely in fresh water, brackish water and moist soil. Some species are symbiotic. *C. lichinia*, for example, is an algae symbiont of the lichen *Calicium chlorina*, while *Zoochlorella* grows as a symbiont in *Hydra*. All members of the genus are non-motile and unicellular. The individual cells of *Chlorella* are spherical, subspherical or ellipsoidal, bounded by a wall of cellulose. Each cell has a cup-shaped chloroplast, in which the chlorophyll-containing membranes (thylakoids) lack **grana**-like organisation. Crystalline protein bodies, called **pyrenoids**, sometimes surrounded by stored starch grains, may occur in the chloroplast. A single nucleus, together with mitochondria and Golgi bodies, occurs in the cytoplasm, which may lie mostly within the cavity of the chloroplast, or to one side of it. Under conditions that are favourable for its growth, *Chlorella* reproduces exclusively by the formation of (normally four) **autospores**. Two successive divisions occur within the cell wall of a mother cell. The autospores are released when the cell wall of the mother cell gelatinises or ruptures (Figure 1.16b).

As *Chlorella* occasionally fouls swimming pools, lakes and canals, biologists have for many years used algicides, such as copper sulphate, to control the organism. More recently, though, biologists have begun to view it in a more favourable light. Biochemical analysis of its cells has shown that they contain about 50% protein, 20% carbohydrate and 20% fat, with significant amounts of amino acids, vitamins and minerals. Following from negative toxicity tests, research is currently underway to investigate the feasibility of growing *Chlorella* in mass culture for use as human food or animal feed. Another future use may well be in controlling sewage disposal. *Chlorella* grows and multiplies in raw sewage, liberating oxygen into its surroundings, thereby creating conditions that favour the growth of aerobic sewage-degrading bacteria and fungi. Looking further ahead, another possibility is the use of this fast-growing, photosynthetic organism in the regulation of oxygen and carbon dioxide levels inside space vehicles designed to carry astronauts.

Late blight of potatoes

Late blight of potatoes (*Phytophthora infestans*), responsible for the Irish potato famine of the 19th Century, was formerly classified as a fungus. Its reclassification as a protoctist is based on the structure of the biflagellate motile spores, which are absent from true fungi, and are very similar in appearance to some ciliates and flagellates.

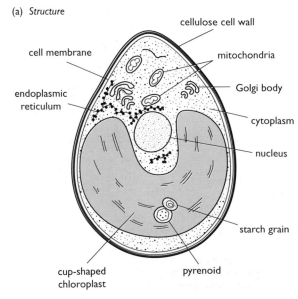

(a) *Structure*

cellulose cell wall
cell membrane
mitochondria
endoplasmic reticulum
Golgi body
cytoplasm
nucleus
starch grain
cup-shaped chloroplast
pyrenoid

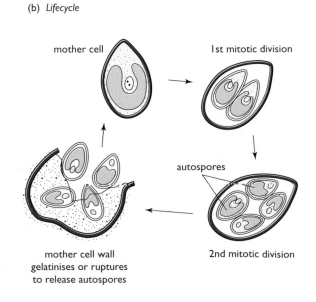

(b) *Lifecycle*

mother cell
1st mitotic division
autospores
mother cell wall gelatinises or ruptures to release autospores
2nd mitotic division

Figure 1.16 *Chlorella*: structure and life cycle

In addition, the **hyphae** have no cross walls, which are diagnostic of true fungi.

The micro-organism attacks mostly mature potato plants in the field, causing destruction of the leaves and tubers. An infection generally begins in the leaves, which blacken and die as the hyphae spread, killing all the cells into which the penetrating branches, called **haustoria**, enter. Dead or necrotic patches appear on infected leaves. Later the disease spreads to the tubers, causing them to rot and emit an offensive odour. Dispersal of the parasite from one crop of potatoes to another most often occurs by means of wind-borne spores, **conidia**, developed at the ends of branched conidiophores, that emerge from the stomata of damaged leaves. If one of the conidia is carried by the wind to the moist surface of a healthy potato leaf, it germinates to form a branched hypha that enters the host, either via an open stoma or by penetrating a cell of the epidermis. Once inside the leaf, the fungus rapidly develops an extensive area of hyphae, with haustoria that penetrate parenchyma cells in the palisade and spongy layers.

Any conidia that are washed into the soil by rain usually form an outgrowth called a **zoosporangium**, in which eight **zoospores** are formed. Each of these is a biflagellate invasive spore, capable of swimming through a film of water to infect a healthy potato.

Under special circumstances, and probably not outside the potato's natural range in South America, a form of sexual reproduction may occur, involving the fusion of nuclei between two different strains of hyphae. Nuclear fusion results in the formation of an **oospore**, a hardy structure that survives the winter.

Potato blight is particularly prevalent during warm, wet summers, when the air temperature exceeds 20°C. Farmers, warned of the risk of blight by weather-forecasters, can take the following measures to prevent the spread of infection.

(i) Treat potato tubers with fungicide before planting.
(ii) Avoid sowing potatoes in the same ground in successive years.
(iii) Spray young crops with Bordeaux mixture, a solution of copper(II) sulphate with lime.
(iv) Burn dead stems and roots of potato plants after digging tubers. This destroys possible reservoirs of infection at the end of each growing season.

'Damping-off' disease of seedlings

Another parasitic organism with motile zoospores is *Pythium*, the cause of 'damping-off' disease in seedlings. There are about 15 species of *Pythium* in the UK, with a wide host range that include members of the cabbage, cucumber and legume families,

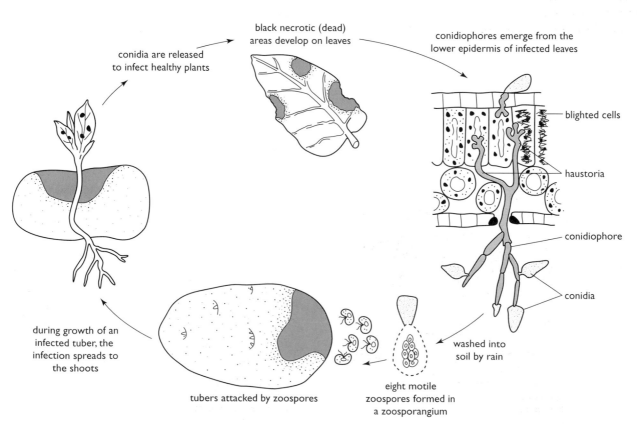

conidia are released to infect healthy plants

black necrotic (dead) areas develop on leaves

conidiophores emerge from the lower epidermis of infected leaves

blighted cells

haustoria

conidiophore

conidia

washed into soil by rain

during growth of an infected tuber, the infection spreads to the shoots

tubers attacked by zoospores

eight motile zoospores formed in a zoosporangium

Figure 1.17 The life cycle of potato blight

together with tomatoes, lettuces and other crop plants. Diseased seedlings are attacked at, or just above, soil level. Hyphae penetrate the stems of young seedlings, growing through the intercellular spaces. **Enzymes** produced by the hyphae break down cell walls, causing stems to collapse under their own weight. Typically, the region that is attacked narrows and softens, producing what is known as a 'wire-stem' effect. The parasite then spreads to other regions of its host, feeding saprobiontically after the host seedling has died. Asexual reproduction is by air-borne spores. Fusion between nuclei of '+' and '−' strains results in the formation of an oospore, which survives adverse conditions.

'Damping off' occurs most commonly when seeds are sown at high density, under conditions of high humidity, high temperature (24–28°C) and acid pH, markedly below 5.2. It may be prevented by sowing varieties of seeds that are *Pythium*-resistant, or by soaking seeds in a systemic fungicide (e.g. Benlate) before sowing them in heat-sterilised soil, made neutral or slightly alkaline by the addition of lime. Seedling vigour is an important factor in host resistance. Sturdy, virile seedlings, grown in full sunlight, are more resistant than spindly, etiolated ones grown at low light intensity.

1.4.2 *Fungi*

The Fungi kingdom consists of eukaryotic heterotrophs, feeding as **saprophytes**, parasites and symbionts. The basic structural unit of a fungus is a multinucleate **hypha**. Nutrients are obtained by absorbing soluble organic and inorganic material into the hyphae. Each hypha is surrounded by a protective wall, with chitin, not cellulose, as a major wall component. No fungus contains chlorophyll, so none are photosynthetic. Asexual and sexual reproduction often results in the formation of **non-motile spores**. There are three phyla – the **Zygomycota** (zygomycetes), **Ascomycota** (ascomycetes) and **Basidiomycota** (basidiomycetes). This classification is based on differences in sexual reproduction and on the nature of the hyphae, illustrated in Figure 1.18.

Zygomycota

The fungi included in this phylum have non-septate hyphae. Their sexual reproduction is by **gametangia** producing **zygospores**. *Mucor hiemalis*, the common bread mould, is a saprophytic zygomycete, the cause of food-spoilage in bread and other moist carbohydrate-containing food products. The branched, multinucleate feeding hyphae of this fungus are of two mating strains, plus (+) and minus (−). All the nuclei are haploid (n). Both strains reproduce asexually by producing spores in aerial, roughly spherical **sporangia**, carried at the tips of long supporting stalks, or **sporangiophores**. If both + and − strains are present in a colony, their nuclei may fuse to form a zygote, the only diploid (2n) phase in the life cycle. Zygote formation results from the fusion of two equal sized gametangia, each with several nuclei. The two gametangia are cut off from other parts of the hypha by complete cross walls. After the tips of the gametangia have broken down, the nuclei of + and − strains fuse in pairs to form zygotes. A thick, resistant wall develops around all the zygotes, forming a resting, overwintering stage in the cycle called a **zygospore**. On the return of favourable conditions, the zygospore germinates to produce a single sporangium at the tip of a sporangiophore. The spores in this sporangium are the products of meiosis. Each zygote (2n) in the

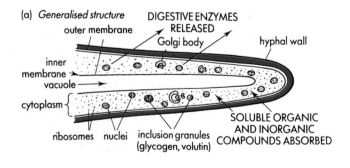

(a) *Generalised structure*

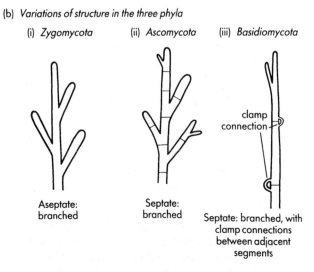

(b) *Variations of structure in the three phyla*

Figure 1.18 Fungal hyphae

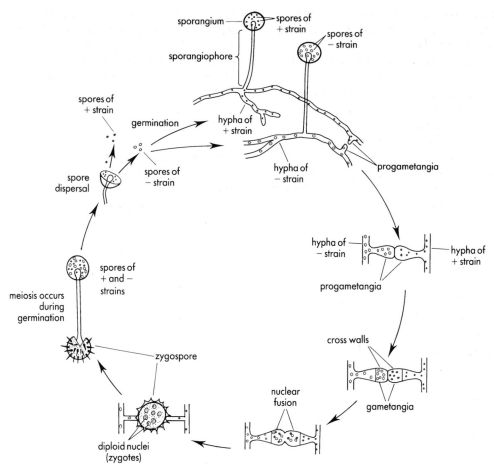

Figure 1.19 The life cycle of bread mould (*Mucor hiemalis*)

zygospore undergoes meiosis to produce four spores, two plus (+) and two minus (−). Meiotic divisions of all the zygotes produces anything from 40–100 haploid spores, which move from the zygospore into the sporangium as it develops.

Ascomycota

Ascomycetes have septate hyphae. Their reproduction involves spore production inside a container, the **ascus**.

The **yeasts** are unicellular ascomycetes, which have evolved from hypha-forming ancestors. Three species, possibly different from one another by no more than a single gene, are of economic importance:

(i) *Saccharomyces cerevisiae* – the yeast of brewing and baking;
(ii) *Saccharomyces ellipsoideus* – the yeast of wine;
(iii) *Saccharomyces carlsbergensis* – the yeast of lager.

Individual yeast cells are ellipsoidal-spherical, encased in a rigid, permeable cell wall composed largely of mannose and glucose polymers. Cell organelles include mitochondria, Golgi bodies and a

nucleus. There is an extensive endoplasmic reticulum throughout the cytoplasm. One or more large vacuoles occupy a central position in the cell. Storage materials, notably glycogen granules and oil globules in the cytoplasm, with polyphosphate granules in the vacuole, may be present. The life cycle (Figure 1.20) involves an alteration of generations between diploid (2n) and haploid (n) phases. Under conditions that are favourable for growth, the diploid vegetative cells undergo meiosis, to form an ascus with four haploid ascospores. These are of different mating strains, two plus (+) and two minus (−). Each ascospore can behave as a gamete, fusing with another of a different strain to form a zygote, from which the next generation of diploid cells is budded. As Figure 1.20 shows, both the diploid and haploid cells are capable of reproducing asexually by budding.

Yeast is a 'facultative anaerobe'; that is, it is capable of respiring both aerobically (when it develops mitochondria) and anaerobically (when it doesn't) depending on the availability of oxygen. Anaerobic respiration, or **fermentation**, uses glucose as respirable substrate and results in the production of alcohol (ethanol) and carbon dioxide.

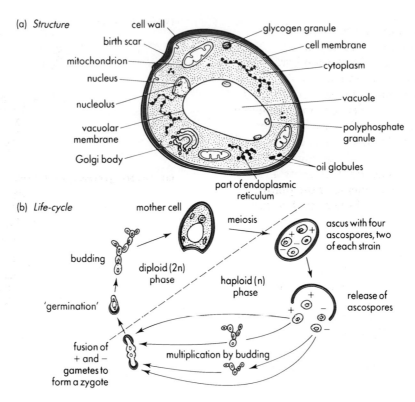

(a) *Structure*

cell wall
birth scar
mitochondrion
nucleus
nucleolus
vacuolar membrane
Golgi body
glycogen granule
cell membrane
cytoplasm
vacuole
polyphosphate granule
oil globules
part of endoplasmic reticulum

(b) *Life-cycle*

mother cell
meiosis
ascus with four ascospores, two of each strain
budding
diploid (2n) phase
haploid (n) phase
release of ascospores
'germination'
fusion of + and − gametes to form a zygote
multiplication by budding

Figure 1.20 *Saccharomyces*: structure and life cycle

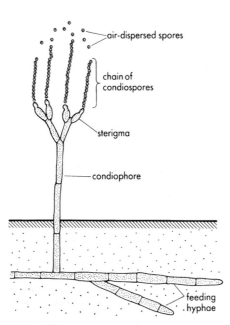

air-dispersed spores
chain of condiospores
sterigma
condiophore
feeding hyphae

Figure 1.21 *Penicillium notatum*

Used for centuries in baking, brewing and wine-making, yeasts have recently become very important organisms in genetic research and biotechnology (see section 3.3.3).

The grey-green mould *Penicillium notatum* bears a superficial resemblance to *Mucor*, and grows on similar substrates such as bread, cheese or fruit. Even so, unlike the bread mould, it has septate hyphae and is therefore classified as an ascomycete. *Penicillium*,

source of the antibiotic penicillin, has feeding hyphae, which divide into branches through its substrate, and aerial hyphae called **conidiophores** that branch dichotomously at their upper ends to form **sterigma**. From the tips of these sterigma, naked cytoplasm oozes, rounds off, and then hardens to form chains of grey-green conidiospores. Following dispersal by air currents to a suitable substratum, each conidiospore germinates to form a hypha. *Penicillium* lacks a method of sexual reproduction.

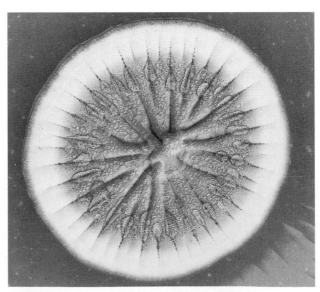

Penicillium notatum growing on an agar plate

Dutch elm disease

Dutch elm disease is caused by the ascomycete *Ophiostoma (Ceratostomella) ulmi* which is transmitted from tree to tree by the elm bark beetle *Scolytus scolytus*. The larvae and adults of this beetle make deep, branching tunnels beneath the bark of elm trees. Some of these tunnels penetrate the living tissues of the tree, including phloem sieve tubes which transport sugars. Fungal spores, carried on the wings and bodies of adult beetles, germinate beneath the bark to produce hyphae. As these grow into the living tissues, conducting elements of the phloem become blocked. The leaves of the trees then turn yellow and fall off. This causes the tree to die over a period of 1–3 months, as its photosynthesising and transpiring systems fail.

Dutch elm disease was introduced into the UK on logs imported from Holland, probably in the 1920s. During the 1960s and 1970s, a particularly virulent strain of the fungus killed more than 25% of all the mature elm trees in the UK. Between 8–10 million trees died during this epidemic. Apart from changing the landscape, this had a marked effect on all elm-dependent food chains and webs.

(a) *An adult beetle*

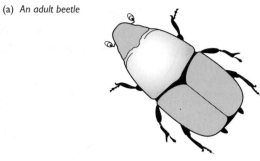

(b) *Bark borings made by beetle larvae*

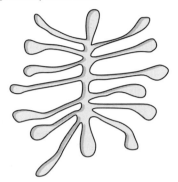

Figure 1.22 The elm bark beetle

Basidiomycota

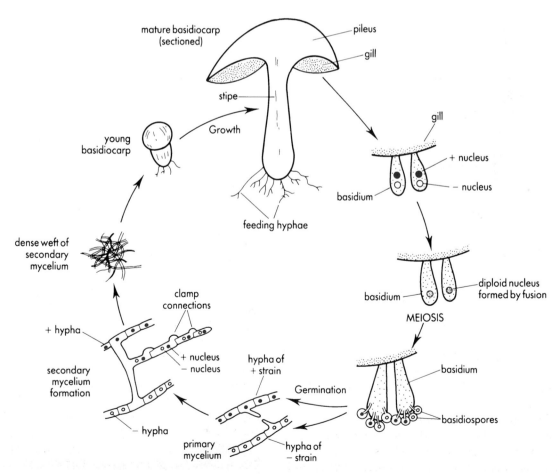

Figure 1.23 The life cycle of *Agaricus campestris*

Fungi classified as basidiomycetes have septate walls. Their sexual reproduction involves spores produced externally on a **basidium**.

The field mushroom (*Agaricus campestris*) is a fleshy, edible basidiomycete, found in grassy meadows with a high organic content. A mushroom's fruiting body, or **basidiocarp**, consists of a cap, the **pileus**, supported by a stalk, the **stipe**. On the underside of the cap are radially arranged gills, lined by spore-producing basidia. The diploid nucleus of each basidium undergoes meiosis to form four **basidiospores**. Again, as in yeast, these are of two different strains, two plus (+) and two minus (−). On germinating, the basidiospores produce a **primary mycelium** formed either from a + or a − hypha. Ultimately, fusion between the two types of hypha produces a **secondary mycelium**, with two nuclei per segment, one of each type. These segments have a characteristic structure, with the formation of swellings called clamp connections around each cross wall. Basidiocarps develop from dense wefts (interlacing threads) of hyphae of the secondary mycelium.

Commercial mushroom production

Commercial production of the cultivated mushroom *A. bisporus* is carried out in mushroom houses equipped to control temperature, humidity and aeration. Modern commercial mushroom production has three preparatory stages: **composting**, **'spawning'** and **casing**. The mushrooms are usually grown in wooden boxes, stacked one above another in tiers of three or four. The most widely favoured substrate is composted wheat straw, fermented by adding horse, pig or poultry manure. By stacking straw-manure mixtures in long narrow piles, about 1 m high and 1.8 m wide, which are regularly aerated by turning, a rapid rise in temperature to 60–80°C is achieved. This, in effect, acts as a form of

Mushroom 'spawn', grown on millet

pasteurisation, killing off any foreign fungal spores, mites, insects and nematodes in the compost. After 3–4 weeks, when the temperature has cooled to around 20°C, the compost is tightly packed into sterilised boxes and 'spawned' with a pure inoculum of *A. bisporus*. The 'spawn' is produced by growing the fungus on sterilised wheat or rye grains with added chalk to maintain alkalinity.

After the 'spawn' has been mixed with compost, its fungal hyphae spread throughout each box, covering the compost with a white weft of hyphae, smelling strongly of mushrooms. After 10–15 days at 25–28°C, the boxes are cased with a 2–3 cm depth of casing soil, added to induce the formation of fruiting bodies. In the UK, peat mixed with granular chalk is often used for casing. This mixture favours the growth of the bacterium *Pseudomonas putica*, which in some obscure way – possibly by removing inhibitors from the compost or by releasing ferrous iron – triggers the production of fruiting bodies from dense clusters of hyphae. Fruiting body formation is favoured by high humidity (95%) and relatively low temperature (15–17°C). Approximately 18–25 days after casing, the first crop is ready for picking. Successive flushes of fruiting bodies appear over the next 30–40 days, providing all the mature fruiting bodies are removed and the compost is kept moist by watering.

Mycorrhizae

Mycorrhizae are associations between fungal hyphae and higher plants. The fungal partner may be a basidiomycete, such as a woodland cap fungus, or a phycomycete, similar to *Mucor*. Sometimes the fungal hyphae may ramify through the entire plant, including the leaves and stems, but more often they are confined to the roots, forming an **ectotrophic** or **endotrophic association**. Ectotrophic mycorrhizae,

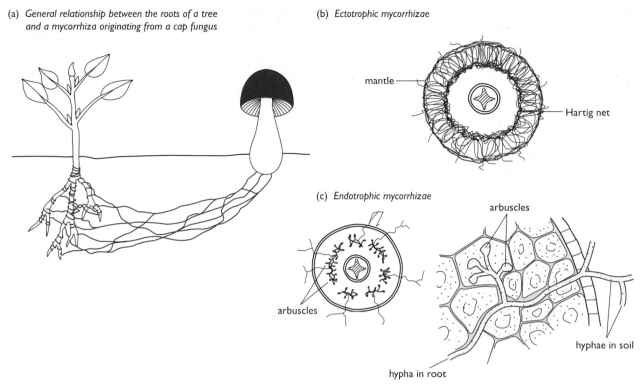

(a) *General relationship between the roots of a tree and a mycorrhiza originating from a cap fungus*

(b) *Ectotrophic mycorrhizae*

mantle

Hartig net

(c) *Endotrophic mycorrhizae*

arbuscles

arbuscles

hypha in root

hyphae in soil

Figure 1.24 Mycorrhizae

seen in pine and larch trees, are the most primitive. After penetrating cortical cells, the fungal hyphae soon disorganise, leaving a network of intercellular hyphae known as the **Hartig net**. As hyphae of the Hartig net grow outwards, forming a mantle that envelops the root tip, cells of the cortex develop tannins and phytoalexins, that probably check the inward penetration of the fungus. Endotrophic mycorrhizae, that occur in many bryophytes, pteridophytes and angiosperms, are more intimate associations, involving the penetration of parenchyma cells by intracellular hyphae, which characteristically form swollen nodules, called **arbuscules**, within the cells.

The relationship between a vascular plant and its mycorrhizae may be obligate or facultative. Orchids have an obligate dependence; that is, without the fungus the orchid dies. Pines and rhododendrons, however, have a facultative dependence, growing rather better with mycorrhizae than without them. It is still not entirely clear how each partner benefits from these associations. The fungus probably utilises some photosynthetic products, especially glucose and sucrose, from the higher plant. Additionally, some fungi may use auxins, gibberellins and cytokinins synthesised by the plants that they penetrate. Equally, the higher plant may derive similar growth stimulants from its fungal partner. More likely, however, the higher plant depends on the fungus for an additional supply of water and mineral ions,

especially phosphorus. Hyphae emerging from the root surface increase the effective absorbing surface of the root. Some researchers believe that the hyphae provide channels for the rapid transport of certain mineral ions into the deep tissues of the root.

QUESTIONS

7 a) Draw and label a named bacteriophage and a named bacterial cell.

 b) What relationship may exist between the bacteriophage and the bacterium?

8 a) Draw and label five features of biological interest in a cell of each of the following organisms:

 Saccharomyces, Anabaena, Chlorella, Paramecium.

 b) Why aren't all the organisms you have drawn placed in the same kingdom?

9 a) Draw and label the spore-producing structures in each of the following organisms:

 Mucor, Penicillium and *Agaricus.*

 b) Why are the organisms you have drawn all classified as fungi?

Biologists have classified micro-organisms in different ways. These groupings, based mainly on structural differences, are subject to frequent revision, as researchers assemble new evidence.

The biological nature of viruses is unique. Although they consist of macromolecular complexes of nucleic acid and protein, and possess the ability to replicate, they do not carry out any of the other physiological processes that are characteristic of living organisms.

All living organisms are composed of cells, produced by pre-existing cells. In the five-kingdom classification, two distinct structural classes of cells are recognised: the prokaryotes, which lack a nucleus, and the eukaryotes, which possess one.

If the three-domain classification is adopted, there are three major groups: Bacteria, Archaea and Eucarya.

Many micro-organisms are of economic importance. Some parasitic species cause damage to crop plants. Others, which are saprobionts, feed on dead organic matter, breaking down complex molecules into simpler ones such as carbon dioxide, water and mineral salts, which are recycled.

An increasing number of micro-organisms are being used by biotechnologists to produce useful products such as food, beverages, fuel and medicines. Effective and efficient cultivation of these species depends on a knowledge of their life cycles and nutritional requirements.

CHAPTER 1   QUESTIONS

(side text, vertical) **Micro-organisms: an introduction**

1 The diagram below illustrates a virus.

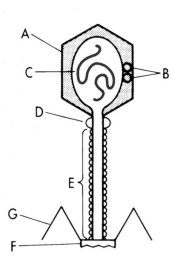

a) Label the parts A–G.

b) Which group of organisms is parasitised by this virus?

c) Name the nucleic acid that the virus carries in its head.

d) What term is used to describe the symmetry of this virus?

e) Cells attacked by this virus may undergo *lysis* or *lysogeny*. Explain how these processes differ.

2 Match the following structures found in viruses, bacteria and fungi with their functions.

Structure	Function
a) Mesosome	cell wall synthesis
b) Cell membrane	ribosomal RNA synthesis
c) Mitochondrion	ATP synthesis
d) Vacuole	maintains cell shape
e) Golgi apparatus	transfer of genetic material
f) Flagellum	chromosome attachment
g) Capsid	adherence to other cells
h) Nuclear envelope	selective permeability
i) Cell wall	encloses DNA or RNA
j) Pilus	stores carbohydrate
k) Glycogen granule	transfer of genetic material
l) Nucleolus	motility
m) Bacteriophage tail	encloses chromosomes
	stores water

3 Critically evaluate the term 'micro-organism', with particular reference to the viruses.
How are 'micro-organisms' classified within the five-kingdom system?
Do you consider that the merits of this system outweigh its shortcomings?

4 By reference to a named bacterium and fungus, explain the meaning of the terms, 'prokaryotic' and 'eukaryotic'. Draw up a table to list the most important diagnostic features of prokaryotic and eukaryotic cells.

5 Describe how you would distinguish between bacteria, algae and protozoa.
Why is *Anabaena*, formerly classified as a blue-green alga, now regarded as a bacterium?

6 Describe and justify the classification of fungi into three phyla (Zygomycota, Ascomycota and Basidiomycota). Why is the late blight of potatoes (*Phytophthora infestans*) now classified as a Protoctistan?

7 Survey the commercial applications of algae and fungi. How may algae and fungi cause economic losses? What measures can be taken to control harmful algae and fungi?

8 a) What do you understand by the 'economic importance' of an organism?

b) Explain why the following organisms are of economic importance: Herpes simplex virus, *Phytophthora*, *Ophiostoma* (*Ceratostomella*), *Saccharomyces*.

9 Write an essay on the similarities and differences between prokaryotic and eukaryotic cells.

BIBLIOGRAPHY

Micro-organisms: an introduction

Anderson, NG (1970) Evolutionary significance of virus infection *Nature* (227) 1346–7

Clegg, CJ (1984) *Lower Plants* John Murray

Deverall, B (1981) *Fungal Parasitism* (Studies in Biology No. 17) Edward Arnold

Fay, P (1983) *The Blue-Greens* (Studies in Biology No. 160) Edward Arnold

Hudson, HJ (1980) *Fungal Saprophytism* (Studies in Biology No. 32) Edward Arnold

Ingle, MR (1986) *Microbes and Biotechnology* (Studies in Advanced Biology No. 4) Blackwell

Ingold, CT (1961) *The Biology of Fungi* Hutchinson Educational

Institute of Biology, Association for Science Education (1989) *Biological Nomenclature* Institute of Biology

Kumar, H and Singh, H (1976) *A Textbook on Algae* The Macmillan Press

Levine, AJ (1992) *Viruses* Scientific American Library, New York

Madigan, MT, Martinko, JM, Parker, J (1997) *Brock Biology of Microorganisms* Prentice Hall International, London

Margulis, L and Schwartz, KV (1988) *Five Kingdoms: An Illustrated Guide To The Phyla Of Life On Earth* 2nd Edn Freeman and Co., New York

Schlegel, HG (1993) *General Microbiology* 7th Ed. Cambridge University Press, New York

Sleigh, MA (1972) *The Biology of the Protozoa* Edward Arnold

Woese, CR (1987) Bacterial evolution *Microbial Rev* (51) 221–71

Micro-organisms: an introduction

CHAPTER 2

Micro-organisms – growth & action

Viruses, and all living organisms, possess the ability to increase their numbers through reproduction. In addition, all other living micro-organisms feed, respire, grow, excrete, move and respond to stimuli. Biologists are currently showing great interest in micro-organisms because of their growth rates and metabolic activities. In a hungry world, where many are starving, new food sources offer new hope. Many micro-organisms can double their biomass in hours or days, whereas the more traditional foods, namely plants and animals, may take weeks, months or years. As they grow, micro-organisms synthesise an enormous number of complex organic molecules, they modify some of their products, and break down others. Increasingly, micro-organisms are being used to synthesise useful products, modify the structure of chemicals and break down harmful waste substances.

This exploitation of micro-organisms to enhance the quality of human life owes its current boom to two technical advances. Firstly, new techniques in **gene manipulation** have made it possible for genes to be transferred from one organism to another. Used as recipients for foreign genes, the cells of certain bacteria and yeasts behave admirably, expressing the novel genes and secreting their products. Secondly, advances in **chemical engineering** have led to the production of stainless steel containers for the mass cultivation of micro-organisms, together with machinery for the extraction of their products. Taken together, these two technical advances provide a basis for new microbial products and processes, both in the immediate future and for many decades to come.

This exciting possibility, however, should not obscure the fact that micro-organisms can be harmful as well as beneficial. For instance, among bacteria that regulate the nitrogen cycle, there are some that fix nitrogen, making it available to crops, and others that break down nitrates, depriving crops of a nitrogen supply. More seriously, from a human viewpoint, some bacteria, protoctists and fungi are pathogens, causing infectious diseases in humans, farm animals and crops. **Biotechnology** is the exploitation of organisms in ways that benefit the human situation. It encompasses many of the diverse activities of micro-organisms, both good and bad.

2.1 Respiration

ATP is the immediate energy reservoir in any cell, and it can be tapped for growth, movement or any other activity. All organisms synthesise ATP during a series of oxidation–reduction reactions, known as biochemical pathways. These pathways may be divided into three major types, depending on the nature of the electron acceptors: aerobic respiration, anaerobic respiration and fermentation.

During **aerobic respiration** electrons, removed from a substrate molecule such as glucose, are shunted, in turn, along a chain of acceptors. The acceptors are reduced and reoxidised. Oxygen is the final electron acceptor in the chain. Water is the end product. Micro-organisms that can only synthesise their ATP in this way are called **obligate aerobes**, because they cannot live in the absence of oxygen.

Anaerobic respiration occurs in the absence of oxygen, but requires the presence of nitrates, sulphates or carbonates. These compounds substitute for oxygen as electron acceptors, and are subsequently reduced.

Fermentation not only occurs in the absence of oxygen, but also in the absence of any added electron acceptor. Reduced nicotine adenine dinucleotide (NADH) plays an important role in fermentation pathways, acting as a hydrogen donor. Yeasts cause the reaction:

$$\text{Glucose} + \text{NADH} \rightarrow \text{ethanol} + \text{NAD}$$

This is **alcoholic fermentation**. Conversely, some bacteria have enzymes that enable them to convert pyruvate into lactic acid:

$$\text{Glucose} + \text{NADH} \rightarrow \text{lactic acid} + \text{NAD}$$

This is **lactate fermentation**.

Other similar biochemical pathways in different species of bacteria end with the formation of a wide range of organic acids, alcohols and ketones. Micro-organisms that obtain their energy by anaerobic respiration or fermentation may be either obligate or facultative anaerobes. An **obligate anaerobe**, such as the bacterium *Clostridium*, which lives in the soil, may die in the presence of oxygen because one or more of its enzyme systems is inactivated. **Facultative anaerobes**, on the other hand, such as yeasts, are able to obtain energy either by aerobic respiration or by fermentation, and do not require oxygen for **biosynthesis**.

2.2 Nutrition

Described in terms of their nutritional requirements, micro-organisms are either autotrophs or heterotrophs.

Autotrophs

Autotrophs have the ability to synthesise all of their nutritional requirements from just three sources: carbon dioxide, a hydrogen donor and mineral salts. Two types of autotroph, photoautotrophs and chemoautotrophs, are recognised.

Photoautotrophs use radiant energy from sunlight, absorbed and made available to the cell by photosynthetic pigments which act as intermediates. In the cyanobacteria and algae, as in higher plants, the hydrogen donor is water. Here, photosynthesis may be represented by the general equation:

$$2H_2O + CO_2 \xrightarrow[\text{chlorophyll}]{\text{light}} (CH_2O) + O_2 + H_2O$$

Photosynthetic bacteria such as *Chlorobium* and *Chromatium* do not use water as a hydrogen source. Neither do they release oxygen as a by-product. Instead, they oxidise hydrogen sulphide to sulphur, which is retained as granules within the cell cytoplasm:

$$2H_2S + CO_2 \rightarrow (CH_2O) + 2S + H_2O$$

Chemoautotrophs, the second group of autotrophic bacteria, use atmospheric oxygen to oxidise inorganic molecules. As a result of these oxidations, energy is released and then trapped by adenosine triphosphate (ATP), to drive synthetic processes in the cell.

Nitrosomonas, for example, oxidises ammonia to nitrites:

$$2NH_3 + 3O_2 \rightarrow 2HNO_2 + 2H_2O + \text{energy}$$

Nitrobacter oxidises nitrites to nitrates:

$$2HNO_2 + O_2 \rightarrow 2HNO_3 + \text{energy}$$

Thiobacillus oxidises sulphur to sulphate:

$$2S + 3O_2 + 2H_2O \rightarrow 2H_2SO_4 + \text{energy}$$

Heterotrophs

Heterotrophs, by far the largest group of bacteria, together with all the fungi, must be supplied with complex organic molecules, such as carbohydrates, lipids and proteins. They obtain energy from the oxidation of these macromolecules into smaller, simpler compounds. Again, the energy released from these oxidations is utilised, via ATP, to drive cellular processes. Most heterotrophs feed as saprobionts, releasing enzymes into their environment and absorbing the soluble products of enzyme action. Some heterotrophic bacteria and fungi feed as **symbionts**, in close physiological association with other organisms, a relationship that gives benefit to both partners. Finally, a relatively small number of bacteria and fungi feed as **parasites**, obtaining their nutrients from a living organism of a different species. As a result of this relationship, only the parasite benefits, while the host invariably suffers some degree of cell or tissue damage.

Nutritional requirements

Micro-organisms can be grown in the laboratory, either in liquid media, known as **broths**, or on **solid media**, hardened to a jelly-like consistency by adding agar. The nutritional requirements of photoautotrophs and heterotrophs are listed in Table 2.1. These essential nutrients are either added to a broth, or incorporated into a solid medium, depending on the micro-organism that is to be grown. Large conical flasks fitted with cotton wool plugs or rubber bungs and glass tubes – so gas can escape – are suitable for small-scale broth cultures. Alternatively, many micro-organisms can be grown on solid-based media, contained in petri dishes.

Selective media are used to encourage the growth of certain micro-organisms, while suppressing the growth of others. An agar containing sugars and mineral salts, without a nitrogen source, can be used to select free-living nitrogen-fixing bacteria from soil. Unlike other soil bacteria, these organisms can synthesise their N-requirements from atmospheric nitrogen.

Indicator media are used to detect some bacteria. Purple McConkey agar turns red when *Salmonella* bacteria are present in human faeces.

Table 2.1 The nutritional requirements of micro-organisms feeding as photoautotrophs and heterotrophs

Nutrient	Sources required by photoautotrophs	Sources required by heterotrophs
Carbon	carbon dioxide	carbohydrates
		amino acids
		peptides
		lipids
Nitrogen	ammonium (NH_4^+) ions	ammonium (NH_4^+) ions
	nitrate (NO_3^-) ions	nitrate (NO_3^-) ions
		amino acids
		peptides
		nucleotides
		proteins
		(some basidiomycota)
Mineral salts (Macronutrients)	phosphorus	phosphorus
	potassium	potassium
	magnesium	magnesium
	iron	iron
	sulphur	sulphur
	calcium	calcium
	chlorine (algae)	sodium (bacteria)
(Micronutrients)	boron	boron
	cobalt	cobalt
	manganese	manganese
	copper	copper
	zinc	zinc
	molybdenum (cyanobacteria)	molybdenum (bacteria)
	vanadium (cyanobacteria)	vanadium (bacteria)
Growth factors		some vitamins of B-complex (required as coenzymes)

(a) *In liquid (broth) media*

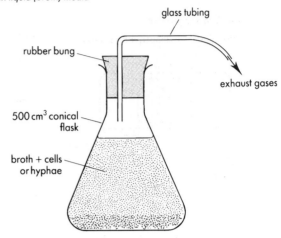

Unit samples are withdrawn at regular intervals. Biomass of the micro-organism, after filtration and drying, is recorded.

(b) *On solid media*

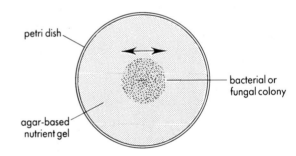

Successive measurements of the bacterial or fungal colony are made, as it spreads from a central point on the agar plate.

Figure 2.1 Two methods for determining the growth rates of micro-organisms

The bacterium converts lactose to lactic acid, causing a colour change in the agar from purple to red as the pH falls below 6.8.

2.3 Population Growth

Rough estimates of growth rates can be made by regularly measuring the diameter of a bacterial or fungal colony, as it spreads from a central point to cover the surface of a solid growth medium (Figure 2.1). More accurate estimates of growth rate, however, are dependent on broth cultures. Unit samples are withdrawn at regular intervals, filtered, dried and weighed. Mass is then plotted against time to produce a growth curve.

Changes in cell density during population growth can be determined by two methods:

(i) total counts, of both living and dead cells, using a haemocytometer;
(ii) viable counts of living cells, made by counting the number of colonies formed after serial dilution and plating onto a solid nutrient medium.

A **haemocytometer** (Figure 2.2), originally designed for counting blood cells, can also be used for counting cells of bacteria, yeasts or algae in liquid media. At the centre of the haemocytometer are one or more grids, overlaid by a specially designed coverglass. Viewed under the high-power of a microscope, an observer sees a central unit of 25

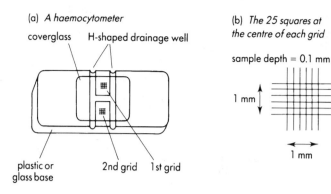

(a) *A haemocytometer*

coverglass H-shaped drainage well

plastic or glass base 2nd grid 1st grid

(b) *The 25 squares at the centre of each grid*

sample depth = 0.1 mm

1 mm

1 mm

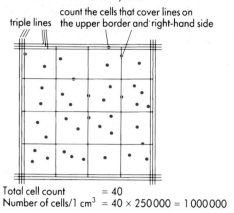

(c) *Magnified view of one of the 25 central squares, each sub-divided into 16 squares*

triple lines   count the cells that cover lines on the upper border and right-hand side

Total cell count   = 40
Number of cells/1 cm^3 = 40 × 250 000 = 1 000 000

Figure 2.2 ▲ Using a haemocytometer for total cell counts

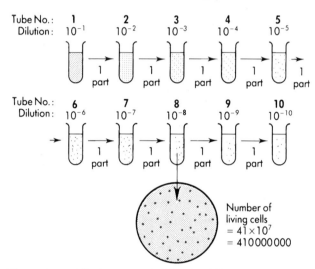

Tube No.:   1   2   3   4   5
Dilution: 10^{-1} 10^{-2} 10^{-3} 10^{-4} 10^{-5}

1 part   1 part   1 part   1 part   1 part

Tube No.:   6   7   8   9   10
Dilution: 10^{-6} 10^{-7} 10^{-8} 10^{-9} 10^{-10}

1 part   1 part   1 part   1 part

Number of living cells = 41×10^7 = 410 000 000

Figure 2.3 ▲ Dilution procedure for serial plating

squares (Figure 2.2b). Each of these 25-squared units usually measures 0.2 × 0.2 × 0.1 mm (depth) and has a volume of 0.004 mm^3. After making a count of the number of cells in one of these units, the observer multiplies the figure by 250 000 to give the approximate number of cells in 1 cm^3 of the cell suspension. Thus in Figure 2.2b, a total count of the 40 cells would give an estimate of
40 × 250 000 = 10 000 000.

Counts of living cells can be made by progressive or **serial dilutions**, carried out as follows. Ten tubes which each contain 9 cm^3 of distilled water, are set up in a rack. A sterile pipette is used to place 1 cm^3 of the original cell suspension in tube 1. After shaking, 1 cm^3 of this suspension is then added to tube 2, and so on. Ten nutrient agar plates are then prepared and numbered. After transferring 1 cm^3 of each suspension to the corresponding plate, and spreading it with an L-shaped spreader, the plates are incubated until colonies of bacteria, yeast or

algae are visible. If 41 colonies grew on plate no. 8, then

No. living cells/1cm^3 suspension =
41 × 100 000 000 = 4 100 000 000

A colorimeter can be used in a **photometric method** for estimating cell density during population growth. Unit samples are withdrawn at regular intervals and transferred to a test-tube. The optical density (absorbance) of the cell suspension is measured and recorded. As cell numbers increase, there is a related increase in light absorption and turbidity. A graph of optical density against time is plotted. This work can be made quantitative if the colorimeter is first calibrated with known masses of a dried micro-organism, such as yeast suspended in unit volumes of water.

2.3.1 Growth curves in liquid media

Bacteria, yeasts and populations of unicellular organisms, grown in liquid media with limited amount of nutrients, show a characteristic sigmoid growth curve, similar to the generalised curve shown in Figure 2.4. This curve has four basic phases:

(i)   the lag phase,
(ii) the log phase, or exponential growth phase,
(iii) the stationary phase,
(iv) the senescent phase, death phase or logarithmic decline phase.

During the **lag phase**, which may last from a few minutes to several days, there is little or no increase in cell numbers. Individual cells show intense metabolic activity, notably enzyme **synthesis**, during this phase. Near the end of the lag phase cells may increase in size, sometimes doubling or tripling their mass and volume. Soon, in the **log phase**, or **exponential growth phase**, the cells begin to divide at a constant rate. Ideally the cell population

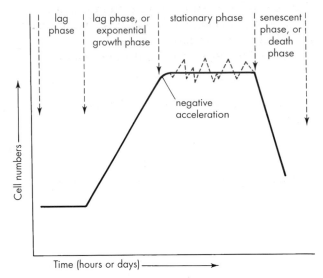

Figure 2.4 The generalised growth curve of a cell population (real populations often fluctuate around an equilibrium level)

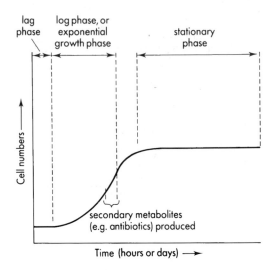

Figure 2.5 The generalised growth curve of a cell population growing on a liquid medium

increases geometrically, in the series 2, 4, 8, 16, 32, 64, 128 etc. This rate of increase, however, is not maintained indefinitely. In substrate-limited growth media, the growth rate slows as nutrients begin to run out. Furthermore, at this stage of their growth, many unicellular organisms produce secondary metabolites (e.g. antibiotics) that have a toxic effect, slowing the rate of cell division. The combined effects of this shortage of nutrients and accumulation of toxins are that the growth rate becomes progressively slower. At a point where the birth rate of new cells is equal to the death rate of old ones, population growth enters the **stationary phase**. In this phase the population is more or less constant. It is drawn as a flat, straight line in Figure 2.4, but may actually be characterised by marked variations in numbers (dotted line), fluctuating on both sides of a mean. When all the food in a nutrient solution has been used up, the number of cell deaths exceeds the number of new cells produced. This marks the beginning of the **senescent phase**, or **death phase**, a period of logarithmic decline. At the end of this period only a few extremely resistant cells may remain, or the population might die out entirely.

If fungal hyphae are grown in liquid media, a flatter growth curve, without a senescent phase, is usually obtained (Figure 2.5). Again, there is a lag phase, followed by exponential growth, but fungal hyphae rarely grow as rapidly as unicellular organisms. Secondary metabolites, such as antibiotics, are produced towards the end of exponential growth. Mycelial mats, formed from intertwined hyphae, are removed during the stationary phase, so that the mass of the hyphae, rarely falls after exponential growth is complete.

2.3.2 Exponential numbers

When biologists plot a growth curve to show changes in cell density, they often plot cell numbers on a logarithmic rather than an arithmetic scale. One reason for this is that actual cell numbers, which can increase in a few hours from tens to billions, are difficult to plot on standard graph paper. Another reason is that exponential growth is shown as a straight line on a logarithmic scale, whereas it would be shown as a curve on an ordinary scale. Straight line graphs are much easier to draw and interpret accurately than curved ones.

A logarithmic scale is based on exponential numbers. The number 100, for example, can be written as 10^2. Here, 2 is its **exponent** or **logarithm to base 10**. Similarly, the logarithm of 10 (or 10^1) is 1 and of 1000 (or 10^3) is 3. Numbers between 100 and 1000 have logarithms between 2.0 and 3.0. Numbers between 10 and 100 have logarithms between 1.0 and 2.0. So an increase of one unit (or log 10) on a logarithmic scale represents a multiplication by ten on an ordinary scale. Likewise, an increase of log 2 on a logarithmic scale represents a multiplication by two on an ordinary scale. Figure 2.6 shows the approximate shape of the curve of Figure 2.4 to a logarithmic scale.

An understanding of exponential numbers is essential in the operation of industrial processes involving the growth of micro-organisms. In such processes, operators need to predict approximate times for cultures to reach required levels of cell density.

During the log or exponential growth phase shown in Figures 2.4 and 2.6, the cells are dividing at a constant rate. Cell numbers will double in a unit

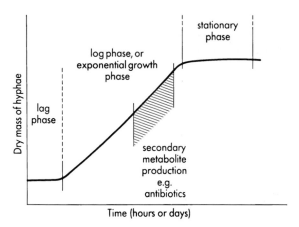

Figure 2.6 The generalised growth curve of fungal hyphae plotted on a logarithmic scale

period of time, known as the **mean generation time**. Each species has its own mean generation time, which is genetically determined. If we know the mean generation time in minutes, t, we can calculate the number of generations per hour, k, by using the equation

$$k = \frac{60}{t} \qquad (1)$$

The name given to k is the **exponential growth rate constant**, and it, too, varies from species to species. A species with a mean generation time of 20 minutes would have an exponential growth rate constant of 3. An initial population of 500 individuals of this species would have increased to 1000 (500×2) after 20 minutes, to 2000 (500×2^2) after 40 minutes, and to 4000 (500×2^3) after one hour. If we call the initial population N_o, we can therefore calculate N_{1H}, the population one hour later, using the equation

$$N_{1H} = N_o \times 2^k$$
$$= 500 \times 2^3 = 4000$$

(note that k will not always be a whole number)

If we want to calculate the population after some other length of time we need a more general equation. If T is the time in hours between the first and second measurements, we can use

$$N_T = N_o \times 2^{Tk} \qquad (2)$$

Alternatively, if g is the number of generations (or mean generation times) which have occurred between the two measurements, we can use

$$N_g = N_o \times 2^g$$

Suppose now that we have a population of an unknown species, and we wish to calculate its mean generation time. We could measure the initial population density and then take a second measurement some known time later. The two measurements and the number of hours between

them could be substituted in equation 2, and then k could be calculated. However k must first be made the subject of the equation:

First taking logs of both sides of equation 2:

$$\log N_T = \log N_o + Tk \log 2$$

Rearranging to make k the subject of the equation,

$$k = \frac{\log N_T - \log N_o}{T \log 2} \qquad (3)$$

The mean generation time is then found by substituting for k in equation 1.

Example 1

A certain species has an exponential growth rate of 2.5. If an initial population of 1000 individuals undergoes exponential growth for six hours, what is its final population?

As we need to find N_T, the population after given time T (in hours), we use equation 2. Substituting the values we know for the initial population, the time elapsed and the exponential growth rate constant:

$$N_{(6\ hours)} = 1000 \times 2^{(6 \times 2.5)}$$
$$= 1000 \times 2^{(15)}$$
$$= 1000 \times 32\ 724$$

The final population can therefore be calculated to be approximately 32.8 million individuals.

Example 2

A population of a species with an unknown exponential growth rate constant is left to grow exponentially for $2\frac{1}{2}$ hours. At the beginning of the period a population of 550 individuals is measured, and at the end it is found to have grown to 16 000. Find the exponential growth rate constant for this species, and use it to calculate the mean generation time.

In this case we know the values of T, N_T and N_o, and we need to find k, so we use equation 3. Substituting the known values into the equation, we obtain

$$k = \frac{\log(16\ 000) - \log(550)}{2.5 \log 2}$$

We can therefore calculate that k is approximately 1.94.

To find t, the mean generation time in minutes, we substitute for k in equation 1.

$$\text{This gives } t = \frac{60}{1.94}$$

So the mean generation time is approximately 30.9 minutes, or 30 minutes and 54 seconds.

2.4 Ecology

Micro-organisms play a more important role in food chains and biogeochemical cycles than their small size might at first suggest. Cyanobacteria and algae are important **producers** in many aquatic food chains. Protozoans are **consumers**, while saprobiontic bacteria and fungi are **decomposers**, breaking down dead organisms into simpler compounds that can be recycled back to the producers (Figure 2.7).

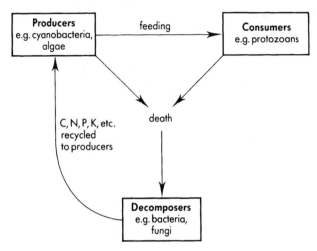

Figure 2.7 The ecological roles of micro-organisms

Each micro-organism has a minimum temperature (below which it cannot grow), an optimum temperature (at which growth is most rapid) and a maximum temperature (above which growth is not possible). Interestingly, the optimum temperature is always nearer to the maximum than the minimum (Figure 2.8). On the basis of their optimum temperatures, it is possible to distinguish three ecologically distinct groups of micro-organisms:

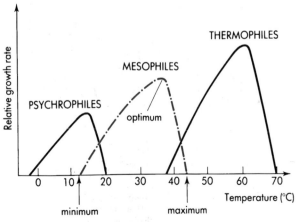

Figure 2.8 Temperature limits and growth rates of psychrophiles, mesophiles and thermophiles

(i) **psychrophiles** (cryophiles), with low optimum temperatures, occur mainly in Arctic and Antarctic regions. Some bacteria belonging to this group may contaminate refrigerated foods, in which they can multiply at a relatively rapid rate.
(ii) **mesophiles**, with medium optimum temperatures, live in tropical and sub-tropical regions, or in warm-blooded animals.
(iii) **thermophiles**, with high optimum temperatures, live in thermal springs, or pools fed by geysers.

These three groups of micro-organisms are of great interest to biotechnologists, because their enzymes are adapted to operate most efficiently at specific temperatures close to their optima.

Just as each micro-organism has a temperature range within which growth is possible, so it also has its own pH range, with minimum, optimum and maximum points. In general, micro-organisms are better adapted to acid environments than plants or animals. For instance, some green algae, including *Chlorella*, have a lower pH limit of 1–2, while some bacteria and fungi will survive below pH 0.8. Cyanobacteria, on the other hand, are never found in habitats in which the pH is less than 4.0. This means that they are one of the first groups of micro-organisms to be killed when lakes become acidified.

QUESTIONS

1 What are the differences between a) autotrophs and heterotrophs, and b) photoautotrophs and chemoautotrophs?

2 Heterotrophs feed on complex organic molecules. Name three different modes of nutrition that occur within this group.

3 What are the end products of a) aerobic respiration, b) alcoholic fermentation and c) lactic acid fermentation?

4 Describe three different methods for measuring the growth rate of a population of yeast cells.

5 Name a micro-organism that acts as a) a producer, b) a consumer and c) a decomposer.

2.5 Nitrogen Cycle

The nitrogen cycle is shown in Figure 2.9. All four stages of the nitrogen cycle: nitrogen fixation, ammonification, nitrification and denitrification depend on micro-organisms. This illustrates the importance of micro-organisms in terrestrial and

Micro-organisms – growth & action

34

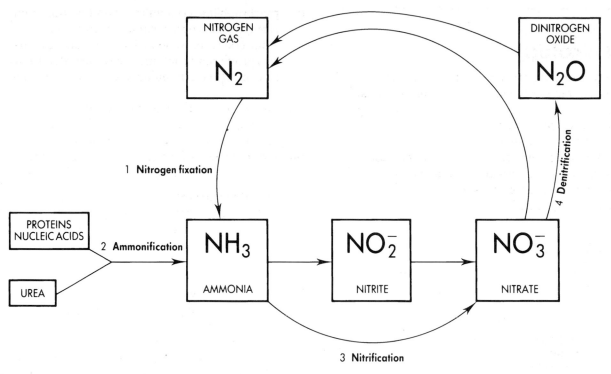

Figure 2.9 Four processes in the nitrogen cycle controlled by micro-organisms

aquatic environments. From a chemical viewpoint, the micro-organisms that drive the nitrogen cycle synthesise nitrogenous compounds, transform one nitrogenous compound into another, and degrade N-containing macromolecules into simpler compounds which are recycled. We will look at the four processes in turn.

Nitrogen fixation

This is the reduction of nitrogen by hydrogen to form ammonia (NH_3). A wide range of free-living soil bacteria are capable of carrying out this reaction. They include aerobes such as *Azotobacter* and *Pseudomonas*, together with anaerobes such as *Clostridium*, *Chromatium* and *Chlorobium*. Bacteria of the genus *Rhizobium* are of particular interest, because they can fix nitrogen when in a symbiotic relationship with the roots of legumes.

The biochemistry of nitrogen fixation is similar in all organisms that have been studied. It depends on the enzyme nitrogenase, which has either molybdenum or vanadium as one of its components. Indeed, some bacteria such as *Azotobacter chroococcum* can make both types of nitrogenase, each with a different heavy metal. ATP is required for nitrogen fixation, which results in the simultaneous oxidation of ferredoxin, a hydrogen acceptor.

$$\text{Reduced ferredoxin} \curvearrowright \text{Oxidised ferredoxin}$$
$$N_2 + 3H_2 \xrightarrow[\text{ATP} \curvearrowright \text{ADP}]{\text{nitrogenase}} 2NH_3$$

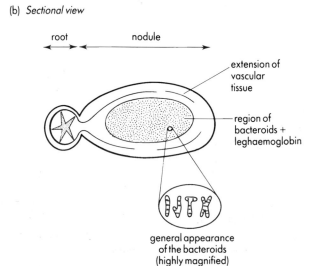

(a) *General appearance*

(b) *Sectional view*

Figure 2.10 Root nodules in legumes

Most legumes, grown in their natural habitats, form symbiotic associations with bacteria of the genus *Rhizobium*. In most cases each species of legume has its own nitrogen-fixing organism, present in swellings called **root nodules** that develop on the roots of infected plants. Thus *R. japonicum* occurs in soya bean, *R. trifolii* in clover and *R. meliloti* in alfalfa. Soon after entering a root hair, the rod-shaped *Rhizobium* loses its cell wall, and multiplies to form Y, X, T or J-shaped **bacteroids**, typically with dark transverse bands. The legume responds to the invasion by producing indole acetic acid (IAA) and cytokinins, growth hormones which stimulate surrounding root tissue to swell, forming a nodule. Nitrogen fixation involves the transfer of hydrogen ions from carbohydrates, such as glucose, to nitrogen. The site of transfer is the enzyme nitrogenase, located in the cytoplasm of bacteroids, in regions of the cell that are protected from oxygen. Ammonia is the initial product of the reaction, but this is soon combined with glutamate, in a reaction catalysed by glutamine synthetase, to form the amino acid glutamine.

$$N_2 \rightarrow NH_3 \rightarrow \begin{array}{c} \text{Glutamate} \\ (\\ \text{Glutamine} \rightarrow \text{Other} \\ \text{amino acids} \rightarrow \text{Proteins} \end{array}$$

The bacterium benefits from receiving a supply of carbon compounds from the legume, together with an anaerobic environment in which its nitrogenase can function. This environment is provided largely by the presence of a red pigment, **leghaemoglobin**, that surrounds the bacteroids, absorbing oxygen molecules from the surrounding soil in a manner similar to the binding between animal haemoglobin and oxygen. The legume, of course, benefits by receiving a supply of NH_3 from the bacterium, without being dependent on a supply of ammonium or nitrate ions from the soil. This means that legumes can survive and produce crops in nitrogen-deficient soils which are unable to support other crop plants.

The ability of symbiotic *Rhizobium* bacteria to fix atmospheric nitrogen as ammonia, and make it available to legumes, is a biological feature that genetic engineers would like to transfer to other crop plants, notably cereals. Such a transfer would greatly reduce the need for nitrogenous fertilisers, and help solve the problem of water pollution by nitrates. Nitrogenases, the enzyme systems responsible for nitrogen fixation, have two components. One of these, 'dinitrogenase', binds N_2. The other 'dinitrogenase reductase' converts N_2 to NH_3. Genes which code for these nitrogenase proteins are called **nif-genes**. Between 17–21 *nif*-genes are believed to code for the molybdenum-containing Mo-

nitrogenase. A different set of *nif*-genes codes for the vanadium-containing V-nitrogenase. It appears that by having both enzyme systems, the bacterium can fix nitrogen over a wide range of temperatures, V-nitrogenase being more efficient when the weather is cold. The complexity of *nif*-genes, both in their numbers and the fact that they may occur scattered throughout the genome, presents difficult problems for the genetic engineers who are working to transfer the capacity for nitrogen fixation to other crop plants with a 'built in' capacity for nitrogen fixation.

Certain cyanobacteria also fix nitrogen. *Anabaena* (see section 1.3) is a free-living genus, abundant in rice paddies and other shallow areas in tropical and temperate wetlands. Biologists are currently searching for strains which fix N_2 in excess of the bacterium's own requirements, and which release excess nitrogen as ammonia. *Nostoc*, another nitrogen-fixer, forms symbiotic associations with a small number of eukaryotic species. In lichens, where it associates with ascomycete fungi, *Nostoc* synthesises photosynthetic products and ammonia, which can pass to its fungal partner. The fungus, in return, provides *Nostoc* with a moist, shaded, well-aerated habitat, together with a supply of water and mineral salts. Liverworts of the genus *Anthoceros* have gall-like structures on the underside of their thalli. The presence of *Nostoc* in these swellings makes the liverworts greener in appearance, more metabolically active, and faster-growing. Certain cycads carry colonies of *Nostoc* in their coralloid roots. These specialised respiratory roots, formed at the soil surface, receive just enough light for photosynthesis and nitrogen fixation. Again, the cycads probably gain ammonia from their association with *Nostoc*. So does one angiosperm, the so-called giant rhubarb, belonging to the genus *Gunnera*. The enormous leaves of this plant, originating at ground level from a short rhizome, carry colonies of *Nostoc* intracellularly in cells at the base of their petioles.

Ammonification
This is the process by which proteins, amino acids, nucleic acids and nucleotides from dead organisms, together with urea from living animals, undergo degradation to form ammonia. Aerobic bacteria and fungi are among the many heterotrophic soil micro-organisms that hydrolyse N containing molecules, liberating NH_3 as an end product.

Nitrification
This is the oxidation of ammonia to nitrite (NO_2^-) and nitrate (NO_3^-) and is achieved by two different genera of soil bacteria, *Nitrosomonas* and *Nitrobacter*.

Nitrosomonas, an obligate aerobe, converts ammonia to nitrite, in the overall reaction:

$$2NH_3 + 3O_2 \rightarrow 2HNO_2 + 2H_2O$$

Nitrobacter, another obligate aerobe, completes the oxidation by converting nitrite to nitrate:

$$2HNO_2 + O_2 \rightarrow 2HNO_3$$

Green plants are able to take up and assimilate the nitrate that this bacterium produces.

Denitrification

This is the reduction of nitrate in the soil to oxides of nitrogen and nitrogen gas and has a detrimental effect on soil fertility. It occurs chiefly in waterlogged soils, with a high organic content, and is caused largely by the anaerobic bacterium *Pseudomonas denitrificans*, and some species of *Thiobacillus*.

The stages in the reduction of nitrates are as follows:

$$NO_3^- \rightarrow NO_2^- \rightarrow N_2O \rightarrow N_2$$

| Nitrate | Nitrite | Dinitrogen oxide (Nitrous oxide) | Nitrogen |

2.6 Human Pathogens

A number of micro-organisms cause human diseases. These are called **human pathogens**. In response to large reactive molecules, **antigens**, on the surface of these pathogens, humans produce protective proteins called **antibodies**. Each antibody is antigen-specific, and gives protection against further attack by that antigen. The principal of the protective procedure known as vaccination is to induce antibody protection without causing symptoms or disease, and so make the vaccinated person immune. **Vaccines** are made from killed, inactivated or genetically modified micro-organisms, or their active products. One major aim of biotechnology is to increase the range of vaccines available and to improve their effectiveness.

Mumps

Mumps is an acute contagious disease caused by an enveloped helical virus containing single-stranded RNA. After entering the respiratory tract, it multiplies in the mouth and oropharynx. About 16–21 days after exposure to the virus, the first symptoms appear. One or both parotid glands – the salivary glands located just below and in front of the ear – swell up and become painful. Virus particles appear in the saliva, then several days later in the urine. Complications may include inflammation of the testes or ovaries, in those who have reached puberty, the pancreas and the membranes surrounding the brain. The disease is transmitted in droplets of fluid that originate in the oropharynx, and are expelled during breathing, speaking, coughing and sneezing. Transmission of the virus is helped by moist, warm conditions, and close contact with infected persons. Full recovery may take 2–3 weeks. A vaccine, measles-mumps-rubella (MMR), is available.

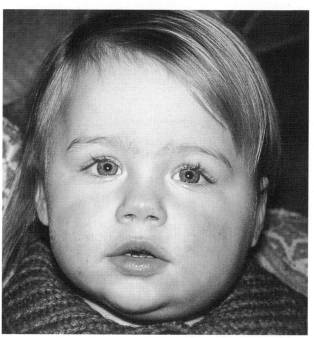

A child suffering from mumps

AIDS

Acquired immune deficiency syndrome (AIDS) is caused by **human immunodeficiency virus (HIV)**. This is a **retrovirus**, one that synthesises DNA using its RNA as a template. All carriers of the disease have virus particles in various cells, notably in T-helper lymphocytes and cells of their nervous system. As the disease progresses, viruses also appear in the blood, saliva and tears, along with semen in men and vaginal secretions in women. On entering a cell, the virus may behave in any one of three different ways:

(i) it may integrate a DNA copy of its genome into the host cell chromosome. Viral DNA is then replicated as a chromosomal gene, without any obvious ill effects on the host cell.

(ii) from the DNA copy of its genome on the host cell chromosome, it may transcribe a few molecules of viral RNA. These become surrounded by part of the host cell membrane to form complete viruses. This process may damage the host cell, but rarely kills it.

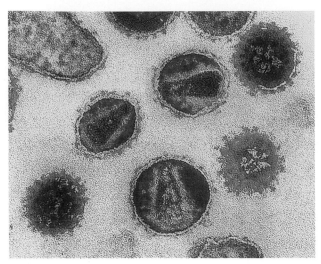

C2 Human immunodeficiency virus (HIV), the causative agent of AIDS *(see Colour Section on inside cover)*

binding protein (binds to a binding site on T-helper lymphocyte)

envelope, containing two protruding (spiked) proteins

core, containing two structural proteins

RNA

Figure 2.11 Cross-sectional view of a human immunodeficiency virus (HIV), the cause of AIDS. An outer coat with binding proteins, and two layers of structural proteins, surround two strands of RNA

(iii) again, from its DNA copy on the host cell chromosome, the virus transcribes large numbers of viral RNA molecules, together with the kinds of mRNA needed to make viral coats, which are the protein coverings of a virus. Many viruses are produced in this process. The cell dies when it bursts to release viruses into the body fluids.

HIV is transmitted principally by contact during heterosexual or homosexual intercourse. It may also be passed from person to person during blood transfusions with contaminated blood, or via re-used hypodermic needles.

This disease has an unusually long incubation period. It can be up to nine years before those who are infected with the virus develop 'full-blown' AIDS. Symptoms such as fever, weight loss,

diarrhoea, night sweats and a persistent cough develop. Progressive destruction of the T-helper lymphocytes affects all the other cell types in the immune system. This is because the T-helper lymphocytes play a central role in co-ordinating other cells of the immune system, by secreting activating substances called **lymphokines**. The consequences of the failure of this activation, are as follows:

(i) phagocytes, notably neutrophils and monocytes, which normally ingest viruses cannot remove them from the body fluids.

(ii) B-lymphocytes, responsible for producing antibodies, do not reproduce themselves in response to antigens. As a result a B-lymphocyte cannot make enough of its antibody to neutralise the complementary antigen.

(iii) T-killer cells, which seek out and destroy any foreign cells, including those responsible for causing cancer, become less efficient.

As the disease progresses there is an added complication – because any cells infected with HIV may become a target for T-killer cells, the immune system often becomes self-destructive. Furthermore, tissues may also be destroyed because HIV randomly 'switches on' clones of antibody-producing **B cells**

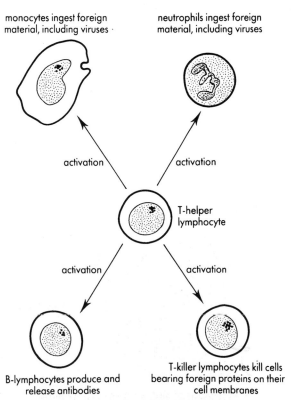

monocytes ingest foreign material, including viruses

neutrophils ingest foreign material, including viruses

activation

activation

T-helper lymphocyte

activation

activation

B-lymphocytes produce and release antibodies

T-killer lymphocytes kill cells bearing foreign proteins on their cell membranes

Figure 2.12 The central role of T-helper lymphocytes in the human immune system. Activation is by means of hormone-like compounds called lymphokines

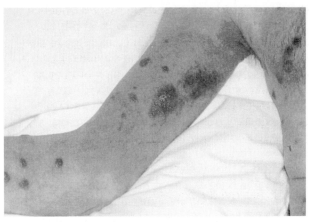
Kaposi's sarcoma

Some of these antibodies attack the host's own tissues, causing muscle wastage and general loss in body mass. 'Opportunist' infections may set in. One of the most common is *Pneumocystis carnii*, an otherwise rare form of pneumonia. An equally rare form of cancer, Kaposi's sarcoma, also occurs in AIDS sufferers. Such conditions are found only in people who have had their immune systems severely damaged.

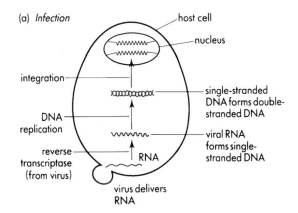

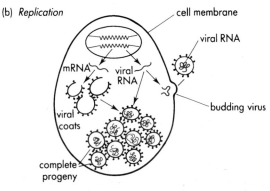

Figure 2.13 Behaviour of HIV, a retrovirus, in a host cell. The virus may remain integrated in the host cell's nucleus, bud off progeny from its cell membrane or form many progeny in its cytoplasm

At present, there is no cure for AIDS. Only preventative measures are available. These include screening all blood samples for HIV antibodies before using them in blood transfusions. Sexually active people are urged to remain with one partner. Men who have more than one sexual partner are advised to wear condoms. For those who are infected, a drug known as zidovudine, formerly called AZT, slows the progress of the disease by inhibiting the enzyme reverse transcriptase, used by the virus to make DNA from RNA (Figure 2.13).

HIV has a high mutation rate, which allows drug-resistant strains to appear within several weeks. As a result, it is common practice to treat AIDS sufferers with a cocktail of two or more drugs to avoid this problem. Zidovudine (AZT), for example, is often given together with a second drug, 3TC. Such **combination therapies** are currently the treatment of choice. Attacks by HIV are limited to those cells that have **CD4 receptor protein molecules** on their surface membrane. These receptors bind specifically to protein gp120 on the envelope of HIV. The cells that carry these CD4 receptors include T-helper cells, **monocytes**, **macrophages**, some brain cells and some intestinal cells. CD4–gp120 binding allows a nucleocapsid (nucleic acid + reverse transcriptase) of the virus to enter a cell, where it replicates. This replication, which produces thousands of new viruses, results in the slow destruction of human host cells, with the development of symptoms that result from the loss of normal function in these cell types.

No effective AIDS vaccine is currently available. One promising approach uses **anti-idiotypic antibodies**. These are protein molecules, similar in configuration to CD proteins. Researchers hope that binding between the antibody and HIV would prevent the virus from binding to cells, and therefore slow the rate at which healthy CD4-carrying cells are attacked and destroyed.

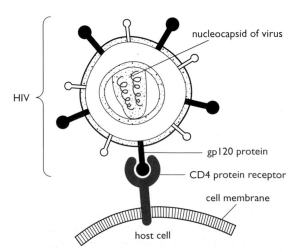

Figure 2.14 CD4-gp120 binding in HIV infection

Micro-organisms – growth & action

Salmonellosis

Salmonellosis, otherwise known as 'food poisoning' or gastroenteritis, is an acute intestinal infection caused by bacteria of the genus *Salmonella*. It is important to realise that there are many different species of *Salmonella*. For example, *S. typhii* causes typhoid fever, a virulent intestinal disease that may cause the small intestine to perforate. In untreated cases, the death rate may be as high as 10 per cent. Uncooked meat, together with unpasteurised milk and cheese made from it, may contain *S. typhinurium*. Chickens and eggs are a source of *S. enteriditis*. It is the disease caused by the last two organisms that is normally called salmonellosis. The symptoms, such as fever, diarrhoea and vomiting, occur after swallowing a very large dose of about 100 million bacteria. These bacteria invade cells lining the small intestine. Typically, recovery takes from 1–3 days, but infants and elderly people may die, following invasion from the intestine into the blood stream. Those who recover continue to shed the organism in their faeces for up to six months.

During the late 1980s there was a particular concern about infections caused by *S. enteriditis*. This bacterium lives in the intestine of chickens and turkeys without causing any obvious ill effects. Intensive methods of poultry farming, in which large numbers of birds are kept together in batteries or deep-litter houses, provided ideal conditions for the bacterium to spread. Furthermore, the practice of processing the heads, legs, feathers and guts of slaughtered chickens, so that they could be added to chicken meal as an additional source of protein, compounded the problem. Inadequate sterilisation often failed to kill off bacteria in slaughtered birds, which meant that some of the food fed to laying birds had been contaminated at source. After slaughter, contamination from the gut and soiled skin frequently transferred infection from one carcass to another. Between 26 and 65% of all carcasses were believed to be infected.

Although thorough cooking destroyed the bacterium making the meat safe to eat, birds that had been deep frozen were often inadequately cooked. When cooking these birds complete pre-thawing is essential, otherwise meat at the centre of the bird may not reach the temperature of 68°C (145°F), which is required to kill off the bacteria.

In 1989 the incidence of salmonellosis reached epidemic proportions. The major source of infection was believed to be eggs, especially uncooked eggs or lightly cooked eggs, used for making marzipan, cake icing, mayonnaise and some alcoholic drinks. Interestingly, the bacterium had spread from the gut of some birds, where it was a fairly harmless parasite, into other tissues, where it became a symbiont. This change in its location, again without any obvious ill effects on the birds, enabled the bacterium to pass directly from parent birds to their chicks via eggs. For the consumer it now means that only hard-boiled eggs, in which all the proteins have been denatured, can be guaranteed free from infection.

Government policy has been to advise consumers about egg consumption, test eggs for *Salmonella*, slaughter infected flocks, and pay compensation to farmers. In the future a solution may lie with a vaccine, a drug or a completely effective method of sterilisation.

E. coli 0157:H7

Recent outbreaks of food poisoning in Scotland and elsewhere in the UK have been caused by a pathogenic foodborne strain of *E. coli* known as 0157:H7. The major source of this infection appears to be raw beef. In humans, this strain of the bacterium causes a disease characterised by blood diarrhoea and sometimes kidney failure, especially in young children and the elderly. The bacterium releases a specific type of **exotoxin** known as an **enterotoxin**, which acts on the small intestine and causes massive secretion of fluid into the intestinal lumen. Among the most effective ways of preventing infection by this organism are ensuring that meat is properly cooked, and that raw meats and cooked meats are not served together at the same counter, or cut with the same knife.

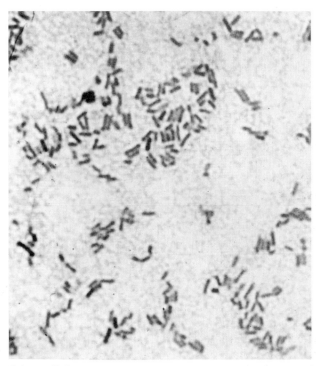

Salmonella bacteria

Tuberculosis

Mycobacterium tuberculosis is the micro-organism that causes tuberculosis, one of the most important infectious diseases of humans, and one that causes many deaths each year worldwide. **Primary infection** occurs when an individual inhales the bacteria via an aerosol, containing contaminated droplets from an individual with an active pulmonary infection. A mild chest infection may result, followed by recovery. Residual bacteria, however, remain in the lungs. In some individuals, but by no means all, these residual bacteria undergo slow growth and become surrounded by clusters of macrophages, called **tubercles**, which are characteristic of the disease. This is called a **postprimary infection**. The enlarging tubercles erode surrounding lung tissue and destroy alveoli. Damaged lung tissue becomes more susceptible to secondary infections such as pneumonia.

A diagnostic test, called the **tuberculin test**, is used to determine whether individuals have been infected by the bacterium. Tuberculin, a protein extracted from *M. tuberculosis*, is injected beneath the skin. The development of a red, hard, raised nodule indicates a positive test. Such individuals may be perfectly healthy, but must at some time have had a previous encounter with the disease.

In the UK, children are normally given anti-TB vaccination from an early age. The antibiotic **streptomycin**, widely used in the 1950s to treat tuberculosis, has been replaced by a drug called **isoniazid**, a nicotinamide that inhibits the formation of cell wall components. Regrettably, the bacterium that causes tuberculosis is rapidly becoming resistant to several forms of chemotherapy. Drug-resistant strains have emerged in parts of London and other large cities, especially among those who sleep rough, are under-nourished, or live in damp, overcrowded conditions.

Tetanus

Tetanus is caused by the bacterium *Clostridium tetani*, an obligate anaerobe. This bacterium is an **opportunist pathogen**. Normally found in soil, it may enter deep wound punctures that become anaerobic, following poor blood supply. Although it rarely spreads from the site of infection, it grows and releases a powerful exotoxin, which enters the blood stream and circulates freely. On reaching the nervous system, this toxin binds to nerve synapses. Here, it prevents the normal relaxation of one set of antagonistic muscles while the other set contracts. Instead, in the presence of tetanus toxin, both sets of antagonistic muscles attempt to contract simultaneously. The result is paralysis, agonising pain and muscle spasm (shaking). Victims die if no treatment is given.

As *C. tetani* is endemic in many soils throughout the UK, and elderly people with poor circulatory systems are particularly susceptible, anti-tetanus vaccination is routinely given to people who have deep skin cuts. Mild infections respond to a number of antibiotics.

Malaria

Malaria is caused by a parasitic protozoan (*Plasmodium*), transmitted from one person to another by an insect carrier, the female anopheline mosquito. Once quite common in low-lying parts of the UK, the disease occurs today in tropical Asia, Africa and in Central and South America. Sufferers experience periodic chills and fever, with vomiting and severe headache. A bite from an infected mosquito injects a form of the parasite called a **sporozoite** into the bloodstream.

Female anopheles mosquito (*Anopheles albimanus*) feeding on human blood

On arrival at the liver the sporozoite enters liver cells and multiplies to form cysts. When a cyst bursts it releases thousands of spherical spores, called **merozoites**, into the bloodstream. Others, however, remain in the liver, forming a reservoir from which they emerge months or even years later to cause a recurrence of the disease. The role of each merozoite is to enter a red blood cell where it grows to form an amoeboid stage called a **trophozoite**.

Rapid growth of the trophozoite is followed by its division into eight, 16 or 32 more merozoites, depending on the species. Release of these merozoites, normally at 1–3 day intervals, is accompanied by an intensification of the symptoms. In addition to the recurrent symptoms, the long-term effects of malaria include anaemia through loss of red blood cells. There may also be degenerative changes in the liver and spleen.

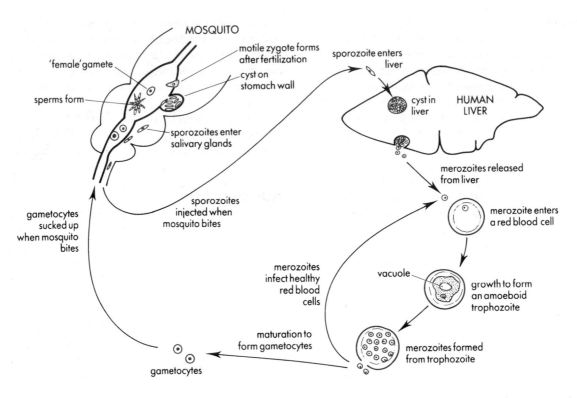

Figure 2.15 The life cycle of the malarial parasite (*Plasmodium*). Three stages (merozoite, trophozoite and gametocyte) are formed in the human host, and two stages are formed in the mosquito (gametes and sporozoites)

The parasite's life cycle continues when a mosquito bites an infected person and sucks up blood containing merozoites that have matured into **gametocytes**. From these, small male and larger female gametes develop as soon as the blood meal reaches the mosquito's stomach. Here, the male gamete divides to form eight **sperms**. Fusion between a sperm and female gamete produces a motile **zygote**, which bores outwards through the stomach wall. On the outside of the stomach the zygote grows into an **oocyst** in which thousands of sporozoites form. When the oocysts burst and the sporozoites pass via the blood into the salivary glands, the life cycle is complete. Note that the mosquito is not merely a passive carrier of the micro-organism; rather, it acts as a primary host. Reproduction of the parasite inside its vector increases the number of individuals that can infect a new host. The mosquito therefore brings about an active or **biological transmission**.

Malaria is one of the commonest of the tropical diseases. Before specific control measures were introduced there were about 250 million cases worldwide, with an annual death rate toll of around 2.5 million.

Interestingly, in some parts of the world where malaria is common, a form of genetic resistance to the disease has evolved. **Sickle cell anaemia** is a single-gene defect, caused by a recessive gene (*a*). Homozygous recessive individuals (*aa*) often die in infancy. Heterozygous individuals (*Aa*) generally survive, although their red blood cells tend to become sickle-shaped, which reduces their oxygen-carrying capacity. As the malarial parasite requires large amounts of oxygen, it cannot live for long in these sickle-shaped red cells. Heterozygous carriers of the sickle cell gene therefore have some innate protection against malaria, a fact that accounts for their prevalence in malaria-ridden regions of the world.

Malaria control is directed either against the malarial parasite in its human host, or against the mosquito that transmits the disease. Drugs such as

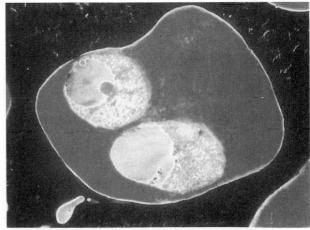

A red blood cell parasitised by two malarial parasites (*Plasmodium falciparum*)

amodiaquine, chloroquine, proguaril, primaquine and pyrimethanine have been used since the late 1950s. In that time some strains of *P. falciparum* have become resistant to chloroquine, a drug that prevents the merozoite stage from replicating by fitting between base pairs in the DNA. More recent drugs include fansidar, maloprim and mefloquine, but again there is some evidence that resistant strains are emerging.

A better long-term solution appears to lie with vaccines. A two-step approach has been adopted. First, antigens on the surface of the parasite's four stages (sporozoite, trophozoite, merozoite and gametocyte) have been identified. Next, the genes that code for these proteins have been used to transform bacteria, so that they secrete the proteins in large amounts. From these specific antigens, against which the human immune system reacts, it is hoped to produce an effective vaccine against the pathogen.

The second line of attack, against the *Anopheles* mosquito, has taken many forms. Wetlands were drained to destroy the insect's breeding grounds. Insecticides, including DDT and pyrethrum, were sprayed on the walls of houses. People slept in mosquito nets at night, to avoid being bitten. *Gambusia affinis*, a fish that feeds on mosquito larvae, was introduced into ponds. Numerous other predators and parasites of mosquito larvae were also used in mosquito-ridden waters. These have included viruses, the bacterium *Bacillus thuringiensis* (p. 132), protozoans, fungi and a nematode worm. Surfactants and oils, sprayed over the water surface, have been used to suffocate the larvae. Chitin inhibitors and juvenile hormones, dissolved in the water, have been utilised in an attempt to prevent the larvae from metamorphosing. Despite this onslaught against the parasite and its vector, malaria remains a widespread and common tropical disease. Containment and control appear to be more realistic aims than eradication.

Candidiasis

Candida albicans is a yeast-like fungus which often lives in a harmless 'commensal' partnership with humans. It occurs chiefly in the mouth, intestines and vagina. Although 20–30 per cent of healthy persons pass the organism in their faeces, it can cause acute or sub-acute infections, known as **candidiasis**, if it enters the bloodstream via broken skin. Infections of the mouth, commonly known as 'oral thrush', are especially common in infants. Mucous membranes lining the tongue, palate and throat become red and raw, spotted with white patches. Similar infections in adults may follow diabetes, leukaemia, alcoholism or friction from badly-fitted false teeth. Vaginal thrush

occurs most commonly in pregnancy and in persons suffering from diabetes, when there is glucose in the urine. Transmission from person to person may occur during intercourse. It is also quite common for *Candida* infections to follow a course of treatment with **antibiotics**. The antibiotic kills off the normal commensal bacteria, allowing *Candida* to take over.

Iodine-based preparations are used to treat infections that have not spread beyond the mucous membranes.

Athlete's foot

Athlete's foot is a **mycosis** of the skin caused by a fungus called *Trichophyton*. The fungus thrives on moist, warm skin, and frequently causes itching, cracking and peeling between the toes. In severe infections, the protective barrier of the skin is broken and fungal growth becomes subcutaneous. Occasionally, the epidermis and dermis of the skin are destroyed, exposing bones of the toes. Superficial infections are treated with Whitfield's ointment, a preparation containing benzoic acid. The antibiotic **griseofulvin**, taken orally, is used to treat severe infections.

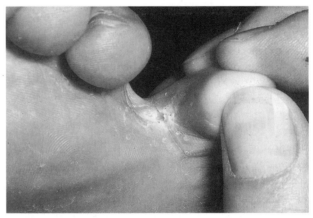

Athlete's foot fungus between the toes

A number of precautionary measures can be taken to prevent the spread of athlete's foot infections, which can be picked up from the damp floors of locker rooms and the wet walkways around swimming pools.

(i) Wear shoes that permit air to circulate. Leather shoes permit better air circulation than plastic ones.
(ii) Wear moisture-absorbing cotton socks. Avoid nylon socks and others that contain man-made fibres.
(iii) Do not share gym shoes or towels.
(iv) After swimming and taking a shower, dry the feet thoroughly, especially between the toes.
(v) Apply a fungus-killing powder, cream or lotion.

Micro-organisms – growth & action

Aseptic techniques

When bacteria and fungi are grown in the laboratory, aseptic techniques must be used in order to prevent **contamination** of pure cultures by other micro-organisms present in the air, on human skin or on the bench surface.

a) To prepare a sterile agar gel

A domestic pressure cooker is required, with a heat source such as a gas ring.

1 Mix the agar powder with water, according to the manufacturer's instructions. Pour the agar/water mixture into screw-topped McCartney bottles (for agar slopes) and/or into 250 cm³ screw-topped medical flats (for agar plates). Do not pour more than 2–5 cm³ agar/water mixture into each McCartney bottle, or more than 200 cm³ mixture into each medical flat. **Loosely replace the screw-tops.**

2 Pour tap water to a depth of about 1 cm into the pressure cooker. Replace the perforated plate, then stand the bottles on it. Replace the lid of the pressure cooker, ensuring that an effective seal is achieved.

Place the pressure cooker, without its weight, on the gas ring. Ensure that the valve, in the lid of the cooker, is open. Apply gentle heat until steam begins to emerge from the valve. Shut the valve by applying the weight. Leave the weight in position for about 20 minutes. During this time pressure within the pressure cooker builds up to more than 100 kNm⁻², raising the temperature of the water above 120°C.

Turn off the gas. Remove the weight after 10–15 minutes. Allow the pressure cooker to cool for a further 2–3 hours. Open the cooker slowly and carefully. Be aware that steam may emerge from the pressure cooker when it is opened. After opening the pressure cooker, tighten the screw-tops of the bottles. Allow the agar to cool and harden (unless it is required for immediate use).

3 Next day, set up a water bath. Slowly increase the temperature of the bath to reach a range of 90–100°C, or until the agar has melted.

Remove the McCartney bottles and place them on the bench surface at an angle of about 45°, using plasticine for support. Once the agar has cooled and hardened, the bottles can be stored at 5–10°C until required.

4 Use molten agar in the medical flats to prepare agar in petri dishes. Carefully pour the molten agar into each dish to a depth of about 0.5 cm. Allow the agar to cool and harden, before removing the dishes for storage at 5–10°C.

b) To sterilise apparatus

A technique known as **flaming** is used to sterilise the instruments, such as needles, wire loops and glass spreaders, which are used to transfer bacteria and fungi from one growth medium to another. Always wear **safety spectacles** when flaming instruments.

1 Set up a small screw-topped bottle, filled with 95% ethanol. Dip the instrument into the ethanol. Replace the screw-top of the bottle (ethanol is flammable).

2 Put on safety spectacles. Holding your hand **above**, and well away from, a gentle Bunsen flame, pass the dipped part of the instrument rapidly through the flame. Wait until the alcohol has burned off.

After waiting for a further 30 seconds, use the flamed instrument to transfer bacteria from one growth medium to another.

3 After use, flame the instrument once more before returning it to the bench surface.

Note the necks of bottles can also be flamed, but this is a more skilled procedure that should be demonstrated and sanctioned by your teacher before it is attempted.

Never place contaminated apparatus onto the surface of the bench and never eat while engaged in a microbiology practical.

c) To obtain bacteria and fungi from the wild

There is always some degree of risk in growing bacteria and fungi from the wild. Many of the colonies obtained will be difficult to identify. Some of the species obtained may cause allergies, others, especially any that are grown from soil, may be human pathogens. If cultivation from the wild is attempted, sources should be limited as follows.

- **Air** – expose agar plates to the air for 5–15 minutes.

- **Soil** – take a very small piece of top-soil, mix it with a drop of distilled water, and spread it over an agar plate with a flamed glass spreader.

- **Pond water** – spread one drop over an agar plate with a flamed glass spreader. Incubate the plate in light to obtain growths of chlorophyll-containing micro-organisms.

- **Leaves** – use green or brown (dead) leaves. Either press the underside of the leaf against the agar plate, or suspend the leaf from the lid of the petri dish using sticky tape, so that bacterial and fungal spores can fall directly on to the agar. Remove suspended leaves before the plates are incubated.

d) To incubate agar plates containing bacteria and fungi

Before incubation, seal each plate with two short strips of sticky tape, one end of each piece stuck to the top and the other to the base of the dish.

This method of sealing maintains aerobic conditions within the dish. If the space between the lid and base of the dish is sealed with a continuous band of sticky tape, anaerobic conditions may develop, and this could encourage the growth of harmful anaerobic micro-organisms.

1 Set up an incubator at 20–25°C.
The incubator should **not** be set up at a temperature of 30–40°C. This might encourage the growth of pathogens, especially in soil samples.

2 Incubate the plates in an **inverted** position.
If the plates are not inverted, moisture from the agar collects on the lid of the plate, forming droplets. These then fall on to the plate, dispersing and diluting the colonies.

3 Incubate the plates for 2–5 days, or until colonies of bacteria and/or fungi have formed.
If pure colonies of bacteria and/or fungi are to be obtained from the mixed cultures, proceed as indicated in the next set of instructions. Alternatively, if cultures are to be examined by a class, seal each dish with a further piece of sticky tape, attached to form a horizontal band securing the lid to the base. This will prevent liquid, containing bacteria and fungi, from spilling out if a petri dish is tipped from a horizontal to a vertical position. Adding this third strip of sticky tape is **very important**, as it prevents very large numbers of micro-organisms from spilling into the laboratory.

e) To obtain pure colonies of bacteria and fungi from a mixed culture

A technique known as the **quadrant streak method** is used as a first step in obtaining pure cultures of bacteria and fungi from mixed cultures.

1 Take a petri dish containing a mixed culture and remove the sticky tape. Place the petri dish on the bench surface. With one hand, gently lift a part of the lid so that a small area of the agar plate is exposed. Do not lift the lid any further than is necessary to insert a wire loop. **Under no circumstances should the lid be removed from the plate.**

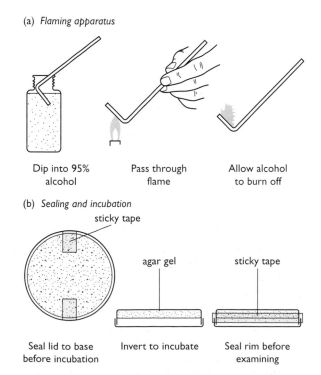

(a) *Flaming apparatus*

Dip into 95% alcohol | Pass through flame | Allow alcohol to burn off

(b) *Sealing and incubation*

sticky tape

agar gel | sticky tape

Seal lid to base before incubation | Invert to incubate | Seal rim before examining

Techniques used when growing bacteria and fungi

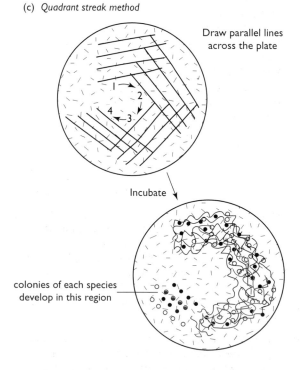

(c) *Quadrant streak method*

Draw parallel lines across the plate

Incubate

colonies of each species develop in this region

Micro-organisms – growth & action

GROWING BACTERIA AND FUNGI *continued*

2 Using a flamed wire loop, take up a small quantity of the desired colony. On a sterile agar plate, draw several short parallel lines with the wire loop on the surface of the agar (see diagram on page 45). Do not puncture the gel (anaerobic micro-organisms may grow if the gel is punctured).

3 Flame the wire loop. Draw a second set of short parallel lines at approximately 100° to the first set (see diagram on page 45).

Repeat the previous procedure on two more occasions, to obtain four sets of parallel lines, filling the plate. Seal, invert and incubate the plate at 20–25°C.

After incubation, pure cultures of bacteria and fungi should be apparent. These may then be isolated and grown.

f) To find the most suitable substrate for growing bacteria and fungi

Saprobiontic bacteria are usually grown on nutrient agar, whereas malt agar or potato-dextrose agar generally proves best for growing saprobiontic fungi.

1 Prepare the following agars according to the manufacturer's instructions: nutrient agar, malt agar and potato-dextrose agar.

In addition, prepare M/10 solutions of glucose, fructose, galactose, sucrose, maltose and lactose. Add bacteriological agar to each of these sugar solutions at the rate of 2 g/100 cm sugar solution.

2 Follow the procedures outlined in investigation a) to prepare sterile agar gels. Pour the molten agar into petri dishes to a uniform depth of 0.5 cm. Allow the agars to cool and harden.

3 Select a bacterium, yeast or mould fungus. Using a flamed wire loop, transfer some of the living micro-organism to a central position on six or more different agar plates. Take care not to break the surface of the gels. Flame the loop. Seal and incubate the plates as specified in investigation d).

4 Compare growth rates by measuring the area (πr^2) covered by the micro-organism in a given time, such as 6, 12 or 24 hours. Extend the investigation to find out how temperature, depth and concentration of the agar, and the addition of nutrients such as vitamins and mineral salts affect the growth rate.

g) Safe disposal of petri dishes containing living bacteria and fungi, and other safety measures

Safe disposal is an essential part of growing bacteria and fungi. **Under no circumstances should untreated petri dishes, containing living cultures, be thrown into the waste paper bin.**

Plastic petri dishes should be **incinerated** or **autoclaved**. The incinerator should have a hot flame (400–600°C), with a vent for waste gases that disperses fumes at chimney height. Autoclaving should be carried out in a pressure cooker. Before dishes are autoclaved, they should be placed into an autoclavable bag. The mouth of the bag should be tied loosely with string, sufficient to retain the dishes, but without impeding the escape of steam. A full sterilising procedure should be carried out, heating to 120°C, under pressure. After the pressure cooker has cooled, the autoclavable bag should be tied tightly and can then be treated as rubbish.

Household bleach, one of the most powerful antiseptics against micro-organisms, can be used to cover spillages or to kill colonies. Bench tops should be washed with a dilute solution of bleach before **and after** any practical work with bacteria and fungi.

Petri dishes containing living micro-organisms should not be stored in refrigerators that are also used to store food. Do not consume any edible products made in the laboratory.

Open wounds on the hands should be covered with plasters before working with micro-organisms. Plastic medical gloves can be worn to give further protection.

Micro-organisms – growth & action

QUESTIONS

6 Write simple word equations to represent each of the following processes.

a) nitrogen fixation, b) nitrification, c) denitrification and d) ammonification.

7 By what stages does a legume, with *Rhizobium* bacteria in its root nodules, convert atmospheric nitrogen into proteins?

8 The relationship between legumes and *Rhizobium* bacteria is a symbiotic (mutualistic) one.

What advantage is gained by a) the legume and b) the bacterium?

9 To which group of organisms do each of the following belong?

a) HIV, b) *Salmonella*, c) *Plasmodium*, d) *Candida* and e) *Trichophyton*.

10 List, in sequence, those stages in the life history of *Plasmodium* that occur in a) humans and b) the anopheline mosquito.

CHAPTER 2 SUMMARY

Biotechnology is the exploitation of organisms in ways that benefit the human situation. As they grow, micro-organisms synthesise an enormous number of complex molecules, modify the structure of others and break down harmful waste products. Biotechnologists aim to take full advantage of these aspects of microbial physiology and metabolism to produce useful products (e.g. antibiotics) and provide services, such as waste disposal.

The metabolic activities of micro-organisms – their nutrition, respiration, growth etc. – have been outlined in this chapter. Methods have been described for growing bacteria and fungi and for measuring their growth rates.

The importance of micro-organisms in terrestrial and aquatic environments is illustrated by the nitrogen cycle. Those micro-organisms that fix atmospheric nitrogen as ammonia begin a process that leads to the synthesis of N-containing compounds, such as amino acids, proteins and nucleic acids in other organisms.

Some micro-organisms, such as nitrogen-fixing bacteria, are beneficial to humans. Others, such as denitrifying bacteria and human pathogens, are harmful. From an intimate knowledge of the life histories of these pathogens, and of their metabolism, biotechnologists hope to develop effective remedies for infectious human diseases.

CHAPTER 2 QUESTIONS

1 Using dry yeast, you prepare 100 cm³ of a 10%$^{w/v}$ suspension of yeast cells.

  a) What volume of water would you add to produce a 0.5%$^{w/v}$ suspension? Show your working.

  b) A circular fungal colony, measuring 1.2 cm in diameter, increases to 1.8 cm diameter after 24 hours.

    (i)   What was the initial area covered by the fungus?

    (ii) What was the final area covered by the fungus?

    (iii) Calculate the percentage increase in area. Show all your working. (Area of circle = πr^2)

2 AIDS is caused by a virus which severely damages the human immune system.

  a) What is the full name of the disease for which AIDS is an abbreviation?

  b) Name the virus that causes AIDS.

  c) List all the routes by which the disease may be transmitted from one person to another.

  d) By the end of 1986 the disease affected mostly men in America, but both men and women in Africa. How would you account for this?

  e) Outline the principal ways in which AIDS affects the human immune system.

  f) What secondary diseases are commonly seen in AIDS sufferers whose immune systems have been severely damaged?

  g) Explain the problem biologists have experienced in attempting to find a vaccine against the AIDS virus.

  h) Until a cure can be found, what preventative measures should be adopted to reduce the spread of the disease?

3 The diagram below shows some stages in the nitrogen cycle.

$$N_2 \longleftarrow N_2O$$
$$\text{Proteins} \longrightarrow NH_3 \longrightarrow NO_2^- \longrightarrow NO_3^-$$

(with labels A, B, C, D)

  a) Name the processes **A–D**.

  b) Which of these processes are carried out by bacteria?

  c) In what forms does nitrogen occur in legumes?

  d) What are the special features of legumes that enable them to carry out process **A**?

4 A population of cells, growing in a liquid medium in which nutrients are limited produces a characteristic growth curve.

  a) Draw a diagram to show principal phases in this growth curve, and briefly explain what is happening to the cells in each phase.

  b) What is a logarithmic scale?

  c) Explain the advantages of plotting changes in cell density on a logarithmic scale.

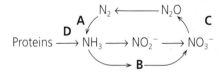

Micro-organisms – growth & action

5 Give a full account of two different methods you could use to measure changes in cell density in a population of bacterial or yeast cells, growing in a liquid, nutrient-limited medium.
Which method produces the most accurate data? Give one or more reasons in support of your view.

6 How do bacteria differ with regard to their

a) nutrition,

b) respiration?

Explain how the various differences you describe have been exploited by biotechnologists.

7 What is a pathogen?
Write a full account of one human pathogen that is a virus, bacterium or fungus. What precautions should be taken to prevent the pathogen you have described from spreading?

8 Describe the life cycle of the malarial parasite (*Plasmodium*).
How does an intimate knowledge of the life cycle of this parasite enable biologists to take effective measures against (i) the parasite and (ii) its insect vector?

BIBLIOGRAPHY

Micro-organisms – growth & action

Brock, TD (1979) *Biology of Microorganisms* 3rd Edn Prentice/Hall International, New Jersey

Dunkerton, J (1989) *Biotechnology – a Resource Book for Teachers* Association for Science Education, Hatfield

Garbutt, JW and Bartlett, AJ (1972) *Experimental Biology with Microorganisms* Butterworths, London

Grace, ES (1997) *Biotechnology Unzipped* Joseph Henry Press, Washington DC

Jennings, DH and Lee, DL eds (1975) *Symbiosis* Cambridge University Press

Postgate, JR (1978) *Nitrogen Fixation* (Studies in Biology No. 92) Edward Arnold

Williams, J and Shaw, M (1976) *Micro-organisms* Mills and Boon

Winstanley, M (1995) *Microbial Friends and Allies* Biotechnology and Biological Sciences Review Council

Micro-organisms – growth & action

CHAPTER 3

Gene expression & manipulation

Humans share the earth with some 3–4 million other kinds of living organisms. All, from the smallest micro-organism to the blue whale, are alike in that the information determining their characteristics is encoded in long molecules of nucleic acids, either **deoxyribonucleic acid (DNA)** or **ribonucleic acid (RNA)**. Most organisms use DNA as their information-carrying genetic material, but certain viruses, such as the mumps virus, use RNA. Along the length of these nucleic acids are short active segments called **genes**. Most genes act as a code for the proteins in the body of an organism. The proteins are assembled from amino acids that are linked into chains, forming protein subunits called polypeptides. As Figure 3.1 shows, each and every protein, regardless of its function, is a direct representation of a particular gene. Furthermore, the protein synthesising machinery in all cells is capable of interpreting a gene in terms of the protein for which it is the code.

3.1 Genes in Eukaryotes

DNA is a molecule that contains all the information that a cell needs to synthesise polypeptides from amino acids. Stretched out, a DNA molecule resembles a long, spiral ladder. The two side pieces, or strands, are made from a chain of nucleotides (sugar + base + phosphate), joined end to end. Rungs across the ladder are formed by pairs of nucleotide bases. There are four types of base: adenine (A), guanine (G), cytosine (C) and thymine (T). You will see from Figure 3.2 that adenine always pairs with thymine (A-T) and guanine with cytosine (G-C). The two strands run antiparallel to one another, and are twisted to give the complete molecule the form of a double helix. The variable part of a DNA molecule, which is the biological

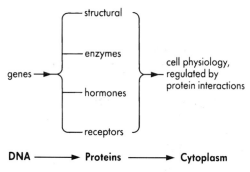

Figure 3.1 The relationship between genes, proteins and cell physiology

basis of the diversity of living things, is the linear sequence of bases along the molecule. This linear sequence differs quite markedly between species, and to a smaller extent between individuals of a species.

Structural genes

A **structural gene** is a length of DNA, anything from 450 to tens of thousands of bases in length, that acts as a code for one polypeptide. The relationship between structural genes and the traits that they determine, may be summarised in the following way.

Structural DNA
↓   **Transcription**
Messenger RNA
↓   **Translation**
Polypeptide
↓
Proteins (e.g. enzymes, hormones)
↓
Metabolic products
↓
Traits

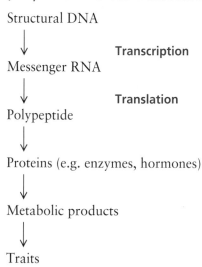

Both strands of a DNA molecule may contain structural genes. These genes are read in one direction in one strand and in the opposite direction in the other. The direction in which a strand is read is determined by the shape of the deoxyribose molecules that form part of the DNA molecule.

Deoxyribose is a five-carbon (pentose) sugar. Biochemists have numbered its five carbon atoms from 1–5 in a clockwise direction (see Figure 3.3a). As Figure 3.3b shows, the arrangement of the deoxyribose molecules gives opposite polarity to each strand of the double helix, with the 5' end of one strand opposite the 3' end of the other strand. The structural genes in each strand are always read in the **5'–3' direction**. Nucleotides or base sequences nearer the 5' end than the 3' end are said to be **upstream**.

(a) *Component nucleotides*

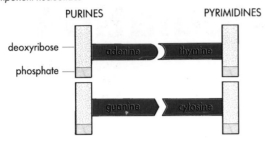

(b) *Double helix*

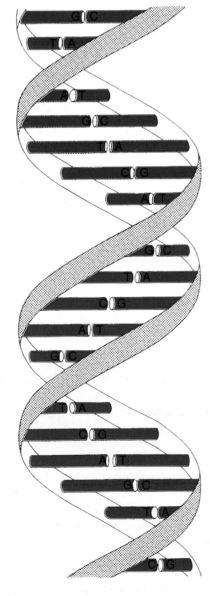

Figure 3.2 The structure of DNA

(a) *Diagram of a deoxyribose molecule, showing the position of the 5' and 3' carbon atoms*

(b) *Polarity of the double helix*

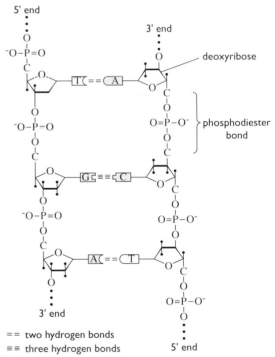

== two hydrogen bonds
≡ three hydrogen bonds

(c) *Direction in which the DNA molecule is read*

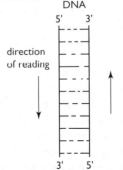

Figure 3.3 The 5' and 3' ends of a DNA molecule

Transcription

Transcription is a process whereby one strand of a DNA molecule directs the synthesis of a type of RNA called **messenger RNA** (abbreviated to **mRNA**). This process is catalysed by the enzyme **RNA polymerase**. Messenger RNA is a single-stranded molecule, of the same length as the structural gene on which it forms, in which the base **uracil** (U) substitutes for thymine (T). The base pairing rules between DNA and mRNA are:

DNA   mRNA
A = U
T = A
G ≡ C
C ≡ G

Figure 3.4a shows how an mRNA molecule forms on a so-called **sense strand**, or **template strand**, of DNA, after it has uncoiled from the double helix.

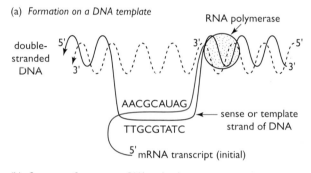

(a) *Formation on a DNA template*

RNA polymerase

double-stranded DNA

AACGCAUAG
TTGCGTATC
← sense or template strand of DNA
mRNA transcript (initial)

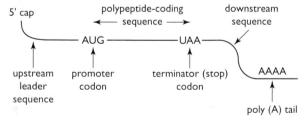

(b) *Structure of a mature mRNA molecule*

5' cap

polypeptide-coding sequence

downstream sequence

AUG — UAA

AAAA

upstream leader sequence

promoter codon

terminator (stop) codon

poly (A) tail

Figure 3.4 Messenger RNA

The structure of a mature mRNA molecule is shown in Figure 3.4b. This molecule carries the genetic code from the nucleus of a cell into its cytoplasm. The genetic code consists of triplets of bases, such as CGA, ATC, TCC etc. Each triplet, called a **codon**, codes for one amino acid. All of the known codons, read in a 5'–3' direction on mRNA, are shown in Table 3.1, together with the amino acids for which they code. Some of the amino acids are specified by more than one codon. As a result of this, the code is described as **degenerate**, which means that some of the codons, and their products, are synonymous. In addition to codons, the genetic code also contains **stop signals** that terminate a polypeptide sequence, and genes that code for two other types of RNA:

Table 3.1 The genetic code

Codon [5' → 3']	Amino acid	Codon [5' → 3']	Amino acid
UUU	Phe	AUU	Ile
UUC	Phe	AUC	Ile
UUA	Leu	AUA	Ile
UUG	Leu	AUG	Met
UCU	Ser	ACU	Thr
UCC	Ser	ACC	Thr
UCA	Ser	ACA	Thr
UCG	Ser	ACG	Thr
UAU	Tyr	AAU	Asn
UAC	Tyr	AAC	Asn
UAA	Stop	AAA	Lys
UAG	Stop	AAG	Lys
UGU	Cys	AGU	Ser
UGC	Cys	AGC	Ser
UGA	Stop	AGA	Arg
UGG	Trp	AGG	Arg
CUU	Leu	GUU	Val
CUC	Leu	GUC	Val
CUA	Leu	GUA	Val
CUG	Leu	GUG	Val
CCU	Pro	GCU	Ala
CCC	Pro	GCC	Ala
CCA	Pro	GCA	Ala
CCG	Pro	GCG	Ala
CAU	His	GAU	Asp
CAC	His	GAC	Asp
CAA	Gln	GAA	Glu
CAG	Gln	GAG	Glu
CGU	Arg	GGU	Gly
CGC	Arg	GGC	Gly
CGA	Arg	GGA	Gly
CGG	Arg	GGG	Gly

(i) **transfer RNA (tRNA)**, which carries amino acids to the ribosomes for protein synthesis;
(ii) **ribosomal RNA (rRNA)**, a constituent of ribosomes, the sites of protein synthesis.

In most eukaryotic genes, including those from humans, there are stretches of non-coding DNA that alternate with coding sequences. These non-coding regions are called **introns**. Functional regions, that actually encode an amino acid sequence, are called **exons**. During transcription, the first mRNA transcript contains introns and exons. The second transcript, however, is much shorter. Introns are removed by nuclear enzymes and degraded, while all the exons are retained and spliced (joined) together.

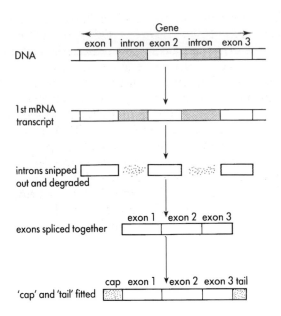

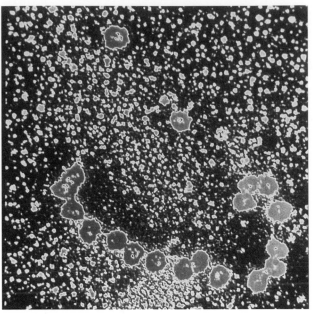

Figure 3.5 Stages in the processing of eukaryotic mRNA

Ribosomes and polyribosomes in the cytoplasm of a cell

The mature mRNA molecule consists of these joined exons, together with a cap and tail.

Translation

Soon after its formation the mRNA molecule leaves the nucleus and enters the cyotplasm. Here it attracts **ribosomes** and tRNA molecules, while serving as a template for joining togcther a particular sequence of amino acids. In a process called **translation** each ribosome attaches to one end of the mRNA molecule, then moves along its length, from one end to the other. As it travels, a chain of amino acids

builds up. This chain, a polypeptide, is released into the cytoplasm when the ribosome has completed its run. Amino acids are brought to the ribosome by molecules of tRNA. There are several different types of tRNA, each carrying a different amino acid. Each type of tRNA has a triplet of bases, called an **anticodon**, which finds and joins up with its complementary codon on the mRNA strand. As a result, amino acids are placed in an appropriate position in the polypeptide chain, and held in position by peptide bonds. After delivering its amino acid, each tRNA molecule moves away to make

(a) *Each ribosome moves along an mRNA molecule to form a polypeptide. Ribosomes may return to make further runs, depending on the needs of the cell*

(b) *Each triplet of bases (codon) on mRNA codes for one amino acid; anticodons on tRNA molecules are complementary*

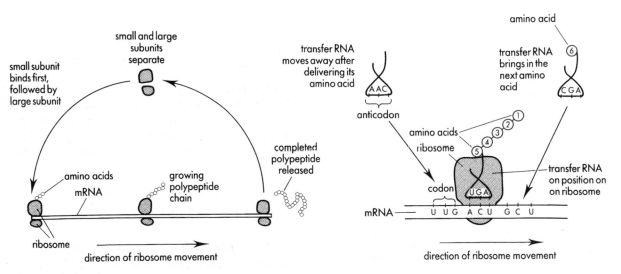

Figure 3.6 Translation

room for the next. The process is repeated from one end of the mRNA molecule to the other until a polypeptide has been synthesised.

Signal sequences in eukaryotes and prokaryotes

The genes of eukaryotes are surrounded by a collection of **signal sequences** that are recognised by the cell. At the 'upstream' end of a gene is the **promoter,** a short sequence of nucleotides, to which RNA polymerase binds at the beginning of transcription. Slightly downstream of the promoter is another short nucleotide sequence, the **ribosome binding site,** where binding to a ribosome takes place. At the opposite end of a gene is the **terminator** (or stop codon), marking the end of the gene, where transcription stops.

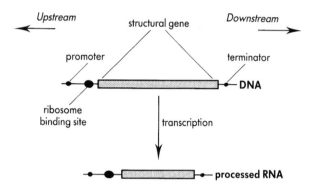

Figure 3.7 Some of the signal sequences associated with a structural gene

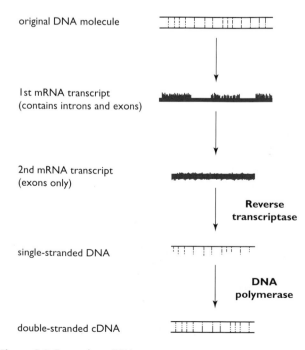

Figure 3.8 Preparing cDNA

The nature of transcription in eukaryotes presents difficulties for genetic engineers. Eukaryotic DNA cannot be expressed successfully in bacteria, because bacteria do not possess the enzymes for removing the introns. Instead, genetic engineers use mature mRNA as their starting point. An enzyme called **reverse transcriptase**, obtained from retroviruses, is used to produce single-stranded DNA from mRNA. In a second step, **DNA polymerase** is used to prepare double-stranded DNA from the single-stranded molecule. After removing mRNA with alkali, a double-stranded molecule of **complementary DNA,** or **cDNA,** is produced. It is this molecule which is transferred into a bacterial plasmid.

QUESTIONS

1 What do you understand by each of the following terms?

Exon, intron, codon, cistron, operon.

2 Which of the following statements is the most accurate?

Each gene codes for one a) enzyme, b) protein, c) polypeptide, d) nucleotide, e) base.

3 Which of the following bases occur in both DNA and RNA?

a) guanine, b) cytosine, c) adenine, d) thymine, e) uracil.

4 a) Write the complementary DNA base sequence for the following single DNA strand.

5' ATTGGCAGCAG 3'

b) What would be the base sequence on an mRNA strand formed on this DNA template?

5 Name three different types of RNA.

3.2 Genes in Prokaryotes

Bacteria have a single circular chromosome. It has been estimated that this chromosome contains about 5×10^6 base pairs, has a total length of around 1 mm, and contains several thousand genes. The relationship of DNA to bacterial proteins can be represented as follows:

$$\text{DNA} \xrightarrow{\text{transcription}} \text{mRNA} \xrightarrow{\text{translation}} \text{PROTEINS (POLYPEPTIDES)}$$

When researchers began to map the distribution of bacterial genes, they were surprised to find that genes with related functions were clustered together.

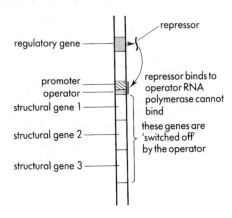
(a) *When lactose is absent*

regulatory gene

repressor

promoter
operator
structural gene 1

repressor binds to
operator RNA
polymerase cannot
bind

structural gene 2

these genes are
'switched off'
by the operator

structural gene 3

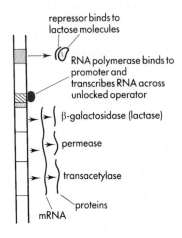
(b) *When lactose is present*

repressor binds to
lactose molecules

RNA polymerase binds to
promoter and
transcribes RNA across
unlocked operator

β-galactosidase (lactase)

permease

transacetylase

proteins

mRNA

Figure 3.9 Gene regulation in the *lac*-operon of *E. coli*

These clusters, now known as **operons**, regulate the rate at which certain structural genes produce proteins. For instance, the bacterium *E. coli*, an inhabitant of the human intestine, can produce lactase, an enzyme that splits lactose in milk into the monosaccharides glucose and galactose. Its access to lactose, however, depends on the amount of milk that its host drinks. Clearly, it would be wasteful for a small organism such as a bacterium to secrete lactase when it was not needed. The problem is

overcome by **regulatory genes**, acting together with signal sequences to 'switch on' or 'switch off' the structural genes for lactase production.

The **lac operon**, illustrated in Figure 3.9, has three structural genes, a **regulator** gene and two signal sequences, the promoter and **operator**. If there is no lactose in the bacterium's environment, the regulator gene produces a protein, the **repressor**, that binds to the operator site. When bound, this protein covers the operator and overlaps the promoter. Neither the

Gene expression & manipulation

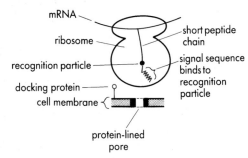
(a) *A ribosome approaches a docking protein in the cell membrane*

mRNA

ribosome

recognition particle

docking protein

cell membrane

short peptide chain

signal sequence binds to recognition particle

protein-lined pore

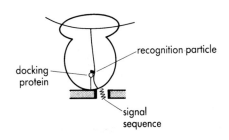
(b) *A recognition particle binds to the docking protein; the signal sequence binds to the membrane*

recognition particle

docking protein

signal sequence

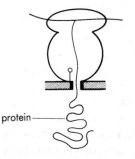
(c) *Cell enzymes digest the signal sequence. Removal of the signal sequence allows protein synthesis*

protein

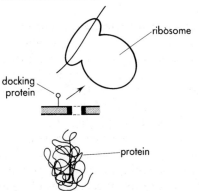
(d) *Release of the protein. The membrane repairs while the ribosomes moves off*

ribosome

docking protein

protein

Figure 3.10 Stages in the secretion of an extracellular protein by a bacterium

operator nor promoter can function when blocked by the repressor. Under these conditions little, if any, lactase is produced. When lactose is present in excess the repressor binds to lactose molecules, thus exposing the promoter and operator sites. The enzyme RNA polymerase can then pass over the unlocked operator site and transcribe the three structural genes. In fact, it does this by transcribing a single mRNA molecule encoding the information for all three genes, which is subsequently translated into three separate proteins.

Unlike the structural genes of eukaryotes, bacterial genes do not have exons and introns. Instead, they produce mRNA transcripts that go into action as soon as they are produced, without the need for secondary processing (see Figure 3.5). Furthermore, although bacterial genes are associated with signal sequences, these are different from those found in eukaryotes. All this means that if a eukaryotic gene, along with its signal sequences, is transferred to a prokaryote, no eukaryotic proteins will normally be produced. Firstly, the bacterium does not possess the cellular machinery required to remove the introns and splice the exons. Secondly, it cannot bind or read the eukaryotic signal sequences. These are problems that have to be overcome before prokaryotes can function as recipients of human, or other eukaryotic genes. Bacteria do, however, possess one important feature that relatively few eukaryotic cells possess, namely the ability to secrete proteins into their external medium. Figure 3.10 shows possible stages in a process that is still not well understood. The ability of any cell to secrete proteins into its surroundings greatly simplifies the process of harvesting gene products, which can be collected from the external medium without killing off the cells that produced them.

3.3 Genetic Engineering

All cellular organisms contain the two nucleic acids DNA and RNA, which together make up their genetic material. Any deliberate manipulation of this material, that changes the natural sequence of nucleotides in nucleic acids, is called **genetic engineering**, **gene manipulation** or **recombinant DNA technology**. More specifically, the technique may involve the addition, modification or deletion of one or more genes in a cell. To date, most genetic engineering has consisted of putting one or more extra genes into cells, so that they acquire an additional property, such as the ability to make a new protein. A successful gene transfer, from a donor organism to a recipient cell, takes place in four main steps, as follows:

(i) removal of DNA from the donor organism, and its fragmentation to extract a particular gene or genes. Alternatively, the enzyme reverse transcriptase may be used to make DNA copies of mRNA molecules.

(ii) incorporation of the desired gene into a **vector**, such as a bacteriophage or plasmid, which carries it into the recipient cell.

(iii) incorporation of the new gene into the recipient cell's **genome**. (Cells of the bacterium *E. coli* and yeast (*S. cerevisiae*) are widely used as recipients by biotechnologists.)

(iv) asexual reproduction of the recipient cells that have been transformed by incorporating the foreign gene. This important stage is called cloning. A **clone** is an exact copy of a bacterial cell, eukaryotic cell or gene.

3.3.1 Extraction and Preparation of Genes

Cells containing the desired gene may be identified by testing for the protein that the gene makes. Any cell making this protein must have the desired gene clone. To extract the desired gene, cells may be broken down by either of two methods:

(i) disruption by ultrasound;
(ii) digestion in a solution of lysozyme, an enzyme that breaks down cell walls.

Disrupted cells are centrifuged to remove insoluble debris. Phenol is added to remove proteins. The slow addition of an ethanolic solution of sodium acetate precipitates strands of nucleic acid at the water–ethanol interface. These strands may be removed by winding them onto a sterile glass rod by slow rotation. After extraction, the DNA is dissolved in dilute saline-citrate solution and purified by reprecipitation with ethanol. At the end of this process the operator obtains purified, crude DNA, probably containing numerous copies of each gene.

Gene selection begins when purified DNA is cut into shorter segments by adding enzymes called **restriction endonucleases**. Around 500 of these enzymes, extracted from bacteria, have been identified and made available to genetic engineers. Each one cuts DNA at specific recognition sites, consisting of anything from 4–10 paired nucleotide sequences. Cuts are either vertical, known as **blunt ends**, or staggered, known as **sticky ends**. The generation of sticky ends is particularly useful because fragments with complementary sticky ends readily join together to form larger molecules.

The material that results from DNA fragmentation may contain the whole genome of an organism, or **genomic library**. From this library a genetic engineer can select a desired gene.

Gene expression & manipulation

Table 3.2 Restriction endonucleases. Each enzyme is named according to the bacterium from which it has been isolated (e.g. *Eco R1* is from *E. coli*)

Enzyme	Recognition sequence		Type of cut
Alu 1	A T C G T A T A G C A T		Blunt
Hha 1	A T C G C A T A G C G T		Sticky
Eco R1	C A A T T T C G T T A A A G		Sticky
Bam H1	C G A T C G G C T A G C		Sticky

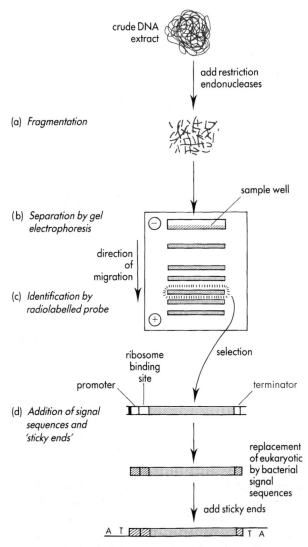

Figure 3.11 Stages in the preparation of a eukaryotic gene for cloning in a bacterium

(a) *Fragmentation*

(b) *Separation by gel electrophoresis*

(c) *Identification by radiolabelled probe*

(d) *Addition of signal sequences and 'sticky ends'*

Figure 3.11 shows the method most commonly used. Firstly, **gel electrophoresis** is used to separate the various DNA fragments, all of different lengths, into horizontal bands, each band containing fragments of approximately the same length. (Since small fragments travel through the gel faster than large ones, the fragments separate according to their length.)

Next, radioactively-labelled single-stranded DNA is added, with at least some of its base sequence complementary to the base sequence of the desired gene. Binding occurs between the radiolabelled DNA, called a **DNA probe**, and a part of the desired gene. From this binding the position of the desired gene can be located on the gel. DNA from this region is removed. After its signal sequences have been replaced by those of the cell into which it is to be inserted, sticky ends are attached, so that it can be carried by a vector.

An alternative approach to preparing genes for incorporation into a vector consists of synthesising the desired gene from its template mRNA. The enzyme **reverse transcriptase** catalyses the production of DNA from mRNA.

$$\text{mRNA} \xrightarrow{\text{reverse transcriptase}} \text{cDNA}$$

Many copies of complementary or copy DNA (cDNA) may result from this reaction.

3.3.2 Vectors

Some species of bacteria are able to take up DNA molecules from the medium in which they grow. Molecules of DNA taken up in this way are mostly degraded, but some may survive and become incorporated into the bacterium's genome. A more reliable method of achieving uptake and incorporation of foreign DNA depends on the use of cloning vectors. Thousands of different vectors, mostly bacteriophages and **bacterial plasmids**, can be used for DNA transfer. The choice, however, depends mainly on the nature of the recipient cell into which the DNA is to be transferred. Bacteria are widely used as recipient cells because there are several bacteriophages, such as λ and M 13, and a large number of bacterial plasmids, that can be used as vectors for foreign DNA. The essential requirement for a cloning vector is that it has a means of replication in its host cell. Another consideration is the amount of space available in a vector for additional (foreign) DNA. In some bacteriophages this space is very limited, especially in M 13, where the ten viral genes are tightly packed within the capsid. Nevertheless, this bacteriophage is popular with genetic engineers, because genes cloned with this vector can be obtained in the form of single-stranded DNA.

Bacteriophages, when used as gene vectors, require elaborate preparation. After removing their DNA from its surrounding capsid, cutting it, and inserting foreign DNA, the hybrid DNA must be returned to the capsid. λ Bacteriophage infection, for

(a) λ *Bacteriophage*

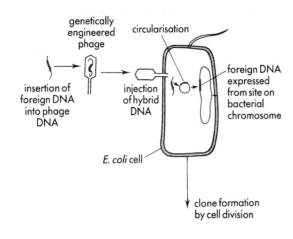

(b) *M13 Bacteriophage*

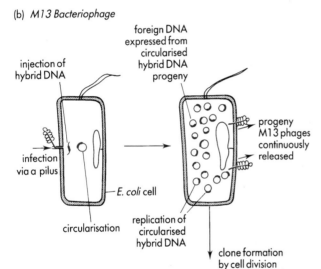

Figure 3.12 Bacteriophage gene vector

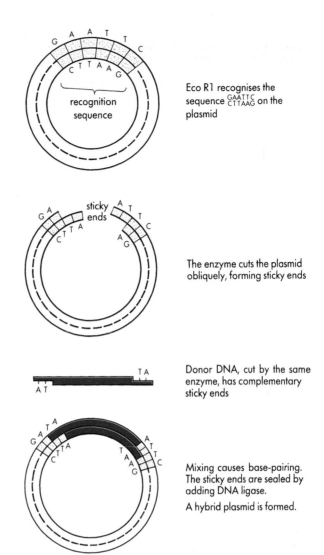

Eco R1 recognises the sequence $\begin{smallmatrix}GAATTC\\CTTAAG\end{smallmatrix}$ on the plasmid

The enzyme cuts the plasmid obliquely, forming sticky ends

Donor DNA, cut by the same enzyme, has complementary sticky ends

Mixing causes base-pairing. The sticky ends are sealed by adding DNA ligase.
A hybrid plasmid is formed.

Figure 3.13 Using *Eco R1* to splice donor DNA into a plasmid

example, is characterised by retention of the phage DNA molecule in the host bacterium, possibly for many thousands of cell divisions. The DNA of this phage, after circularising, becomes integrated into the bacterial chromosome, where it remains quiescent for many generations. Eventually, however, it becomes active again, producing viral progeny. M 13 bacteriophage attaches to a pilus of *E. coli* and injects its DNA. This DNA circularises and replicates in the cytoplasm of its hosts. It does not integrate with the bacterial chromosome. New phage particles are continuously assembled and released by the cell.

Plasmids are small self-replicating double-stranded circles of DNA, found in many bacteria. They carry genes that a bacterium needs only under special circumstances, such as those for antibiotic resistance, or resistance to heavy metals. The bacterium *E. coli* is the main source of plasmids used for transferring genes into bacteria. Plasmids may be categorised in several different ways, notably as **conjugative** or **non-conjugative**, depending on whether or not they carry a set of transfer genes, called *tra*-genes, that promote bacterial conjugation. A second grouping, based on other types of genes carried by plasmids, is given in Table 3.3. Thirdly, plasmids that are maintained as a limited number of copies per cell are called **stringent plasmids**, whereas those that replicate freely are called **relaxed plasmids**. Genetic engineers cut plasmids with the same restriction endonucleases used to cut the donor DNA. This results in the formation of sticky ends on the plasmids that are the same as the sticky ends on the DNA segments. When mixed together the DNA segments tend to base-pair with the sticky ends of the plasmids. They are sealed together by adding **DNA ligase**. This results in the production of a hybrid plasmid, carrying a segment of foreign DNA. It should be noted that the foreign gene usually

Table 3.3 The five principal types of plasmid

Plasmid type	Genetic characteristics
R (resistance)	carry genes for resistance to one or more antibiotics and some heavy metals (e.g. mercury)
F (fertility)	carry *tra*-genes, which promote the formation of a conjugation tube, through which plasmids are transferred to other bacteria
Degradative	carry genes for the degradation of uncommon toxin such as naphthalene, toluene, salicylic acid etc.
Col	carry genes which code for colicins, proteins which kill other bacteria
Virulence	carry genes which transform the host bacterium into a virulent form

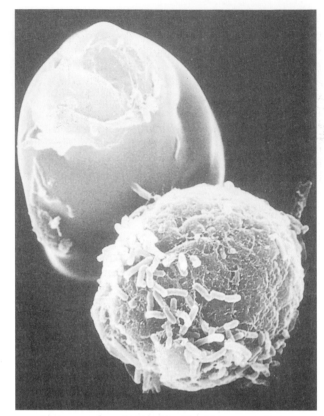

Agrobacterium tumefaciens (small bacilli) on tobacco cells

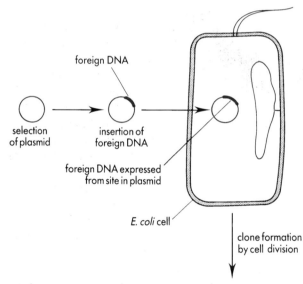

Figure 3.14 Plasmid gene vectors

Crown gall (*Agrobacterium tumefaciens*) growing on a rose bush

requires both a promoter – to indicate the start of mRNA synthesis – and a terminator – to mark the end of transcription – before it will function. Once inside a bacterium, however, the plasmid becomes a functional part of the bacterium's genome. The foreign gene is expressed from its position on the plasmid, without being incorporated into the bacterial chromosome.

As many species of bacteria, including *E. coli*, will not readily take up plasmids, genetic engineers have devised treatments that improve the success rate. By soaking bacterial cells in an ice cold solution of calcium chloride ($CaCl_2$), plasmids can be made to stick to the cell walls. Their ingestion into the cytoplasm is achieved by raising the temperature to 42°C. Neither effect is fully understood.

Another vector of major importance in genetic engineering is the bacterium *Agrobacterium tumefaciens*, used to introduce foreign DNA into plant cells. This bacterium is a soil micro-organism, the cause of crown gall disease in many dicotyledonous species. Infected tissues swell to form tumour-like growths. The ability of the bacterium to cause this condition is associated with the presence of **Ti (tumour inducing) plasmids** within the bacterial cell. It is this plasmid that has been used as a gene vector to introduce foreign DNA into plant cells.

Other cloning vectors for higher plants include the cauliflower mosaic virus (CaMV), and other small plant viruses, like caulimoviruses and also geminiviruses, a recently discovered group. Simian virus 40 (SV40) and bovine papilloma virus (BPV) have been used to introduce foreign DNA into mammalian cells. BPV is of particular interest because it acts as a **shuttle vector**, with the ability to replicate its plasmids in both bacterial and mammalian cells. It can also be used to introduce quite large pieces of DNA into mammalian cells.

A closer look at plasmids

Plasmids normally exist as double-stranded DNA molecules. Figure 3.15 shows the gene map of plasmid pBR322, a type that has been widely used for gene cloning. The plasmid carries two genes for **antibiotic resistance**, one for ampicillin resistance and the other for tetracycline resistance. Other genes are carried in other parts of the plasmid. Arrows in the diagram indicate that the genes in the two DNA strands are read in opposite directions, from 5' to 3' in each strand. The outer DNA strand also carries a number of **binding sites** for restriction endonucleases. After binding, these enzymes cut through both strands, producing short DNA segments with blunt or sticky ends. From a knowledge of plasmid gene maps, which show the position of both genes and endonuclease binding sites, a genetic engineer can select the most suitable restriction endonucleases for cutting the plasmid. If, for example, the desired gene were located in the region between the two antibiotic resistance genes, a genetic engineer would use enzymes that cut on each side of this region. The most suitable would probably be enzymes *Cla* 1 and *Pst* 1.

Restriction endonuclease *Bam* 1 could be used to cut the gene for tetracycline resistance, allowing the insertion of a foreign gene into that region. Once inserted, the foreign gene would prevent the tetracycline resistance gene from exerting its effect; that is, any bacterium that carried it would lose its resistance to tetracycline.

Another widely used plasmid is the Ti (tumour inducing) plasmid of *Agrobacterium tumefaciens*. This plasmid carries quite a large number of genes, each controlling one or more aspects of tumour formation in those plants that develop crown gall disease: **oncogenes** encode compounds that initiate tumour formation; **opine genes** encode amino acid-like compounds, on which the bacterium feeds; while **virulence genes** control the severity of the disease in plants that are attacked. It is the ability of the Ti plasmid to enter living plant cells and introduce foreign DNA into their genome, that makes it an important tool in recombinant DNA technology.

3.3.3 Recipients for foreign DNA

The bacterium *E. coli* and the yeast *S. cerevisiae* are widely used as recipients for foreign DNA. These unicellular, quick-growing micro-organisms are ideal for the large-scale production of bulk proteins, such as industrial enzymes, for which the economics of production are critical. Extensive studies of *E. coli* have provided a lot of information about this organism. For instance, it has several bacteriophages, and different types of plasmid, that can be used to introduce foreign DNA. Furthermore, foreign DNA introduced via a plasmid can account for up to 60 per cent of its total protein production. This bacterium, on the other hand, occurs naturally in the intestines of humans and, under certain circumstances, can cause disease.

Yeast is rarely a human pathogen. Although it is a unicellular organism, it is also a eukaryotic cell, in which the genes are organised, expressed and controlled in ways that are similar to human genes. Another advantage of yeast over *E. coli* is that it can add sugar side-chains to proteins, a common feature of some human proteins. Yeast, like *E. coli*, is very amenable to genetic engineering. Some strains of yeast have naturally occurring plasmids. Vectors derived from these are called **yeast episomal plasmids**. The word 'episomal' means that the plasmids can replicate independently, or become integrated into one of the yeast chromosomes. Moreover, some are capable of acting as shuttle vectors, replicating in both yeast and *E. coli*.

3.3.4 Transformation and cloning

From a population of 1000 or more treated cells, only one or two may take up foreign DNA and

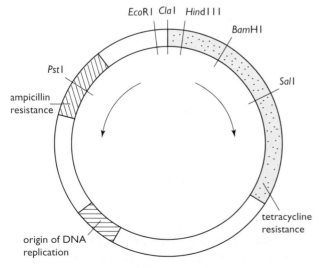

Figure 3.15 Plasmid pBR322, a typical cloning vector

EcoRI ClaI HindIII
BamHI
PstI
SalI
ampicillin resistance
tetracycline resistance
origin of DNA replication

become **transformed**. Finding out which bacteria have taken up a plasmid containing foreign DNA is a two-stage process (Figure 3.16). *E. coli* cells treated with $CaCl_2$ are incubated with plasmids that, in addition to foreign DNA, carry genes for resistance to two antibiotics, ampicillin and tetracycline. Note that the foreign DNA is inserted into the middle of the gene for tetracycline resistance.

(i) After incubation, cells are spread out on a plate of nutrient agar containing ampicillin. Only those cells which have taken up plasmids grow on this medium. After 2–3 days the colonies of these cells are harvested. (All of the cells in these colonies will have taken up the plasmid, but not all will contain the foreign gene in active form.)

(ii) Harvested cells are then spread out on a plate of nutrient agar to which enough tetracycline has been added to prevent growth of the cells, but not to kill them. The cells that fail to grow on this medium are likely to be those that have the desired DNA segment incorporated into the gene for tetracycline resistance.

An alternative procedure identifies cells containing active foreign DNA from the protein that the new gene produces. Sometimes it is possible to apply a specific diagnostic chemical test for this protein. Another approach is to apply antibodies, coupled to dyes or radioactively labelled. As antibodies are protein-specific, and bind only to their target protein, this provides a highly specific test for cells that have acquired new functional genes.

After identification, transformed bacteria are isolated and transferred to a suitable growth medium, where they grow and multiply. This process is called **gene cloning**, and the genetically identical offspring are called clones. The plasmids also replicate as a bacterium multiplies, so producing many copies of any plasmid carrying foreign genes.

3.4 Examples of Protein Production by Engineered *E. coli*

Insulin, secreted by the pancreas, is a hormone that regulates glucose concentration in the blood. About 1–2 per cent of the population in the UK suffer from a deficiency of insulin, which causes diabetes mellitus. Roughly 20 per cent of these are dependent on insulin injections.

For many years the source of insulin for injection was the pancreases of slaughtered pigs and cows. Used over many years, however, these insulins proved 'immunogenic'; that is, they caused injected persons to produce antibodies against them. Human insulin was the first human hormone to be genetically engineered and produced commercially. The gene for the protein precursor of insulin, **proinsulin**, was inserted into a plasmid and cloned in *E. coli*. Following on from this treatment the bacterium produced and secreted the protein proinsulin, which required further treatment before insulin was formed. This treatment, carried out in the laboratory, consists of preliminary exposure to

Gene expression & manipulation

gene for ampicillin resistance (Ap^r)

gene for tetracycline resistance (Tet^r)

plasmid vector

inserted DNA

insertion of new DNA into Tet^r region (inactivates Tet^r gene)

E. coli, treated with $CaCl_2$

incubation

plating (i)

ampicillin-resistant *E. coli* colonies (contain plasmid)

nutrient agar + ampicillin

plating (ii)

tetracycline-sensitive colonies (contain inserted DNA)

nutrient agar +tetracycline

Figure 3.16 A common strategy for cloning DNA in *E. coli*

Samples of insulin

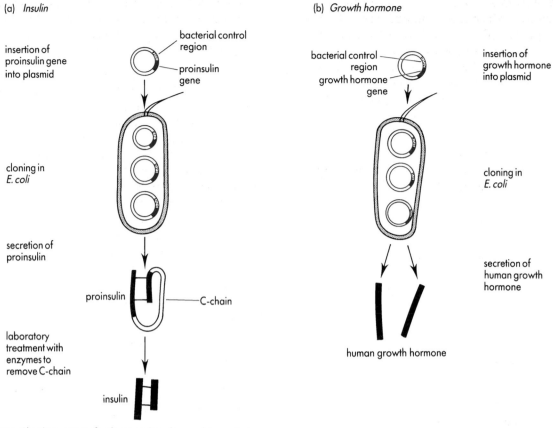

(a) *Insulin*

insertion of proinsulin gene into plasmid

bacterial control region

proinsulin gene

cloning in *E. coli*

secretion of proinsulin

proinsulin

C-chain

laboratory treatment with enzymes to remove C-chain

insulin

(b) *Growth hormone*

bacterial control region

growth hormone gene

insertion of growth hormone into plasmid

cloning in *E. coli*

secretion of human growth hormone

human growth hormone

Figure 3.17 Cloning genes for human insulin and growth hormone

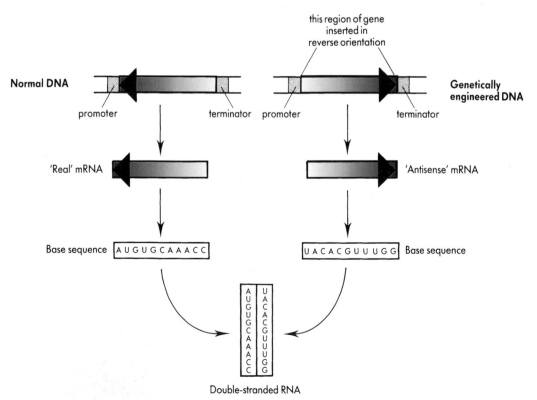

this region of gene inserted in reverse orientation

Normal DNA

promoter   terminator   promoter   terminator

Genetically engineered DNA

'Real' mRNA

'Antisense' mRNA

Base sequence AUGUGCAAACC   UACACGUUUGG Base sequence

AUGUGCAAACC
UACACGUUUGG

Double-stranded RNA

Figure 3.18 The use of 'antisense' mRNA to block expression of a gene

Gene expression & manipulation

cyanogen bromide, followed by the use of enzymes, notably trypsin and carboxypeptidase B, to remove the so-called C molecule, as shown in Figure 3.17.

Human growth hormone (HGH), secreted by the anterior pituitary gland, is needed during childhood for longitudinal growth of the skeleton. Approximately ten people per million suffer a deficiency of this hormone, leading to dwarfism. The DNA sequence that codes for this hormone was prepared in the laboratory on a DNA synthesising machine, base pair by base pair. It was then inserted into a plasmid, next to its bacterial control region. Cloned in *E. coli*, populations of transformed bacteria secreted HGH into their surroundings.

Other important proteins that can be made by genetically engineered micro-organisms include enzymes, which have many industrial applications (see section 7.1) and adhesives, such as the protein that sticks barnacles to rock surfaces.

3.5 Possible Future Developments

Apart from introducing new genes into cells, there are many other genes that genetic engineers would like to block or eliminate. Cucumbers, for example, have genes that produce yellow-skinned fruits, fruits with spines (prickles), bitter-tasting fruits, and fruits that cause indigestion. Eliminating any of these genes would produce 'improved' fruits, of greater commercial value to anyone who grew them.

Humans, too, suffer from single-gene disorders, the cause of diseases such as sickle cell anaemia, cystic fibrosis and Tay-Sachs disease. Here, among biomedical researchers, the immediate aim is to map the human genome to discover the precise location of the DNA that causes these conditions. Once located, it may be possible to block the gene, so that sufferers can be offered some relief from their symptoms.

At the present time, effective methods of achieving these aims are still a long way off. Even so, one potentially powerful technique for blocking gene transcription is through the use of **antisense mRNA**. This is the product of a synthesised DNA molecule in which the sequence of bases, between the promoter and terminator, is the exact reverse of the 'real' gene. Introduced into a cell, and integrated into one of its chromosomes, it produces antisense mRNA (Figure 3.18). Contact between the two types of mRNA results in the formation of double-stranded RNA. This, in effect, locks up the 'real' mRNA molecule, so that it cannot play its normal role in translation. As a result, the polypeptide that is normally synthesised from it cannot be produced.

3.6 Concerns About Biotechnology

Like many other technological advances, from the introduction of anaesthetics to the use of electricity, recombinant DNA technology could be used to harm humans as well as help them. Since the 1970s there has been public concern about the possible escape of a genetically-engineered pathogen from a laboratory. Most of this concern has centred around *E. coli*, a natural inhabitant of the human intestine, which has virulent strains. The worst fears are that strains carrying plasmids with genes for human hormone synthesis, antibiotic resistance or cancer induction might escape and wreak havoc among human populations. Aware of such possibilities, however unlikely, genetic engineers have acted in the public interest by working with strains that are poorly adapted for life in the human intestine. These engineered strains may include bacteria that:

(i)   grow more slowly than normal wild-type intestinal bacteria, and so would have difficulty in replacing them,

(ii) have a minimum temperature above body temperature (36°C),

(iii) contain 'suicide genes' that are activated outside certain pH or temperature limits, or

(iv) die if they lose their plasmids.

Legislation provides a further public safeguard. In the UK, guidelines for recombinant DNA work have been laid down by the Ashby Report (1975), the Godber Report (1975) and the Williams Report (1976). Work on potentially dangerous pathogens is generally restricted to isolated, purpose-built laboratories employing only highly-qualified staff. Containment is achieved through strict hygienic measures, highly efficient air filters, and regular monitoring of the atmosphere within such buildings. To date, there is no evidence that genetically-engineered strains of *E. coli* have been able to colonise the human alimentary canal.

Fears about the possibility that genetically-engineered organisms might escape into the environment, enter food chains, and disrupt the existing balance of nature are also probably exaggerated. While it is possible that genes for herbicide resistance, say, could spread from crops to weeds, making them more difficult to kill, the effects would probably be more economic than ecological.

Humans probably have most to fear from the application of genetic engineering to biological warfare. Lethal agents that might be used in biological warfare include genetically-engineered

Gene expression & manipulation

anthrax, cholera and plague bacteria. Molecular toxins, so-called because they kill or paralyse if ingested in minute quantities, can also be produced in genetically-engineered bacteria and yeasts. During a war they might be released into the atmosphere or dropped into water supplies. Botulinus and tetanus toxins are extremely poisonous bacterial products that can now be made in large quantities. Other extremely toxic substances such as ricin (from castor oil seeds), saxitoxin (from fish) and tetrodoxin (from snake venom) could be made in large amounts by transferring appropriate genes to bacteria.

Influential pressure groups with both religious and non-religious affiliations, have reservations about tinkering with the human genome. Strong opposition is likely to be expressed if genetic engineers attempt the genetic manipulation of human embryos, the addition of genes from other species to the human germ line, or fusions between human cells and those of other species. Behind such opposition is the supposition that these practices transgress the natural integrity of species, or the sanctity of the individual. On that issue, everyone has to make their own judgement.

Creative cloning

In the plant kingdom, cloning – the production of genetically-identical offspring – is a common phenomenon. Bulbs, corms and rhizomes all produce genetically-identical offspring, from which the next generation of plants is propagated. Gardeners clone their favourite herbs, shrubs and trees by taking 'cuttings'. Among invertebrates there are many groups of animals, such as coelenterates and platyhelminthes, that produce clones. Cloning also occurs in vertebrates. Identical twins are clones. Although human identical twins may look alike, it is important to appreciate that each twin is a unique individual. Individuality is preserved because the personality of each individual is not only determined by genotype, but also by a very large number of environmental factors that affect the aims, ambitions, interests and responses of each person.

Recent advances in biotechnology have enabled researchers to produce clones of sheep. In 1997, after 275 attempts, researchers at the Roslin Institute working in association with PPL Therapeutics plc, cloned a sheep called **Dolly**. This animal, produced from udder cells, also contained one human gene. The main objective of cloning is to speed up the rate at which animals with unique genotypes, such as Dolly, can be reproduced. These unique genotypes may include animals which produce therapeutic proteins in their milk, such as antitrypsin, used to treat emphysema. In addition, they may include animals whose organs may one day be used for human organ transplants. This type of animal

cloning, with its associated medical benefits, is widely accepted by the general public, providing the cloned animals do not suffer in any way.

The successful cloning of sheep has brought the possibility of **human cloning** one step nearer. This is an emotive issue, widely regarded as an abuse of human individuality and a violation of the uniqueness of human life. Some countries have introduced legislation to ban research into all aspects of human cloning. Elsewhere, others believe that the technique may have some acceptable applications, such as the cloning of fertilised eggs to help childless couples. There is almost universal agreement that the technique should not be used to clone loved ones who have died, or as a device for perpetuating the genotype of individuals noted for their positive or negative contributions to society.

The creation of genetically-modified organisms and their successful cloning, has resulted in applications for **patents** by biotechnology companies and individuals. A patent gives an inventor control of a product and entitlement to any financial gains resulting from its use. In 1988, geneticists at Harvard Medical School produced mice with cancer-causing genes inserted into their cells. These mice were used in studies of cancer development and for screening anticancer drugs. Sold under the name *OncoMice*, these patented mice were commercialised by Du Pont in 1989. Within the last decade, patents have been issued for many genetically-altered microbes, genes, plasmids, novel proteins and monoclonal antibodies. One powerful objection to the patenting of living organisms and their products is that it increases the gulf in living standards between people in wealthy countries, who can afford them, and those in poorer countries, who can't. Furthermore, an organism or gene that is patented often originates in one of these poorer countries, which derives no benefit from the present system of patenting.

The darker side

The most important question to ask about gene manipulation is whether its potential advantages outweigh its potential disadvantages, to the extent that it offers a net asset to the human population. All scientific advances carry some degree of risk, threat or hazard. Genetic engineering is no exception to this general rule.

Plant breeders, for instance, aim to produce crop plants with higher yields, greater tolerance to drought and disease, higher protein content and a longer shelf-life. Genetic engineering provides a tool whereby all of these objectives can be achieved. It is a more controllable and direct tool than cross breeding, because it adds a single gene to an already useful genome, without causing the loss of any desirable traits. At the same time there is always the possibility that the addition of a new gene to an organism may have unforeseen consequences. Sometimes a single gene controls more than one trait, or it may suppress the effect of another gene at a different locus (epistasis). Some unexpected features of genetically-engineered crops arise from small, gene-regulated changes in metabolic pathways. Novel compounds, produced as intermediates or end products, may change flavours, reduce nutritional value or even have a toxic effect. As many genes control the synthesis of proteins, the addition of a new gene generally results in the crop plant synthesising one or more novel proteins. Some beans, for instance, produce the protein **lectin**, which deters aphids from feeding on them. The gene for lectin production has recently been transferred to potatoes as a pest defence strategy. Some people are allergic to lectin. In order to protect consumers, suppliers would need to label, with suitable warnings, any products made from these potatoes. There would be very real difficulties for allergy sufferers if hundreds of similar products were to be marketed.

In medicine, the primary aim is to cure disease rather than to alleviate symptoms. Again, genetic engineering is an effective tool that provides a means of curing certain inherited diseases, such as a rare immunological disease caused by a lack of the enzyme adenosine deaminase (ADA). **ADA-deficient people** are homozygous recessive (*aa*) for this condition. By adding a normal (*A*) gene to the T cells of ADA-deficient people and then returning treated T cells to the blood, all symptoms of the disease can be cured. Treated individuals have the genotype *Aaa*. As genes produce proteins, and some of these proteins regulate metabolic pathways, it is possible that individuals with this novel *Aaa* genotype may develop problems as they grow older, caused by the formation of abnormal metabolic products.

Stated in very general terms, one possible disadvantage of this type of gene therapy is that adverse effects may take many years to become evident. What seems at first to be a near miraculous cure may degenerate in the longer term into a chronic, incapacitating condition.

Environmentalists often voice concern about possible errant genetic engineering. Some weeds have a gene which makes them resistant to the weedkiller glyphosate. The transfer of this gene into crop plants, such as strawberries, allows the crops to be sprayed from tractors with glyphosate solution. The **glyphosate-resistant plants** survive this treatment, while surrounding weeds are killed. This novel piece of genetic engineering greatly reduces the time required for weeding. Unfortunately, aphids and other sap-feeding insects have the potential for transferring glyphosate-resistant DNA from strawberry plants to weed species. If this resulted in the production of glyphosate-resistant weed populations, the genetic engineering would have exacerbated the weed problem rather than solved it. It is the fear of this type of problem that makes some scientists very cautious about any unregulated applications of gene manipulation in agriculture. During the last decade, several countries have manufactured and stockpiled **biological weapons**. Some of these contain virulent strains of pathogenic bacteria, such as anthrax (*Bacillus anthracis*) which produces enzymes that liquefy lung, kidney and heart tissues. Others contain ricin and botulin, single-gene products which are toxic in molecular concentrations. The application of scientific knowledge to 'kill or cure' is not new. What are new, and a cause for legitimate concern, are the indiscriminate and widespread biological effects of these weapons, affecting many animals in food chains in addition to humans. Furthermore, the problem of restoring ecological equilibrium to areas where such weapons had been used would be complex, lengthy and hazardous. Careful monitoring of biological weapons is therefore essential if worst-case scenarios are to be avoided.

QUESTIONS

6 How does transcription differ from translation?

7 In the lac operon, what happens to each of the following regions when lactose is present?

a) structural genes, b) promoter, c) regulator, d) operator.

8 a) What is a DNA vector?

b) Name two types of vector that could be used to transfer human genes into bacteria.

9 Name two different types of plasmid.

10 If a plasmid with ampicillin- and kanamycin-resistant genes has a foreign gene inserted into the kanamycin region, will a bacterium containing it grow on a) ampicillin agar, and b) kanamycin agar?

One of the most powerful tools at the biotechnologist's disposal is an ability to carry out recombinant DNA technology, a process more commonly known as genetic engineering.

Structural genes are lengths of DNA, anything from 450 to tens of thousands of bases in length, that code for one polypeptide. More specifically, a triplet of bases, or a codon on a DNA molecule, codes for one amino acid. Enzymes on the ribosomes join the amino acids together to make proteins, which are important structural and regulatory components of cells.

The genetic code is universal and is found in all living organisms. This means that a gene from one organism can be transferred into any other organism, where, after appropriate treatment, it can be used to produce the polypeptide for which it codes.

The proper functioning of any gene depends on the presence of appropriate signal sequences – short lengths of DNA that promote and terminate polypeptide synthesis. The successful transfer of a human gene into a bacterium requires the addition of signal sequences that the bacterium can interpret. When these requirements are met, the bacterium secretes the product of the human gene.

This technique of transferring human genes into bacteria has been highly successful in the production of human insulin and growth hormone (HGH). Adequate quantities of these hormones, formerly obtained from cadavers and animals, have been made available to the medical profession for the treatment of human diseases.

CHAPTER 3 QUESTIONS

1 Part of a DNA molecule has the following sequence:

ATCCGGTTAAGCCTAGTTACCGATTTAGCA

a) Name the bases represented by the letters A, T, G and C.

b) Which of these bases are pyrimidines?

c) Write out the base sequence of a complementary mRNA molecule.

d) On this mRNA molecule, what is a codon, and why is it so-called?

e) How many codons are there on the mRNA molecule you have drawn?

f) What is the base sequence of the fifth codon?

g) If the first transcript of human mRNA contains exons and introns, how does the final transcript differ?

h) Suppose the first mRNA molecule contained 23 per cent uracil, how much of each base would you expect the original DNA molecule to contain? Explain your answer.

2 The diagram below represents a plasmid before and after the insertion of a structural gene from a mammal.

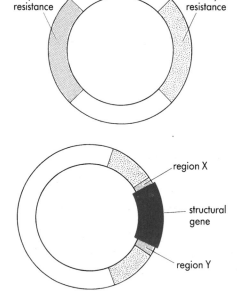

a) What type of plasmid is illustrated?

b) What is the natural function of this plasmid in bacteria such as *E. coli*?

Gene expression & manipulation

c) Among populations of bacteria living in the wild, how is a plasmid transferred from one bacterium to another?

d) What name is given to the regions X and Y on either side of the structural gene?

e) Explain the functions of these regions.

f) Are the regions X and Y of bacterial or mammalian origin?

g) How would you find out if a bacterium, previously without plasmids, had taken up one or more of the bacterial plasmids (untransformed plasmids)?

h) Why has the mammalian structural gene been inserted in the middle of the plasmid gene for kanamycin resistance?

i) What procedure would you follow to find out if the bacterium had taken up one or more of the transformed plasmids?

3 The diagram below shows part of a DNA molecule. Gene X is responsible for breaking down compound X. The binding sites of restriction endonucleases are shown, together with the relative distances between them.

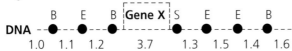

```
        B   E   B  Gene X  S    E    E    B
DNA --●---●---●--[      ]--●---●----●---●---
      1.0 1.1 1.2   3.7   1.3  1.5  1.4  1.6
```

B = *Bam H1*   E = *Eco R1*   S = *Sal 1*

a) What would be the effect of inserting another gene into gene X?

b) What enzymes would you use to cut out gene X?

c) If this piece of DNA were cut with each of the following enzymes, how many DNA fragments would be obtained?

(i) *Sal 1*, (ii) *Bam H1*, (iii) *Eco R1*, (iv) *Bam H1* and *Eco R1*.

d) If the DNA molecule were cut with each of the enzymes listed in **c)**, what would be the relative lengths of the fragments produced?

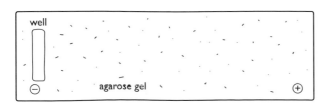

well

agarose gel   ⊖   ⊕

e) If the fragments resulting from a cut with *Bam H1* were separated by gel electrophoresis on an agarose gel, draw the relative positions they would take after applying an electric current.

4 For each of the following, construct sentences, or make annotated diagrams, to show the biological relationship of the terms listed.

a) DNA, mRNA, thymine, uracil.

b) DNA, mRNA, ribonucleic acid polymerase, reverse transcriptase.

c) Codon, anticodon, tRNA, mRNA.

d) Ribosome, tRNA, amino acids, polypeptide chain.

e) Structural gene, promoter, operator, regulator gene.

5 What differences exist between

a) DNA and RNA;

b) transcription and translation;

c) exons and introns?

6 What do you understand by the terms (i) gene vector and (ii) gene cloning? By reference to one or more examples, describe how a genetic engineer working with plasmids and a bacterium such as *E. coli*:

a) isolates and selects a mammalian gene for cloning;

b) inserts the gene into a plasmid;

c) inserts the transformed plasmid into a bacterium;

d) detects transformed bacteria that are expressing the mammalian gene;

e) obtains a clone of transformed cells.

7 Write illustrated notes on the following:

a) plasmids

b) restriction endonucleases

c) gene vectors

d) gene cloning

8 What is genetic engineering?
Evaluate the potential advantages and disadvantages of genetic engineering.

9 Should genetic engineers attempt to manipulate the human genome? Present both sides of the argument.

Some genes, such as the gene for sickle cell anaemia, have undesirable effects. Outline possible future treatments for someone suffering from this condition (see p.105).

Gene expression & manipulation

Gene Expression & Manipulation

Baker, JW and Allen, GE (1982) *The Study of Biology* 4th Edn Addison Wesley

Biotol Project (1994) *Techniques for Engineering Genes* Butterworth-Heinemann, London

Brown, TA (1986) *Gene Cloning* van Nostrand Reinhold

Green, NPO, Stout, GW, Taylor, DJ and Soper, R (1984 and 1985) *Biological Science* (vols 1 and 2) Cambridge University Press

Keevles, DJ and Hood, L (1992) *The Code of Codes: Scientific and Social Issues in the Human Genome Project* Harvard University Press, Cambridge

Kimball, J (1983) *Biology* 5th Edn Addison Wesley

Kornberg, A and Baker, TA (1992) *DNA Replication* 2nd Edn WH Freeman, New York

Old, RW and Primrose, SB (1985) *Principles of Gene Manipulation* 3rd Edn Blackwell Scientific Publications

Prentis, S (1984) *Biotechnology: A New Industrial Revolution* George Braziller, New York

Raven, P and Johnson, G (1986) *Biology* Times Mirror Mosby, St Louis

Starr, C and Taggart, R (1987) *Biology, The Unity and Diversity of Life* 3rd Edn Wadsworth

Villee, CA and Dethier, VG (1976) *Biological Principles and Processes* WB Saunders

Villee, CA, Solomon, EP and Davis, PW (1985) *Biology* Saunders, Holt, Reinhart and Winston

Warr, JR (1984) *Genetic Engineering in Higher Organisms* Edward Arnold

Watson, JD *et al.* (1983) *Recombinant DNA: A Short Course* Scientific American Books, New York

Wheale, PR and McNally, RM (1988) *Genetic Engineering, Catastrophe or Utopia?* St Martin's Press, New York

Williams, JG and Patient, RK *Genetic Engineering* IRL Press Ltd, Oxford

CHAPTER 4

Biotechnology & chemical engineering

Biotechnology is a relatively new name given to the use of living organisms and their products, such as enzymes, in the manufacturing or service industries. The origins of biotechnology lie deep in the mists of prehistory. From the Stone Age, about 10 000 years ago, humans have grown crops and farmed domestic animals, thereby changing their nomadic hunter–gatherer existence for one of more settled agricultural communities. Much later, without any understanding of the role of micro-organisms in the process, they baked bread, brewed beer and made cheeses from stale milk. The current revolution in biotechnology, however, owes its impact to two technological advances.

First, there are the techniques of genetic engineering. These allow organisms to be rapidly modified, without the need for breeding, in ways that enhance their usefulness, or reduce their harmful effects.

Assembly line check on drug capsules prior to their packaging

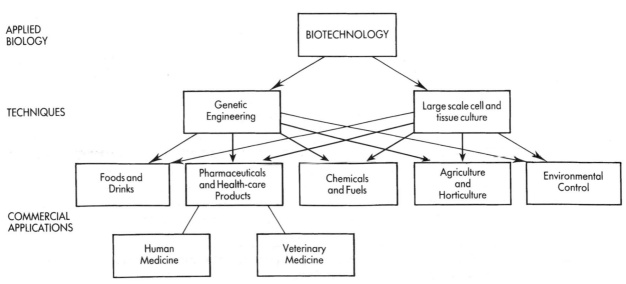

Figure 4.1 The major techniques in contemporary biotechnology, and some of their commercial applications

A large waste tip, Manila, Philippines

Secondly, there are the contributions of **chemical engineering**. The chemical engineers have produced machinery, including fermenters, for the large-scale production of useful cellular products, ranging from drugs to food and agricultural chemicals. The development of the **microchip** has also contributed by making biological fermentations inside large fermenters easier to monitor and control.

4.1 Goods and Services

A major aim of biotechnology is to improve the quality of human life by providing additional goods and services. The goods, mostly in the form of consumables, include food, drugs and fuels. The services include environmental controls such as water purification and waste disposal. As Figure 4.1 shows, there are four production industries and one service industry, that are most likely to benefit from genetic engineering, large-scale fermentation processes, or both. These are as follows:

Table 4.1 Present and potential applications of biotechnology

Area of application	Product/potential application/aim
Food production	bread-making; manufacture of cheese, yoghurt, butter and other dairy products; production of rennet substitutes for cheese-making; production of vinegar; manufacture of monosodium glutamate, a flavour enhancer; extraction of 'natural' colourings from algae; production of single cell protein (SCP)
Alcoholic drinks	manufacture of beer, cider, wines and spirits
Medicines, pharmaceuticals and health-care products	production of antibiotics; synthesis of enzymes with therapeutic value; production of monoclonal antibodies; production of highly specific vaccines to induce specific antibodies in response to pathogen antigens; synthesis of human proteins (e.g. insulin, HGH) by bacteria and yeasts; synthesis of human proteins in the milk and eggs of transgenic animals; use of gene probes to identify harmful genes in human embryos; use of gene therapy to eliminate harmful single-gene traits (e.g. cystic fibrosis); 'genetic fingerprinting' for forensic and medical identification; biosensors for estimating glucose, urea, cholesterol etc. in body fluids
Chemicals	enzymes for industrial, analytical and manipulative processes; production of industrial solvents (e.g. acetone); extraction of copper, nickel and uranium from their ores; production of xanthan gum to assist oil extraction; manufacture of nerve gases and toxins for biological warfare
Fuels	manufacture of ethanol for combustion engines; manufacture of biogas (methane)
Agriculture and horticulture	increased crop plant resistance to disease, drought, frost, herbicides and insects; better salt tolerance (e.g. rice, cereals); transfer of *nif*-genes for nitrogen fixation from legumes to cereals and other crops; introduction of genes for flavour, colour, shape etc. into fruits and vegetables; micropropagation of plants with unique combinations of genes (e.g. oil palms, house plants); increased milk, meat and egg yields in farm animals; faster growth rates in farm animals; better disease-resistance, cold-hardiness and heat-tolerance in farm animals; improved reproduction rates in farm animals by multiple births, surrogate mothering etc.; production of animal feedstocks from single cell protein
Environmental control	removal of heavy metals from water; breakdown of sewage effluent; breakdown of crude oil, tar and petroleum products; biodegradation of plastics

Biotechnology & chemical engineering

Production industries
(i)   The manufacture of foods and drinks.
(ii) The manufacture of drugs, vaccines, diagnostics and health-care products.
(iii) Production of industrial chemicals and fuels.
(iv) Agriculture and horticulture.

Service industries
(i)   Water purification and waste disposal.

The combined applications of genetic engineering and chemical engineering to biotechnology have not only led to improvements in existing manufacturing processes, but to a whole range of applications not previously thought possible. Some of these applications, currently in use or under development, are listed in Table 4.1.

4.2 Cell and Tissue Cultures

The production of useful products, based on the mass cultivation of viruses or living material, normally passes through three stages:

Laboratory model → pilot plant → industrial plant

In the laboratory, the primary objective is to discover the optimum conditions for the growth and reproduction of the material that is to be cultured. These optimal conditions must be defined in terms of nutrient supply, oxygen supply, temperature and pH.

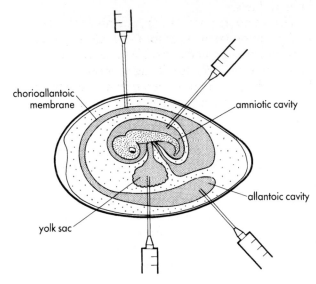

Figure 4.2 Regions in a fertilised egg, where viruses can be grown

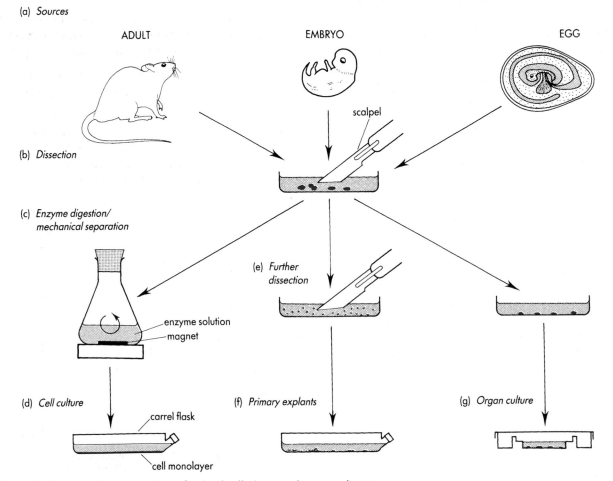

Figure 4.3 Stages in the preparation of animal cell, tissue and organ cultures

Beyond that, a researcher may need to know the mean generation time, the rate at which nutrients are used up, the stage at which useful metabolites are produced and the volume of gas generated by the cells or tissues as they grow. Needless to say, viruses, micro-organisms, plant cells and animal cells all have different requirements and therefore multiply at different rates.

Viruses are required in large numbers for the production of vaccines, or for use as cloning vectors. They present a particular problem, because they cannot multiply outside a living host cell. Bacteriophages may be grown relatively easily on bacterial cultures, either in liquid or on semi-solid media. At one time animal viruses were grown in living animals such as rabbits, mice and guinea pigs. Others were grown in fertilised eggs, widely used in the production of anti-viral vaccines. The virus was injected into one of the embryonic membranes of the developing egg of a hen. Viral growth was indicated either by death of the embryo, or by damage to one or more of its membranes. Today, such methods have been largely replaced by growing animal viruses in animal cell cultures, contained in Carrel flasks (see Figure 4.3) or larger containers. Plant viruses are grown in cultures of plant plastids, which are plant cells from which the cell walls have been digested away.

Plant cells and tissues require media that contain the same macro- and micronutrients as are required by algae (see Table 2.1). In addition, as they cannot usually photosynthesise, they also require sucrose, organic nitrogen sources (e.g. glycine, inositol), vitamins (B_1, B_6 and nicotinic acid) and growth regulators (e.g. auxin, cytokinin and gibberellic acid). Casein hydrolysate (peptide source), yeast extract (vitamin source) and a gelling agent, either agar or gelatin, may be added to media.

Animal cells, especially cells from mammalian tissues, are particularly demanding when grown in culture. They require a supply of complex nutrients, similar to those required by fungi, and a steady supply of oxygen. The growth media must also be buffered, to keep the pH between 7.1 and 7.4, must contain additional vitamins, and must have the same water potential as the cell cytoplasm, equivalent to a 0.9 per cent solution of NaCl. At the beginning of this century, cells from a frog embryo were grown in clotted lymph. Concurrently, other excised animal tissues were cultured in media containing blood plasma and embryo sac fluid. A wide selection of media, such as Liebig's meat extract, is now available for culturing animal tissues. Figure 4.3 shows the three basic techniques that are used to prepare cell culture, primary explants and organ cultures from animals:

(i) **cell cultures** consist of suspensions of separate cells, obtained by the enzymatic and mechanical disruption of a tissue. These cells may be cultured in a suspension in a liquid medium, or as an adherent monolayer on a solid substratum. Skin cells, for example, grow best on a flat, rough surface, in a shallow depth of liquid medium.

(ii) **primary explants** are small pieces of tissue, from which new cells form and break away to form either a suspension or an adherent monolayer.

(iii) **organ cultures** are larger pieces of tissue, in which the structural and functional organisation of cells is maintained, at least in part.

These three tissue culture techniques have been adopted into many applications, including the production of **monoclonal antibodies**, chromosome analysis and the study of animal viruses.

Biotechnology & chemical engineering

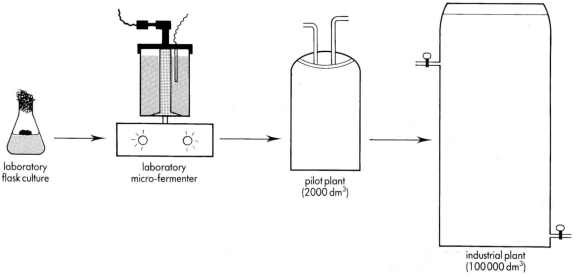

laboratory
flask culture

laboratory
micro-fermenter

pilot plant
(2000 dm³)

industrial plant
(100 000 dm³)

Figure 4.4 Scaling up

4.3 Scaling Up

Modifying a laboratory procedure, so that it can be used on an industrial scale, is called 'scaling up'. Laboratory procedures are normally scaled up via intermediate models of increasing size (Figure 4.4). The larger the plant, the greater the running costs, as skilled people are required to monitor and maintain the machinery.

Large industrial fermenters have to be built to high specifications. Containment of the desired micro-organism, and exclusion of any contaminating organism, is the first objective. Of almost equal importance is the installation of highly sensitive controls that allow pH, temperature and fluid volume to be maintained within narrow limits. Foam formation, at the surface of the culture broth, must also be monitored and controlled.

As cells multiply in the culture broth, the mixture becomes more viscous. This increasing **viscosity**, as cells multiply, can pose serious mechanical problems. Both the motor, and the paddles that it drives, must be large enough to rotate and stir the mixture, even when it reaches a porridge-like consistency. At this stage, when the mixture becomes thick and sticky, cells tend to stick to the sides of the vessel and surface of the paddles. These surfaces have either to be non-adhesive themselves, or coated with a non-adhesive substance, to overcome the problem of cell adhesion.

In cultures of aerobic organisms, **oxygen supply** is the most important limiting factor. For large-scale cultures, forced aeration with small bubbles having a high surface area to volume ratio, is the only way in which the high oxygen demand of cells can be met. Sterile air must therefore be pumped into the container, entering via a 'sparger' with multiple small holes. Micro-organisms and other cells, contained in a

confined space, generate heat as they grow. This must be removed via a heat exchanger in order to maintain a constant temperature. The larger the number of cells in a container, the greater the risk of spoilage through **cell mutations** and contamination with undesirable plasmids. In **batch cultures**, when cells are grown in a fixed volume of a liquid medium in a closed vessel, without making any additions or removals during the period of incubation, the actual time taken for incubation is influenced by the shape and volume of the container. When cells are grown in **continuous culture**, with nutrients added and cells harvested at a given steady rate, the shape and volume of the container also influences the rate at which the process can be operated. The principle of continuous culture is shown in Figure 4.5.

It should be noted that the term 'fermentation' is now applied to industrial processes that are oxygen-independent (anaerobic) as well as to those that are oxygen-dependent (aerobic).

QUESTIONS

1 Name two present or potential applications of biotechnology in a) food production, b) medicine and c) agriculture.

2 Name a site or medium where the following could be grown.

a) viruses, b) bacteriophages.

3 What is an explant?

4 When fermentation processes are scaled up, what factors are most likely to limit the growth of an aerobic micro-organism?

5 How does a batch culture differ from a continuous culture?

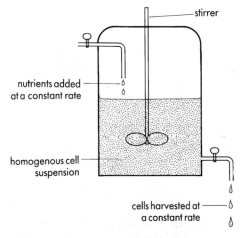

Figure 4.5 A continuous culture system (e.g. chemostat)

4.4 Fermenters

Large-scale fermentations, both aerobic and anaerobic, are carried out in large cylindrical steel containers, commonly called **bioreactors** or **fermenters**. Apart from being able to withstand the high internal pressures resulting from gas production, stainless steel provides a smooth, hard and corrosive-resistant inner surface, from which micro-organisms can be removed by washing. After the inner surface has been disinfected and washed with distilled water, the central cavity is filled to a specified level with a sterile nutrient solution. This nutrient fluid is then inoculated with a pure culture of a bacterium or fungus. **Paddles**, driven by a

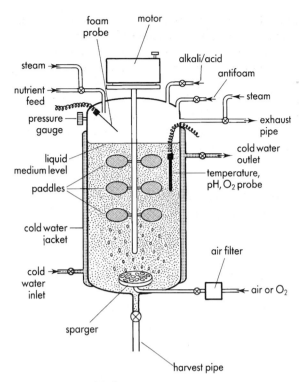

Figure 4.6 An aerobic fermenter

motor, rotate the mixture at about 1000 rpm, so that the cell or mycelium suspension is always homogenous. As nutrients are used up, more are added from the nutrient feed pipe, especially in continuous cultures. There may also be an inlet point for alkali – to counteract increasing acidity as fermentation proceeds – and 'antifoam', to prevent the formation of surface froth. **Electrically-operated probes** monitor the formation of foam at the surface of the mixture, and changes in temperature, pH and oxygen concentration within it. A **water jacket**, surrounding the fermenter, normally contains fast-flowing cold water, used to cool the fermenter since fermentation is a heat-generating (exothermic) process. In a batch process, superheated water at around 120°C may be pumped through the two steam inlets between one batch and the next in order to sterilise the inner surface of the fermenter.

Although some 'fermentations' operate anaerobically, the vast majority are aerobic processes, requiring large volumes of filtered air or pure oxygen. Air entering a fermenter needs to be filtered, otherwise air-borne micro-organisms may enter the culture and produce foreign products that would affect the purity of the end products.

After it has been filtered, air enters the bottom of the fermenter via a **sparger**. This is either a multiholed steel ring or a perforated disc, from which bubbles rise through the mixture. Most of the air, together with carbon dioxide and other gases produced by cell metabolism, leave the fermenter via

an exhaust pipe positioned above the liquid level. As the fermenter is operated under pressure it requires a **pressure gauge** and **safety valve** to prevent dangerous build up of pressure, which could lead to an explosion. At the end of fermentation, when the biomass of cells or mycelia has increased, surplus material may be removed from the fermenter via a **harvest pipe**.

Two variations in fermenter vessel design are shown in Figure 4.7. In a **draught-tube airlift vessel**, a smaller stainless steel cylinder is positioned inside a larger one. Incoming air or oxygen carries the cell suspension upwards. It completes its circulation by returning between the walls of the two cylinders. **Looped airlift vessels**, used for the production of single cell protein (p.83) and mycoprotein (p.84), have two vertical shafts, a 'riser' and a 'downcomer'. An upward draught of air or oxygen from the bottom of the 'riser' causes the contents to rise. At the top of the vessel, after gas has entered the exhaust pipe, solid material sinks down the 'downcomer' under the action of gravity. Neither of these two designs requires a motor or paddles.

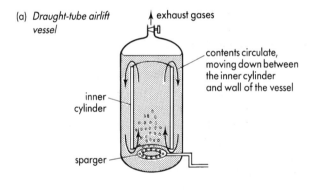

(a) *Draught-tube airlift vessel*

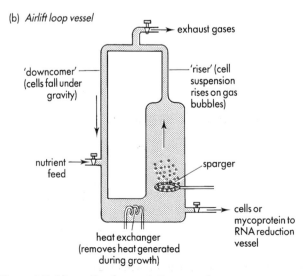

(b) *Airlift loop vessel*

Figure 4.7 Alternative fermentation vessels

4.5 Downstream Processing

Downstream processing, or **'downstreaming'**, is the extraction and purification of the desired end products of fermentation processes. Such products might include cells, solvents or solutes. Various processes are available for the separation of cells from the fermentation broth in which they are grown, including flocculation, filtration, centrifugation, sedimentation or flotation. The procedure adopted depends on whether it is the cells, or the solution surrounding them, that contains the desired end products. Downstreaming to extract cells from liquid cultures may involve the following successive stages:

Flocculation
(to precipitate cells)

↓

Filtration
(to separate cells from solution)

↓

Centrifugation
(to concentrate cell masses)

↓

Drying
(to prepare cells for packaging)

If the solution surrounding the cells is required, as in brewing, or one of the solutes is the required product, as in antibiotic production, any of the following downstream processes might be used:

Flocculation
(to precipitate cells)

↓

Ultrafiltration or
centrifugation
(to obtain a cell-free solution)

↓

Distillation
(to concentrate the solvent, or drive it off)

↓

Drying
(to obtain crude solute)

↓

Purification
(to obtain pure solute)

Later in this book you will find detailed accounts of downstreaming in the production of beer (p.78) and penicillin (p.102).

Biotechnology & chemical engineering

(a) *Spray drying*

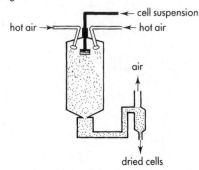

(b) *Fluidised bed drying*

(c) *Freeze drying*

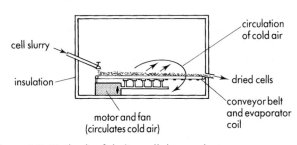

Figure 4.8 Methods of drying cellular products – a stage in downstream processing

QUESTIONS

6 On a fermenter, what is the function of each of the following?

  a) paddles, b) sparger, c) heat exchanger, d) air filter.

7 What types of probe might a fermenter contain?

8 Name three successive stages in a downstream process designed to produce a dry, cellular end product.

9 a) What is distillation?

  b) In what manufacturing processes is distillation an important part of downstreaming?

10 Make a large, labelled drawing of a fermenter.

74

CHAPTER 4 SUMMARY

Genetic engineering has allowed organisms to be modified, without the need for cross-breeding, in ways that enhance their usefulness, or reduce their harmful effects.

Chemical engineers have produced machinery, such as bioreactors, for the large-scale manufacture of useful products, ranging from drugs to food and agricultural chemicals.

Bread, beer, antibiotic and vaccine production all owe something to the work of genetic and chemical engineers. Medicine, agriculture, industry and waste disposal are served by researchers who have studied recombinant DNA technology and chemical engineering.

Bioreactors (fermenters), designed by chemical engineers, are large, cylindrical, steel containers, in which environmental factors, such as pH and temperature, can be controlled. It is in these bioreactors that large-scale fermentations, both aerobic and anaerobic, can be carried out to produce food, beverages and medicines.

The commercial manufacture of useful products involves several developmental stages, notably modifications of small-scale laboratory procedures, so that they can be used on an industrial scale. This is called 'scaling-up'. The effective purification, drying and packaging of commercial products, collectively known as 'downstreaming' is another important aspect of the manufacturing process.

CHAPTER 4   QUESTIONS

1 The diagram below illustrates a large industrial fermenter.

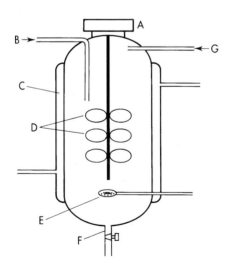

a) Name the parts A–G.

b) Through which parts do sterile materials enter the fermenter?

c) Explain the function of part C.

d) How is part A affected as cell density increases inside the fermenter?

e) Why are the walls of the fermenter usually made from stainless steel?

f) Name two other types of fermenter commonly used in industrial processes.

2 Biotechnologists aim to improve the quality of water by (i) removing heavy metals and (ii) speeding up the rate at which sewage effluent is broken down. For each of the following, state two aims or achievements of biotechnologists:

a) Cereal crops

b) Brewing

c) House plants

d) Vaccines

e) Food colourings

f) Human proteins

g) Therapeutic enzymes

h) Mining

i) Oil extraction

j) Oil pollution

k) Fuel production

l) Biosensors

3 What do you understand by the term 'biotechnology'?

Evaluate the contributions of **a)** biologists and **b)** chemical engineers in developing modern biotechnology.

Biotechnology & chemical engineering

4 What

a) nutritional and

b) environmental conditions are required to grow a bacterium such as *E. coli* in the laboratory?

In what ways do the requirements of

c) viruses and

d) algae differ from those of bacteria?

When large numbers of cells are grown in fermenters, what factors must be monitored and regulated? How is this monitoring and regulation achieved?

5 Draw and describe the gross structure and component parts of a large industrial fermenter. Outline the methods that can be used to separate and purify

a) liquid and

b) solid end products of fermentation processes.

BIBLIOGRAPHY

Biotechnology & Chemical Engineering

Brown, CM, Campbell, I and Priest, FG (1987) *Introduction to Biotechnology* Blackwell Scientific Publications

Gottschalk, G (1986) *Bacterial Metabolism* 2nd Edn Springer-Verlag, New York

Higgins, IJ, Best, DJ and Jones, J (1985) *Biotechnology, Principles and Applications* Blackwell Scientific Publications

Mantell, SH, Matthews, JA and McKee, RA (1985) *Principles of Plant Biotechnology* Blackwell Scientific Publications

Mantell, SH and Smith, H eds (1983) *Plant Biotechnology* Cambridge University Press

Marx, JL (1989) *A Revolution in Biotechnology* Cambridge University Press

Prentis, S (1984) *Biotechnology: A New Industrial Revolution* Orbis

Olejnik, I and Farmer, B (1988) *Biology and Industry* Blackie

Primrose, SB (1987) *Modern Biotechnology* Blackwell Scientific Publications

Sattelle, DB (1988) *Biotechnology in Perspective* Hobsons Publishing

Smith, JE (1981) *Biotechnology* (Studies in Biology No. 136) Edward Arnold

Stanbury, PF and Whittaker, A (1984) *Principles of Fermentation Technology* Pergamon Press

Biotechnology & chemical engineering

CHAPTER 5

Foods & drinks

Bread-making, wine-making and cheese-making are ancient crafts, all dependent on the activities of micro-organisms. In the 20th century these crafts have been transformed into industrial processes allowing the controlled production of foods and drinks on a large scale, and achieving a more predictable end product. In the industrialised countries, biotechnologists have improved the techniques of food processing and developed microbial strains better suited to the jobs that they perform. A future aim of biotechnology is to produce more food that is inexpensive and has a high nutritional value. One way forward may be to produce **single cell protein (SCP)**, prepared from the cells or hyphae of micro-organisms. The fact that many micro-organisms can double their biomass in a day is an attractive feature, promising both rapid and abundant food production in the future.

Conversely, SCP production is expensive and some of the end products aren't particularly palatable.

The following sections outline stages in the manufacture of bread, beer, dairy products and other foods that depend on micro-organisms for their production.

5.1 Bread

The principal dry ingredients used in bread-making are wheat flour, salt, sugar, ascorbic acid, and the yeast *Saccharomyces cerevisiae*. Water or milk is added to produce a thick, sticky dough which is repeatedly folded or **kneaded**, to create nuclei for gas production and expansion. The mixed dough is rested, folded, and moulded into tins.

(a) *Mixing*   (b) *Kneading*   (c) *1st moulding*   (d) *1st proving*

(e) *2nd moulding*   (f) *2nd proving*   (g) *Baking*   (h) *Cooling*   (i) *Wrapping*

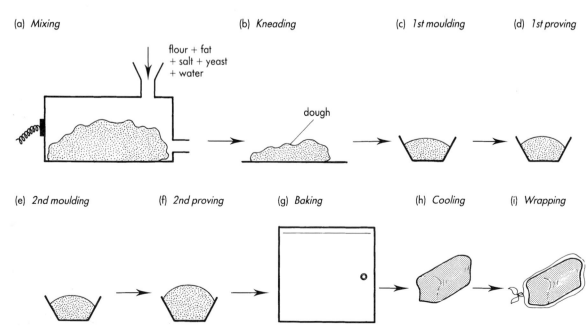

Figure 5.1 Commercial bread production

Foods & drinks

In a humid atmosphere at 34–35°C dough is left for 10 minutes to 'prove'. It is then remoulded and left for a final 'proving'.

During the 'proving' process, fermentation of sugars in the dough, catalysed by enzymes from the yeast cells, produces carbon dioxide. As this gas cannot escape from the sticky mass, it fills the gas nuclei and causes the dough to 'rise', or increase in volume. This process is sometimes called **leavening**. Ascorbic acid (vitamin C) makes gluten in the dough more elastic. As a result, the time required for leavening is greatly reduced, an important consideration in commercial bread production. While the dough is being leavened, proteolytic enzymes from the yeast act on proteins in the flour, changing their textures by making them less tough and stringy. The overall effects of leavening are to make the dough lighter, more digestible and of better flavour, following from the production of organic acids, alcohols and esters by yeast cells.

The role of enzymes in the process may be summarised as follows:

(i) Maltose (in flour) $\xrightarrow[\text{(from yeast)}]{\text{maltase}}$ glucose

(ii) Sucrose (added) $\xrightarrow[\text{(from yeast)}]{\text{invertase}}$ glucose + fructose

(iii) Glucose + fructose $\xrightarrow[\text{(from yeast)}]{\text{'zymase'}}$ alcohol + carbon dioxide

Baking inactivates the yeast, drives off any alcohol that may be present in the dough, and stops enzymic reactions. The bubbles of carbon dioxide persist, however, giving the bread a spongy texture after baking. Genetic engineers are currently attempting to improve strains of yeast used in baking. Their main aims are to produce more active, better-flavoured strains, which can make dough rise at lower temperatures, and in less time.

Table 5.1 Ingredients for bread-making

Ingredients	Parts (volume)
Flour	100
Salt	1
Sugar	1
Yeast	5
Ascorbic acid (vitamin C)	0.5
Milk or water	60

5.2 Beers and Wines

Beer

Beer is produced from barley grains, which contain mostly starch and proteins. There are six major stages in the manufacture of beer, as follows:

Malting
↓
Milling
↓
Mashing
↓
Boiling
↓
Fermentation
↓
Finishing

Brewing: using yeast to ferment 'wort'

Malting results in the conversion of starch to maltose, and proteins to amino acids. This is achieved by steeping the dry grains in water, then layering them in a malting tower or spreading them out on a malthouse floor, and allowing them to germinate until their roots have reached about 0.5–0.75 cm in length (Figure 5.2). Enzymes produced during germination, namely amylases and proteases, degrade stored materials in the grains into compounds that can be fermented by yeast. Germination is stopped by slowly heating the grains at 80°C, a temperature that is sufficient to destroy the enzymes. The grains that emerge from this process are known as malted barley.

Milling breaks each malted barley grain into 2–3 pieces. These crushed grains, or grist, are then fed into a 'mash tun', where **mashing** takes place. Hot water percolates through the grains, softening them, and extracting a nutrient-rich liquid called 'wort'.

Foods & drinks

Boiling is a stage in which 'wort', mixed with hops to give added flavour and some antiseptic properties, is heated to a high temperature in a 'lauter tun'. The resulting sterile liquid, after straining through a 'hop-back', is then allowed to cool.

Fermentation takes place in large conical fermenters, after an appropriate strain of yeast has been added. As the fermentation of the beer proceeds, *S. cerevisiae* builds up at the bottom of the fermenter and at the surface of the 'wort', where it forms a crust. Carbon dioxide is prevented from escaping and so dissolves in the beer, making it effervesce. After 7–10 days fermentation is complete. Downstreaming consists of flocculation, filtration and maturation. A protein called isinglass, from the swim bladders of tropical fish, is added to flocculate yeast cells. Isinglass, which has an opposite electrical charge to that of the yeast cells, causes yeast to be precipitated as a firm deposit, leaving an almost clear liquid.

Malting barley

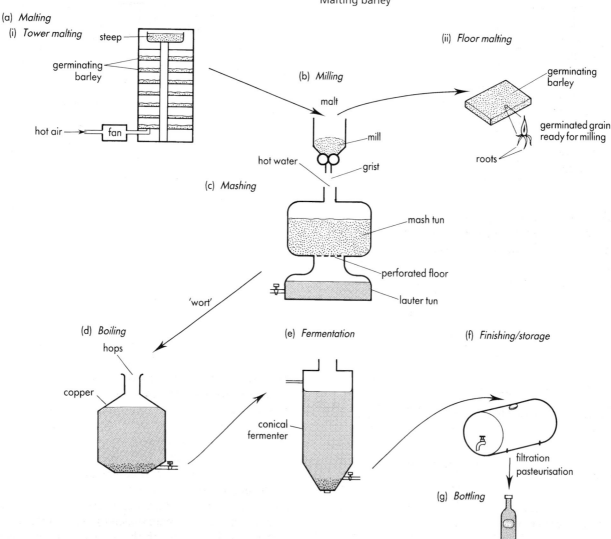

Figure 5.2 Commercial beer production

Hops in flower

Filtration, through a slurry of diatomite rock (fossilised silica shells of diatoms) layered to form a bed, removes any yeast cells that may remain in suspension. Following filtration, the beer is allowed to stand for several weeks at 0°C, until any cell debris or protein haze has cleared.

Finishing, the final stage in beer production consists of packaging beer for sale to the public. Bottled and canned beers are usually pasteurised at 60°C to kill of any yeast cells that may still be present. Some beer is still marketed in wooden barrels, where interactions with the wood give it a more mellow flavour. In general, the alcohol (ethanol) content of beer is around 4–6% volume. 'Low alcohol' beer may either be processed, to remove most of the alcohol by osmosis, or may be a direct product of an engineered strain of yeast that produces alcohol in low concentration.

Wines

Wines are traditionally made from grapes, but can also be made from sugar-rich fruits, flowers or root crops, such as parsnips or carrots. In commercial winemaking, grapes are crushed between rollers then passed into a fermenting vat. Here sulphur dioxide – to prevent the growth of unwanted micro-organisms – and yeast are added. The resulting fermented pulp, known as 'must', passes through a press, where seeds and skins are removed. Finally, following retention in one or more settling vats, the fermented juice is filtered, heated and aged before bottling.

Table wines contain from 6–12% alcohol. Fortified wines, such as sherry, may contain as much as 20% alcohol. Spirits, including whisky and vodka, the products of distillation, contain 30% or more alcohol.

5.3 Vinegar

Vinegar, used to flavour food, contains not less than 4% acetic acid. It is produced by a second fermentation of beer, cider or wine. The second fermentation is aerobic and is dependent on a mixed culture of *Acetobacter*, including *A. scheutzenbachii*, *A. curium* and *A. orleanse*. Providing oxygen is available, these bacteria convert alcohol to acetic acid by the following route:

Alcohol (ethanol) → acetaldehyde → acetic acid

Commercial vinegar producers generally increase the alcohol content of the beer (for malt vinegar) or cider (for cider vinegar) to about 12%. In the traditional vinegar-making process, large wooden vats, made of Columbian pine, were fitted with many bundles of birch twigs (Figure 5.3). Bacteria on the surface of these twigs converted alcohol-enriched beer or cider to vinegar. After it had dripped over the surface of the twigs, the fermenting liquid was collected and recycled, so that it was sprayed over the twigs several times before it was removed and bottled. Today, however, most vinegar is made in aerated fermenters, similar to that shown in Figure 4.6.

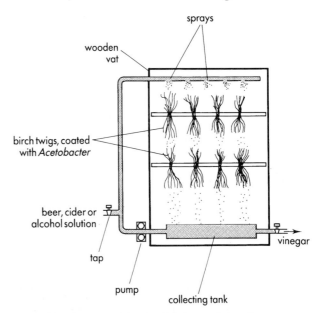

Figure 5.3 Vinegar production by the traditional method

5.4 Cheese

Cheese-making is an ancient craft, originally used to preserve milk from attack by micro-organisms that rendered it unfit for human consumption.

Table 5.2 Bacteria used in cheese-making

Role	Species
Gas production	*Leuconostoc cremoris*
	Leuconostoc lactis
	Lactococcus diacetylactis
Acid production	*Streptococcus cremoris*
	Streptococcus lactis

More recently, however, it has developed into a biotechnology, drawing on specialised machinery, enzymology, microbiology and biochemistry. In both small- and large-scale cheese-making there are four main steps, as follows:

Milk-pretreatment
↓
Milk coagulation
↓
Curd extraction
↓
Salting, pressing and ripening

Milk pretreatment consists of low temperature pasteurisation to kill off any micro-organisms that might be present. Milk coagulation is brought about by adding a 'starter culture', consisting of lactose-fermenting bacteria and rennet, which causes the formation of a solid curd and liquid whey. Cheese is made from the curd, often salted, pressed and ripened before it is eaten. The bacteria used in cheese-making are either gas producers or acid producers. **Gas producers** release carbon dioxide, while **acid producers** form lactic acid from lactose. It is the gas producers that determine the texture of a cheese. Acid producers determine its flavour.

Blocks of cheese curd

Cheddar cheese is made from milk sterilised at 72°C for at least 15 seconds. A starter consisting mostly of subspecies of *Streptococcus lactis* is added. About an hour after adding the starter, the milk is said to 'ripen', as its lactic acid content rises (to more than 0.18%). The milk is then ready for **renneting**. Rennet (previously called rennin) which is a mixture of chymosin and pepsin from the stomach of a calf (or from genetically-engineered bacteria), is added to coagulate casein, the principal milk protein. A semi-solid mass or 'coagulum' is formed, consisting of fat, water and solutes trapped in a casein matrix.

Next, the coagulum is cut into pea-sized pieces, so that it separates into small, creamy particles of curd, suspended in a watery whey. **Scalding** the mixture at a temperature of 30–39°C for about 45 minutes expels more whey, and changes the texture of the curd. After scalding, the curd is allowed to settle under gravity, or **pitch**, and the whey is run off. At this stage the individual pieces of curd begin to knit together into blocks. The blocks are then cut,

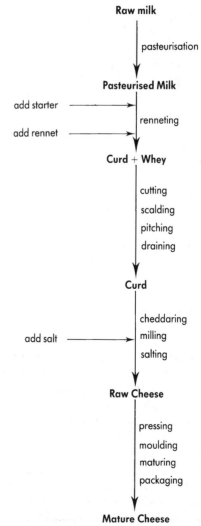

Figure 5.4 Stages in the manufacture of cheddar cheese

Foods & drinks

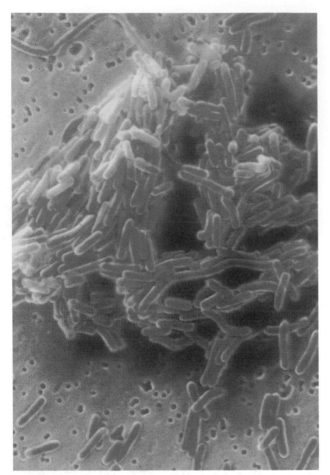

Listeria monocytogenes, a food poisoning organism sometimes found in cheeses

5.5 Yoghurt

Two species of bacteria *Lactobacillus bulgaricus* and *Lactococcus thermophilus*, in approximately equal proportions, are used to make yoghurt.

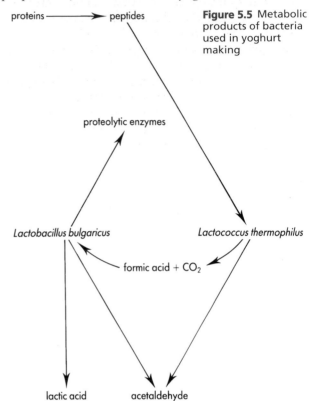

Figure 5.5 Metabolic products of bacteria used in yoghurt making

stacked, drained and turned in a process called **cheddaring**. When 'cheddaring' is complete and the pH has fallen to about 5.2, the curd is **milled** into small pieces. Salting is the final stage of preparation. The addition of salt to about 2% helps preserve the finished cheese and brings out its flavour.

Semi-soft cheeses (e.g. Brie, Camembert), hard cheeses (e.g. Lancashire) and very hard cheeses (e.g. Cheddar) are **pressed** to reduce their water content and bind the curd into a solid mass. The raw cheese is then moulded and usually coated with one or more layers of plastic, to conserve water and prevent colonisation by species of micro-organism living in the wild. **Ripening** consists of storing the cheese under appropriate conditions so that bacteria and other micro-organisms can cause chemical changes in the curd, improving and enhancing its flavour. Mould fungi are used in the ripening of some cheeses. Spores of *Penicillium camemberti* are sprayed over the surface of raw Camembert cheese. Those of *Penicillium roqueforti* are placed deep into the curd of Roquefort cheese by using special needles. The growth of fungal hyphae in cheese gives it a stronger, characteristic flavour.

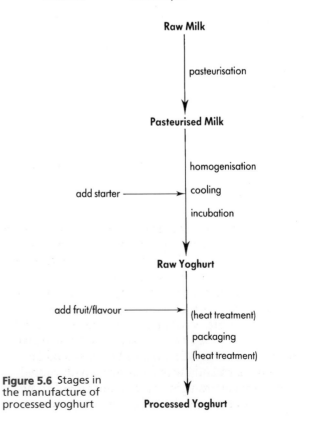

Figure 5.6 Stages in the manufacture of processed yoghurt

Commercial producers pasteurise and homogenise milk before adding the starter. After stirring, the mixture is then incubated for 3–6 hours at 40–45°C. At this temperature, the two bacteria have a mutually-stimulating effect on one another. Proteolytic enzymes from *L. bulgaricus* break down milk proteins into peptides. These stimulate growth of *L. thermophilus* which, in turn, produce formic acid and carbon dioxide, growth stimulants for *L. bulgaricus*. As incubation proceeds, *L. bulgaricus* also converts lactose to lactic acid. At the end of incubation, the pH has fallen to around 4.2–4.4, and the lactic acid has coagulated proteins, causing the yoghurt to thicken. Acetaldehyde, a metabolic by-product of both species, gives raw yoghurt its characteristic flavour. Further processing may involve the addition of flavouring, colouring and fruit pulp. Some yoghurts may then receive additional heat treatment to kill off any living bacteria, before or after being packaged for the consumer.

the butter with a rancid flavour. For this reason, butter is often wrapped in aluminium foil, which excludes light and protects the product from foreign flavours and odours.

QUESTIONS

1 In bread-making, what is the role of each of the following?

a) yeast, b) sugar, c) ascorbic acid

2 In beer-making, what are a) malt and b) wort?

3 a) When vinegar is produced from wine, what chemical transformations take place?

b) What conditions are necessary for these chemical transformations to take place?

4 Name a) three bacteria and b) two fungi that are used in cheese-making.

5 How does the treatment of milk used to make cheese differ from that used to make yoghurt?

5.6 Butter

Butter is made from cream. During churning, tiny droplets of fat coalesce to turn a fat-in-water emulsion (cream) into a water-in-fat emulsion (butter). Rejection of the surplus water solution, or buttermilk, leaves a solid product with 80% or more fat. There are two main types of butter, called 'sweet cream' and 'lactic'.

Sweet-cream butter, the most popular type, is prepared from pasteurised cream, cooled to between 4–5°C. The cream is then passed through a machine called a continuous buttermaker, where it is churned, separated and worked. Churning causes the globules of fat to aggregate into butter granules, while the watery buttermilk is drawn off. The butter granules are then worked to reduce their water content, and compressed into blocks of the desired consistency. Salt, in the form of a slurry, may be added before the final working.

Lactic butter is made from fermented cream. After pasteurisation, a starter is added which contains *Streptococcus lactis*, a diacetyl-producing bacterium, *Leuconostoc citrovorum* or *Leuconostoc dextranicum*. Fermentation by *S. lactis* produces lactic acid, with citric acid as a by-product. The second bacterium in the starter acts on citric acid, converting it to diacetyl, the compound which gives butter its characteristic flavour. Butter should be kept cool, dark and away from strongly-flavoured foods. Exposure to light causes oxidation of some fats, reduces the vitamin A content, and may leave

5.7 Single Cell Protein (SCP)

Single cell proteins (SCPs) are the whole dried cells of bacteria, fungi or algae grown in mass culture. In addition to a high protein content, forming 40% or more of their total dry mass, SCPs have a high content of amino acids, vitamins, lipids, carbohydrates, minerals and nucleic acids. They are used mostly as animal foodstuffs, because humans find the cell walls indigestible and cannot metabolise the high nucleic acid (purine) content.

The basis of SCP production is the continuous culture (or fermentation) of micro-organisms under carefully controlled conditions. In the early 1970s ICI produced SCP from a bacterium called *Methylophilus methylotrophus*, with methanol as the carbon source and ammonia as the sole source of nitrogen. Methanol was chosen because it was relatively abundant, miscible with water, and easily separated from the end product. The fermenter had two vertical shafts, a 'riser' and 'downcomer', through which the contents circulated. Sterilised methanol with dissolved nutrients entered at the bottom of the 'riser'. Bubbles of air and ammonia, entering at the base of the 'riser', assisted the upward flow of cells. At the top of the fermenter bacterial cells, in the form of a cream, were extracted. This extract was flocculated by steam treatment and centrifugation, then dried. After extensive toxicity testing the product was sold as animal feed under the name *Pruteen*. Unfortunately, high production costs made this SCP more expensive than soy bean and fish meal. These economic problems caused the plant to close down in the early 1980s.

One of the earliest uses of yeast for SCP production was by British Petroleum, again in the 1970s. They used *Candida lipolytica*, with n-paraffins as the carbon source. Today, most SCP production is in South America, where yeasts are grown for animal foodstuffs and human consumption. In the future, it is possible that algae and cyanobacteria, such as *Spirulina*, first used by the Aztecs to make cakes, may become major sources of SCPs. The fact that these organisms have a rapid growth rate, and require only water and mineral salt as nutrients, makes them particularly attractive as food sources, especially in tropical and sub-tropical regions. Furthermore, the dried product promises to be more palatable and digestible than bacterial SCP.

The growth of micro-organisms for food has two attractions:

(i) they have a much faster growth rate than agricultural products, with a doubling time measured in hours.

A mycoprotein food product marketed as 'Quorn'

(ii) a wide range of waste materials can be used as substrates, including cheese whey, molasses and starchy wastes.

Table 5.3 Essential nutrients in mycoprotein and beef

Nutrient	% Dry mass	
	Mycoprotein/Nutrient	Beef/Dry mass
Protein	40–45	60–65
Fat	10–15	30–40
Mineral salts	3–4	1–2
Fibre	30–40	none

These advantages, however, have to be balanced against high production costs and the fact that some of the end products are unacceptable to humans, because they are indigestible, bitter-tasting and can cause gout on account of their high RNA content. Perhaps the most promising and commercially successful SCP is **mycoprotein**, a meat substitute made from hyphae of the fungus *Fusarium graminearum*.

The fungus is grown in a looped air-lift fermenter at 30°C, in a liquid medium containing glucose syrup, mineral salts and choline, a growth factor that increases the length of the hyphae. Continuously harvested from the fermenter, the hyphae pass into an RNA reduction vessel, where they are heated to

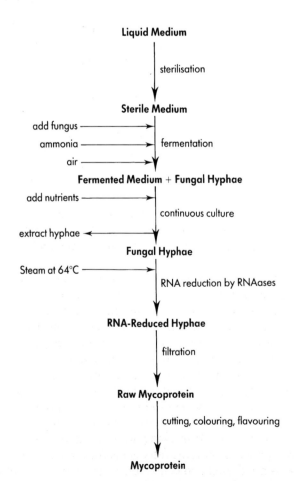

Figure 5.7 Stages in mycoprotein production

Foods & drinks

64°C reducing the RNA content to around 1% of total dry mass. The processed hyphae are then cut, coloured and flavoured to resemble meat. The end product, marketed as 'Quorn', is often added to meat products such as sausages, where it blends well with the other ingredients. As Table 5.3 shows, mycoprotein contains less fat and more fibre than beef – important considerations for those seeking a more healthy diet.

5.8 Food Preservation

Developing effective methods of food storage and preservation helped humans abandon their original nomadic existence as hunter–gatherers. Today, large human populations, like those in the UK, are heavily dependent on effective methods of food preservation. Untreated food always contains some saprobiontic organisms, notably bacteria and fungi, capable of causing 'food spoilage'. In addition some pathogens – the direct or indirect cause of 'food poisoning' – may also be present. If food is stored under conditions in which these micro-organisms can multiply, populations of pathogens may build up to dangerous levels. Most food poisoning organisms, including species of *Salmonella*, *Campylobacter fetus* and *Listeria monocytogenes*, multiply inside the human gut. **Endotoxins**, the cause of diarrhoea, vomiting and fever, are released when these bacteria are engulfed by phagocytes inside the human intestine. Other bacteria, such as *Clostridium botulinum* and *Staphylococcus aureus* multiply in the food that they colonise, and poison it by releasing extracellular **exotoxins**. Anyone eating food containing these exotoxins becomes ill, although they may not necessarily swallow any of the bacteria that have produced them.

Today, the most widely used methods of preserving foods are refrigeration (freezing), heat treatment (sterilisation), chemical inhibition and drying. In the future, irradiation with gamma rays may gain popularity.

5.8.1 Refrigeration and Freezing

Household refrigerators, kept at about 4°C, reduce the growth rate and reproduction of most bacterial pathogens. Freezers, at about −20°C, prevent all known pathogens from growing or multiplying. In fact, at this temperature, populations of bacteria in deep-frozen foods slowly decline. Even so, neither refrigeration nor freezing kills all the bacteria present in a food sample. On thawing, any bacteria in the food are reactivated and often multiply at an increased rate, because freezing has broken down cell walls and increased the food's water content.

Vegetable, meat and fish products are heat-treated before freezing to kill off all of their natural microflora and denature enzymes that might otherwise cause spoilage. An increase in the popularity of chilled straight-from-the-supermarket meals has been accompanied by an increase in infections caused by *Salmonella*, *Campylobacter* and *Listeria*. This has happened because these species grow relatively well at low temperatures in the range 0–15°C. If supermarket chilling cabinets are faulty, allowing temperatures to rise above 5°C, or if the food is allowed to warm up slowly after purchase, the public is at risk from these organisms. This is especially so in food that has passed its 'sell by' date.

5.8.2 Heat Treatment

Exposure to temperature in the range 70–100°C for 15–60 seconds kills most bacteria. Milk, for example, is pasteurised by heating at 72°C for 15 seconds. This temperature is sufficient to denature enzymes and kill bacteria, but it doesn't noticeably affect the milk's flavour.

Canned meats, fruits and vegetables are packed into containers, sealed to the air, and heated to a temperature of around 120°C. This temperature is sufficient to kill off any bacteria in the food, together with heat-resistant **endospores** of species such as *Clostridium botulinum*. The product remains sterile until the can is opened, but it is then colonised by micro-organisms from the environment.

5.8.3 Chemical Inhibition

Growth of pathogens in food is rare below pH 5.0. For this reason, lactic, sulphurous and benzoic acids are added to certain foods and beverages to lower their pH. A number of sodium salts and antibiotics have been used to slow the growth rates of bacteria and fungi, and to prevent germination of their spores. These chemicals include sodium nitrite, sodium chloride, sodium metabisulphite, sodium sorbate benzoate, and the antibiotics nicin and tylosin.

When bacon is cured, the meat is injected with a solution of sodium chloride, sodium nitrate, potassium nitrate and polyphosphate, and then steeped in a similar solution. Salt-tolerant micrococci and lactobacilli reduce nitrate to nitrite. They also assist in the formation of nitrosomyoglobin in muscles, which gives the bacon its attractive pink colour. As an additional treatment, the bacon may then be smoked. Wood smoke contains acids and other chemicals with bactericidal effects. Hence, the ancient practice of smoking meat, fish and cheese has been updated. Volatile fatty acids from the treated foods are thought to contribute to their preservation, inhibiting all but lactic acid bacteria.

5.8.4 Drying

Cereals, pulses and potato products are some of the commonest food items stored for long periods in a dry form. A total water content of below 10–15% inhibits the growth of micro-organisms and prevents enzymes from causing spoilage. Placing fruits in a concentrated solution of sugar, or meat in a concentrated solution of salt, has a similar drying effect. Water is drawn by osmosis from any micro-organisms in the food, so that they are left with insufficient water for growth or reproduction.

5.8.5 Irradiation

Irradiation with gamma rays, which can be carried out after products have been packaged for final distribution, is a powerful technique for killing micro-organisms. Applied to dairy products, cooked poultry, meat and shellfish, it would virtually eliminate food poisoning caused by *Salmonella*, *Campylobacter* and *Listeria*, along with other bacteria that produce endotoxins. Irradiation also extends the shelf-life of fresh vegetables and fruits, keeping strawberries in prime condition for as long as three weeks. Used to treat grain products, dried herbs and spices, irradiation can provide an alternative to the use of insecticides. Usefully, irradiation also prevents stored onions and potatoes from sprouting.

Although irradiated food does not itself become radioactive, the treatment nevertheless causes some nutrients to undergo irreversible changes. Vitamins are destroyed, along with essential fatty acids. A number of untested toxic, mutagenic and carcinogenic agents may be formed. Work on laboratory animals, fed exclusively on irradiated food, has suggested possible long-term damage to the immune system and kidneys, with an increase in genetic disorders of the blood.

At the present time, 21 countries permit food irradiation. Clearly, the technique is still experimental. If irradiated food is a health hazard, any damage may take from 10–20 years to show up.

A more immediate worry to health authorities and consumers, however, is the possibility that stale food, with a high bacterial count, could be irradiated to resemble fresh food.

Table 5.4 The advantages and disadvantages of irradiated food

Advantages	Disadvantages
Reduces risk of food poisoning from endotoxin-producing bacteria	Doesn't reduce risk of food poisoning from endotoxin-producing bacteria
Improved texture and flavour in some foods (e.g. chicken, meat, certain cheeses)	Adverse effects on texture and flavour in some foods (e.g. cucumber)
Longer shelf-life	Loss of vitamins and essential fatty acids Could be used to disguise old and dirty food Formation of toxic chemicals?

QUESTIONS

6 a) What is mycoprotein?

  b) Why is mycoprotein a useful addition to a healthy diet?

7 Why are some foods, such as vegetables, boiled before they are frozen?

8 Some meats are preserved by adding nitrates. State a) one advantage and b) one possible disadvantage of this practice.

9 Name three micro-organisms that cause food poisoning.

10 State a) two advantages and b) two possible disadvantages of irradiating food.

A current and future aim of biotechnology is to produce more food that is inexpensive and has a high nutritional content.

Traditional products of biotechnology – bread, beer, wine, vinegar and cheese – are currently being produced in ways that take full advantage of recent developments in recombinant DNA technology and chemical engineering. Modern technology standardises manufacturing processes, so that the quality of the end product is consistent.

Some micro-organisms have considerable potential as novel and valuable food sources,

because they can double their biomass in a matter of days. Already some commercial success has been achieved with these novel foods. 'Quorn' is a widely available mycoprotein, a meat substitute with high protein and fibre content, yet with a much lower fat content than meat products.

Stored food may become contaminated with pathogenic bacteria, which release exotoxins. Effective methods of preserving food include refrigeration, heat treatment, chemical inhibition and drying. The irradiation of food is effective in killing pathogens, but may possibly have harmful effects on consumers in the long term.

INVESTIGATING INDUSTRIAL BIOTECHNOLOGY

Fermentation

Yeast (*Saccharomyces cerevisiae*) ferments glucose to produce ethanol and carbon dioxide. The process can be summarised by the following equation:

$$C_6H_{12}O_6 \rightarrow 2C_2H_5OH + 2CO_2$$

glucose   ethanol   carbon dioxide

The rate of this reaction can be monitored by measuring the rate at which carbon dioxide is produced. Four methods for determining the rate of fermentation are illustrated in the figure opposite.

a) To determine the rate at which yeast ferments different sugars

Yeast is capable of fermenting monosaccharide and certain disaccharide sugars. When comparing the rates at which different sugars are fermented, it is important to use sugar solutions with the same molar concentration, e.g. M/10 or M/5.

Prepare M/10 solutions of each of the following sugars:

- monosaccharides: glucose, fructose, galactose
- disaccharides: maltose, sucrose, lactose

Add dried, powdered yeast to each sugar solution at the rate of 0.5g/100 cm³

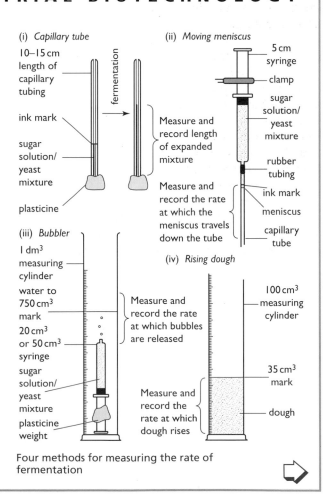

Four methods for measuring the rate of fermentation

Foods & drinks

Method (i) Capillary tube

Yeast does not ferment all of the sugars listed above. Those that are fermented undergo fermentation at different rates. This method, which uses a 10–15 cm length of capillary tubing, provides a useful preliminary guide, indicating whether a sugar is fermented and, if it is, the relative rate of its fermentation.

1 Cut 10–15 cm lengths of 0.5 mm diameter glass capillary tubing. Use a glass marking pen to draw a line 1.5 cm from one end. Dip the marked end of the capillary tube into the sugar solution/yeast mixture to a level above the mark. Let any excess fluid above the mark drain out, or gently blow it out. Hold the level of the sugar solution/yeast mixture at the mark by placing a finger over the open end of the capillary tube.

2 Push the end of the capillary tube containing the mixture into a small ball of plasticine, stuck to the bench surface. Ensure that the glass tubing is upright. Leave the mixture to ferment for 6–12 hours.

3 After 6–12 hours, measure the length of capillary tubing containing the sugar solution/yeast mixture. Use this measurement, and those measurements obtained from other sugar solution/yeast mixtures, to provide a rough indication of relative rates of fermentation. (The longer the sugar solution/yeast column, the faster the rate of fermentation.)

Method (ii) Moving meniscus

The apparatus is constructed from a 5 cm³ or 10 cm³ plastic syringe, attached by a piece of rubber tubing to a 25–30 cm length of 2 mm diameter glass tubing. As carbon dioxide is produced by the sugar solution/yeast mixture, it accumulates at the top of the syringe. This displaces some of the mixture, which flows into the glass tubing. By measuring the distance travelled by the meniscus in a given time, the volume of gas produced can be calculated from the formula $\pi r^2 h$, where $\pi = 3.14$, r = radius of glass tubing and h = distance travelled by meniscus m^{-1} or h^{-1}.

1 Draw sugar solution/yeast mixture in a 5 cm³ or 10 cm³ plastic syringe. Fit a piece of rubber tubing over the nozzle end of the syringe, and then fit the free end over a 25–30 cm length of glass tubing. Depress the plunger until some of the mixture appears at the top of the glass tubing. Mark this position with a glass marking pen.

2 Either clamp the apparatus into a vertical position, or stick it, using sticky tape, to the side of a bench or table. Use one or more pieces of this apparatus to find out how each of the following affect the rate of fermentation:

- different sugar substrates
- variations in the concentration of a sugar
- variations in the concentration of yeast
- different species or varieties of yeast

Method (iii) Bubbler

The apparatus consists of a 20 cm³ or 50 cm³ glass or plastic syringe filled with sugar solution/yeast mixture. After a 1 dm³ measuring cylinder has been filled to the 750 cm³ mark with water, the syringe is inverted, placed into the measuring cylinder, and weighed down with plasticine placed around the handle.

1 Fill a 20 cm³ or 50 cm³ plastic or glass syringe with sugar solution/yeast mixture. Attach plasticine to the handle of the syringe. This must be sufficient to prevent the inverted syringe from rising when it is submerged. Pour water into a 1 dm³ measuring cylinder to the 750 cm³ mark. Invert the syringe and place it into the measuring cylinder.

2 Record the number of bubbles released from the nozzle of the syringe in a given period of time.
Use the apparatus to investigate how each of the following affects the rate of fermentation:

- temperature (place the measuring cylinder into a water bath)
- pH (add a crushed pH tablet to the sugar solution/yeast mixture).

Method (iv) Rising dough

If flour is added to a sugar solution/yeast mixture to form a creamy paste, bubbles of carbon dioxide become trapped by the sticky, elastic dough. This causes the dough to rise. The initial rate at which dough rises is directly proportional to the rate of fermentation. At a certain point, however, enzymes produced by yeast cause gluten molecules in the flour to break down. As a result, some gas escapes and the dough tends to collapse.

1 Produce a dough by adding 70–80 g white flour to 100 cm³ sugar solution/yeast mixture. Use a glass rod to stir the mixture until an homogenous texture has been obtained. Pour 35 cm³ dough mixture into a 100 cm³ glass measuring cylinder, taking care not to spill any down the sides of the glass.

Foods & drinks

2 Place the measuring cylinder into a water bath at 35°C. Record the height of the dough column at 10 or 20 minutes intervals.

Use the apparatus to investigate how each of the following affects the rate of fermentation:

- temperature

- pH

- additions to the dough, such as baking soda, ascorbic acid (vitamin C) and mineral salts.

Small scale laboratory models

Some industrial processes can be illustrated by small-scale laboratory models. In the following example an inverted plastic bottle, from which the base has been removed, forms the main part of the apparatus. The type of micro-organism placed into the bottle, and the type of substrate that is drip-fed through it, determine the nature of the end product that can be extracted from the filtrate.

b) *Making vinegar from beer or cider*

Vinegar, or more accurately its major component acetic acid, is produced from ethanol by an aerobic process, with acetaldehyde as an intermediate product, by bacteria of the genus *Acetobacter*. The ethanol-containing substrate can be beer (for malt vinegar), or cider (for cider vinegar).

1 Mix a dried culture of *Acetobacter* with a 3%$^{w/v}$ suspension of sodium alginate. Use this mixture to coat dry, clean, wood shavings and horticultural grade vermiculite. Solidify the gel by dipping the coated materials into a 3%$^{w/v}$ solution of calcium chloride.

2 Cut the base from a large plastic drinks bottle. Plug the neck of the bottle with cotton wool. Invert the bottle and support the neck in a jam-jar. Fill the inverted bottle with coated wood shavings and vermiculite, but do not compress this material. Ensure that air can circulate between the wood shavings and vermiculite.

3 Place about 250 cm³ of beer or cider into a plastic freezer bag. Clamp the freezer bag above the top of the inverted plastic bottle. Prick the bag with a pin to establish a very slow drip-feed of beer or cider through the apparatus. Examine the filtrate for the presence of acetic acid, which has a characteristic pungent odour.

Never consume any beverage or food prepared in the laboratory.

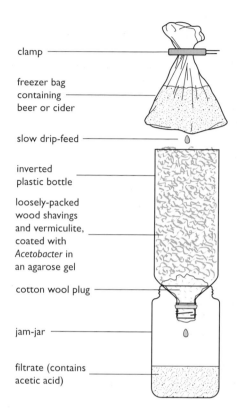

clamp

freezer bag containing beer or cider

slow drip-feed

inverted plastic bottle

loosely-packed wood shavings and vermiculite, coated with *Acetobacter* in an agarose gel

cotton wool plug

jam-jar

filtrate (contains acetic acid)

Small scale vinegar production

Antibiotics and antiseptics

Both antibiotics and antiseptics are used to kill pathogenic micro-organisms. The measurement of the relative efficiency of these compounds in killing bacteria involves similar techniques. Antibiotics are assayed using paper rings called Mastrings, each of which has six different coloured projecting discs that have been dipped into different antibiotics. Dipped filter paper discs, cut with a ring punch, can be used to assay antiseptics.

c) *Measuring the relative toxicity of different antibiotics against the bacterium* Bacillus subtilis

1 Prepare nutrient agar plates and a culture of the bacterium *B. subtilis*.

2 Put on eye protection. Light a Bunsen burner. Flame the bent end of a glass spreader, to destroy any micro-organisms that might be present. Cool the spreader by waving it in the air. Carefully dip the spreader into the culture of *B. subtilis*. Hold one of the petri dishes containing nutrient agar in your other hand. As soon as the agar is

Foods & drinks

exposed, spread the culture of *B. subtilis* thinly and evenly over the surface. Take care not to break the surface of the gel. Use flamed forceps to lay a Mastring in the centre of the agar. Press the coloured paper discs down with the tip of the forceps.

3 Seal the dish with sticky tape. Write your name on the bottom of the dish. Turn the dishes upside-down and transfer them to an incubator at 25°C. Leave them to incubate for about 24 hours.

4 After incubation, examine the petri dishes for translucent zones, but do not remove the lid. Use a ruler to measure the diameter of clear zones surrounding each of the paper discs. Record your results. The greater the area of the translucent zone, the more effective the antibiotic is shown to be. List the antibiotics in order of their effectiveness.

d) To determine the relative toxicity of different antiseptics against B. subtilis

Two or more antiseptics/disinfectants are required. Be aware that some disinfectants are toxic to humans.

1 Use a ring punch to cut discs of uniform size from a piece of filter paper.

2 Proceed, in general, as in investigation (c). Use forceps to dip each paper disc into an antiseptic/disinfectant. Allow excess liquid to drain off before applying the disc to a nutrient agar gel. Treat each agar plate with a culture of *B. subtilis* as before. Place two dipped discs on each agar plate.

(a) *Spread the bacterial culture with an L-shaped spreader, to cover the entire surface of the agar*

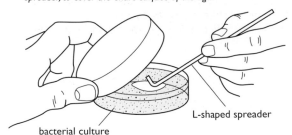

bacterial culture

L-shaped spreader

(b) *Place the Mastring-S in position*

forceps

Mastring-S

(c) *Seal the dish with adhesive tape and write your name on the base*

sticky tape

Investigating the effectiveness of antibiotics against bacteria

Foods & drinks

CHAPTER 5   QUESTIONS

1 Fermentation of glucose to alcohol may be represented by the following equation:

$$C_6H_{12}O_6 \rightarrow 2C_2H_5OH + 2CO_2$$
glucose   alcohol   carbon
                                          dioxide

(H = 1, C = 12, O = 16)

a) From the equation:

   (i)   Calculate the theoretical yield of alcohol from 1 kg glucose.

   (ii) What is the theoretical yield of carbon dioxide from the same mass of glucose?

   (iii) How much glucose would have been fermented to produce 1 dm³ alcohol? What assumption has been made?

b) Why should the home-brewer always ferment 'wort' in thick-walled glass vessels or plastic containers, never in beer bottles?

c) What safety precautions should home-brewers take to prevent their beer being contaminated by other micro-organisms before, during and after fermentation?

d) After fermentation is complete, beer may be treated with

   (i)   pectolytic enzymes and
   (ii) filtered.

Explain the reasons for each treatment.

2 Give a step-by-step account of modern beer production. In what ways does the large-scale production of wine differ from that of beer?

3 Outline the principal stages in the production of a commercial cheese such as cheddar.
Explain the role of micro-organisms, including fungi, in cheese-making.

4 Write illustrated notes on each of the following:

a) single cell protein (SCP)

b) yoghurt production

c) vinegar production

d) bread-making

5 What methods are used to preserve food from attack by saprophytes? Explain the biological principles that make each of these methods effective in food preservation.

Argue the case for and against the use of gamma ray irradiation as a method of food preservation.

BIBLIOGRAPHY

Foods & Drinks
Barnell, HR (1980) *Biology of the Food Industry* (Studies in Biology No. 45) Edward Arnold
Bravery, HE (1976) *Home Booze* Book Club Associates, London
Burch, B (1992) *Brewing Quality Beers – The Home Brewer's Essential Guidebook* 2nd Edn Joby Books, Fulton, CA

Goldblith, SA, Rey, L and Rothmeyer, WW eds (1984) *Freezedrying and Advanced Food Technology* Academic Press
Hough, JS (1984) *The Biotechnology and Malting Brewing* Cambridge University Press
National Centre for Biotechnology Education (1993) *Practical Biotechnology* University of Reading
National Dairy Council (1988) *From Farm to Doorstep: a Guide to Milk and Dairy Products*
Thear, K (1983) *Home Dairying* Batsford, London

Foods & drinks

CHAPTER

6 | Clinical & forensic medicine

Clinical & forensic medicine

Recent advances in biotechnology promise major advances in many different areas of medicine. Mass cell culture techniques, pioneered in the production of antibiotics, are proving equally effective in producing a wide range of other pharmaceutical products. Hormones, vaccines and therapeutic proteins, such as monoclonal antibodies and interferon, are some of the cell products that are already being mass produced. An alternative approach is to use **transgenic** animals as a drug source. Transgenic animals are those which have had genes transferred into them from another organism. Sheep that secrete interferon into their milk, and chickens that produce antibodies in their eggs, could soon become commonplace.

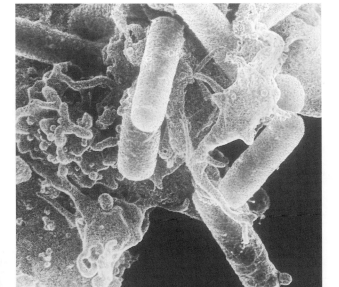

C3 Scanning electron micrograph (SEM) of a white blood cell (leucocyte) attacking and engulfing bacteria (*see Colour Section on inside cover*)

Our ability to manipulate the human genome has led to new diagnostic and therapeutic methods. Gene probes, added to treated blood samples or amniotic fluid from around a developing foetus, can diagnose the presence of viral, bacterial or other pathogens. They can also be used in the diagnosis of genetic disorders such as sickle cell anaemia, cystic fibrosis and Tay-Sachs disease. Gene therapy may soon provide a cure for some of these conditions, by replacing defective genes with normal ones. Genetic fingerprinting, in which an individual's identity can be established from analysis of the DNA in blood or semen, is a powerful tool in forensic science.

6.1 Micro-organisms Versus the Immune System

If pathogenic viruses, bacteria and other micro-organisms penetrate natural barriers such as the skin and mucous membranes, they enter the bloodstream where they encounter the body's immune system. This system consists mainly of white cells circulating in the blood and lymph, together with those contained in the spleen, liver, lymph nodes and tissues. In addition, a number of chemical compounds assist cells of the immune system in keeping cells and tissues free from infection.

6.1.1 Cells of the Immune System

Six different types of white cell are normally found in the blood. These are neutrophils, eosinophils, basophils, monocytes, lymphocytes and plasma cells. Biologists have classified these cells on the basis of structure, source and function. Neutrophils, eosinophils and basophils, with granules in their cytoplasm, are known as **granulocytes**, whereas the non-granular types are called **agranulocytes**. Another classification, based on function, distinguishes **phagocytes** (neutrophils, eosinophils and monocytes), which actively ingest invading micro-organisms and then break them down by secreting digestive acids and enzymes, from other types of non-phagocytic blood cells.

Granulocytes

- **Neutrophils**, with granules that do not stain with acidic or basic dyes, move through the vascular system and tissues by amoeboid motion. They show chemotaxis towards inflamed tissues and bacterial toxins. These cells are powerful phagocytes, attacking and destroying invading bacteria, viruses and other injurious agents. A neutrophil can usually ingest and destroy 5–20 bacteria before it becomes inactivated and dies.
- **Eosinophils**, with granules that stain red with eosin, are weak phagocytes, attracted to tissues by substances present in inflamed tissue. Their most important function is to ingest and destroy antibody–antigen complexes after the immune system has performed its function (see page 95).
- **Basophils**, with granules that stain blue with basic dyes such as methylene blue, secrete inflammatory activators into the blood. These compounds include heparin, which slows blood clotting, histamine, serotonin and bradykinin.
- **Mast cells**, which resemble basophils in structure and function, occur only in tissues. It may be that mast cells develop from basophils once they have entered tissues. Both basophils and mast cells are activated by the absorption of IgE antibodies (see page 95). In response to a specific foreign protein they release relatively large amounts of histamine and bradykinin, which initiate **inflammation**. The massive release of these activators from mast cells is the immediate cause of anaphylactic shock (see page 95).

Phagocytes

In addition to the granulocyte phagocytes (neutrophils and eosinophils) there is an agranulocyte type, known as a monocyte when it is circulating in blood and a macrophage after it has entered tissues.

- **Monocytes** are small, immature phagocytes, found in the blood, with very little ability to fight injurious agents.
- **Macrophages** are mature monocytes. On entering tissues they swell, increasing their size as much as five-fold, while developing numerous lysosomes and mitochondria in their cytoplasm. Mature macrophages are powerful phagocytes, each capable of taking up more than 100 bacteria and destroying them. Macrophages in different tissues are given a variety of names based on differences in form and function. These include Kupffer cells in the liver and reticulum cells in the spleen and bone marrow.

Lymphocytes

Lymphocytes are cells which respond to specific foreign proteins, known as antigens. They are of two types, **B** and **T cells**, differentiated by the distinct way in which each type matures.

- **B lymphocytes** originate in the bone marrow and mature there without the influence of the thymus gland. After contact with a specific antigen, they mature into **plasma cells**. These cells produce Y-shaped protective proteins called **antibodies**. Plasma cells have sticky surface immunoglobulins that trap specific foreign proteins, known as **antigens**. There are millions of different types of B cells, each capable of responding to a different specific antigen.
- **T lymphocytes** also originate in the bone marrow but mature by passing through the thymus gland, which surrounds the blood vessels immediately above the heart.

    This gland, which is believed to be most active shortly before birth, gradually decreases in size during childhood and adolescence. When T lymphocytes pass through the thymus gland, they acquire the ability to distinguish 'self' proteins from 'non-self' proteins. They also undergo differentiation into a million or more different types, each capable of responding to a different antigen. Mature T lymphocytes exist in several different types.

    - **T killer cells**, or **cytotoxic T cells**, attack and destroy whole cells with specific foreign proteins on their surface membranes. Such cells may include those of invading micro-organisms, or cancerous cells that have arisen by mutation.

    - **Natural killer (NK) cells** are large, non-specific lymphocytes that attack tumours of virus-infected cells.

    - **T helper cells** regulate – or help – other cells. As a result of the influence of T helper cells, B cells differentiate into antibody-secreting cells and T killer cells become functional.

    It is currently unclear whether there is a distinct subpopulation of **T suppressor cells**, which may limit or terminate the immune response. Following a successful immune response, in which an invading micro-organism is eliminated, both B and T cells produce **memory cells**. These persist within the immune system.

Clinical & forensic medicine

93

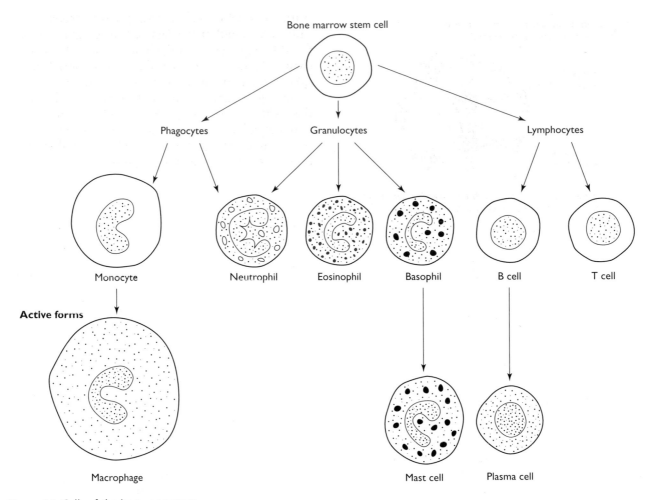

Figure 6.1 Cells of the immune system

Any subsequent exposure to the same pathogen immediately activates the memory cells. A rapid attack is mounted, which generally destroys the invader before it produces any symptoms of disease.

QUESTIONS

1 Name two antibiotics produced by a) fungi and b) bacteria.

2 Name two anti-inflammatory steroid drugs.

3 State two advantages of using vaccines produced only from the surface antigens of pathogens.

4 The human immune system consists of several different groups of cells. Name two different types that are a) phagocytes, b) granulocytes and c) lymphocytes.

5 What types of T cell occur in the immune system?

6.1.2 Antigens and Antibodies

B cells produce protective proteins called antibodies in response to the presence of foreign macromolecules, such as proteins, polysaccharides and lipids, collectively known as antigens. It is important to realise that the cell surfaces of invading micro-organisms contain non-antigenic macromolecules as well as antigenic ones. Furthermore, only parts of an antigen, such as an antigenic protein, may be involved in an antigen–antibody response. Specific regions of antigens, known as **antigenic determinants**, or **epitopes**, are the only parts of these molecules which are capable of reacting with a specific antibody.

Antibodies are Y-shaped proteins, consisting of two identical light (L) and two identical heavy (H) **polypeptide chains**, joined by **disulphide bonds**. These bonds form hinges, which give some flexibility to the molecule at its mid-point. Each of the two arms ends in a **combining site**, where the antibody binds epitopes of an antigen. At the tip of each arm is a **variable region**, which is different for each specific antibody. The stem of an antibody along with the lower part of its arms, form the **constant region**, with the same species-specific sequence of

Clinical & forensic medicine

(a) *The surface membrane contains both antigenic (black) and non-antigenic (white) macromolecules*

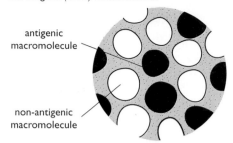

antigenic macromolecule

non-antigenic macromolecule

(b) *The immune system recognises only the antigenic determinants – parts of a molecule where antigen–antibody binding takes place*

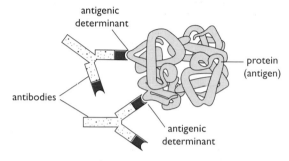

antigenic determinant

protein (antigen)

antibodies

antigenic determinant

Figure 6.2 Antigenic and non-antigenic macromolecules on the surface of pathogenic micro-organisms

amino acids in each type. Each polypeptide chain of an antibody is divided into **domains**, four in each long chain and two in each short one.

Antibodies protect against invading agents in one or more of the following ways.

(i) By a direct attack on the invader. This may involve **lysis** of antigens in the cell membrane of an invader, causing it to rupture, or the **neutralisation** of these antigens, a process by which toxic regions of antigen molecules are covered. **Agglutination**, or clumping, of invading bacteria occurs when antibodies form cross-links with antigens. A fourth process, **precipitation**, occurs when an invading bacterium, such as the tetanus bacterium, produces a soluble toxin. When this binds with an antibody, an insoluble, non-toxic antigen–antibody complex is formed and is precipitated.

(ii) By activating the complement system which then destroys the invader.

(iii) By causing the mast cells to degranulate. This is known as the **anaphylactic response**, which changes the cellular environment in organs that are under attack. Unfortunately, in some individuals the severity of this reaction increases with successive exposures to specific antigens – a process that can result in sudden death.

Antibodies, which belong to a group of proteins called **immunoglobulins (Igs)**, can be separated into five different classes on the basis of their physical, chemical and immunological properties: **IgG, IgA, IgM, IgD** and **IgE**. IgG is the major circulating immunoglobulin, present in blood and lymph, with the ability to cross the placenta. IgM is the first immunoglobulin to appear after vaccination (immunisation). IgE, with the ability to bind mast cells, is involved in allergic responses.

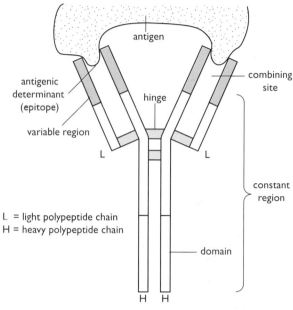

antigen

antigenic determinant (epitope)

combining site

variable region

hinge

L

L

constant region

L = light polypeptide chain
H = heavy polypeptide chain

domain

H   H

Figure 6.3 An antibody

6.1.3 The Immune Response

Infectious diseases, caused by micro-organisms, initiate a sequence of events in the immune system that is summarised in Figure 6.4. An invading micro-organism, carrying surface antigens, is ingested and broken down by a macrophage. The macrophage, a large phagocytic cell, then displays fragments of the antigen on its surface. This attracts an **antigen-presenting cell**, which accumulates antigen on its surface, before presenting it to B cells, T helper cells and the precursors of T killer cells. Only those lymphocytes with the specific antigen receptors on their surfaces respond. Their response, known as **clonal selection**, consists of a rapid multiplication, by mitosis, of those lymphocytes capable of dealing with the specific antigen. After a successful attack has been mounted by the B and T lymphocytes, T suppressor cells slow the rate of lymphocyte multiplication. Finally, when an invading micro-organism has been cleared from cells and tissues, memory cells persist. These are capable of mounting a rapid, effective and efficient attack against subsequent invasions by the same micro-organism.

Clinical & forensic medicine

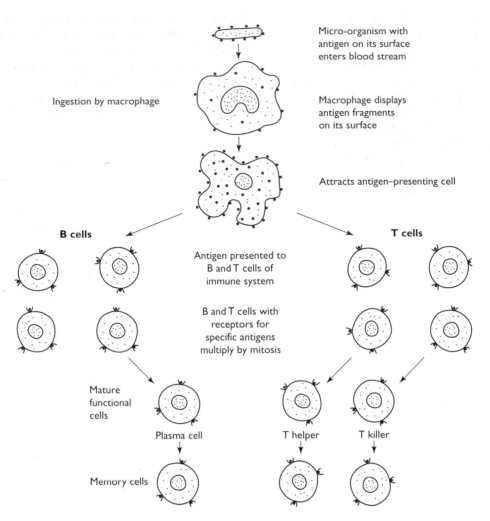

Figure 6.4 The immune response

6.1.4 Chemical Compounds of the Immune System

Two distinct groups of compounds, the lymphokines and complement, are important in achieving an effective immune response.

- **Interferon**, a lymphokine, is produced by cells which are attacked by viruses. It has little or no effect on any host cell that is under attack, but increases the resistance of neighbouring cells to the virus. Interferon does this by diffusing out of damaged cells and binding to receptors on the cell surface membrane of neighbouring healthy cells. Once bound, the healthy cells synthesise a protein that gives some protection by slowing or inhibiting viral replication.
- **Interleukins**, also lymphokines, are hormone-like compounds that pass between cells of the immune system. Interleukin secretion by T helper cells, for example, which can be suppressed by T suppressor cells, transforms B lymphocytes into plasma cells and activates T killer cells.

- **Complement** is the collective name for a series of 18 plasma proteins. These proteins assist in protecting the host primarily against bacterial infections. Some act as chemotactic agents, attracting neutrophils to areas of injury. Others, known as **opsonins**, become attached to bacteria, marking them in some way for rapid uptake by phagocytic cells. A third group kill bacteria directly by lysing their surface membranes. When antibodies react with antigens, **immune complexes** are formed. Complement marks these immune complexes for uptake and destruction by phagocytes.

6.1.5 Allergy

Sometimes the immune response is inefficient or defective. The result is an exaggerated and inappropriate immune reaction, called an **allergy**, usually against a foreign compound, that causes damage to body tissues or exerts other unpleasant effects. Some people show allergic reactions to the antibiotic penicillin, which is given as a drug to help the immune system combat bacterial infections.

During the 1950s, benzyl penicillin was used widely in the treatment of streptococcal infections. Solutions of penicillin were injected every 4–6 hours, over a period of several days. As a result of this high exposure to penicillin, a significant number of patients developed an allergy to penicillin. In some of these patients, penicillin, possibly in combination with a protein, acted as an antigen. Antibodies reacted with it forming an immune complex, which was not cleared by complement and phagocytes. Instead, these immune complexes settled in different parts of the body causing inflammation, for example in the skin (urticaria), joints (arthritis) and kidneys (nephritis). A much more severe type of allergy, known as **anaphylactic allergy**, also occurred in some patients. A sensitising dose of penicillin in these patients produced no adverse symptoms. Subsequent doses, however, produced allergic reactions of increasing severity. The reasons for this are now understood. In response to the initial dose of penicillin, IgE antibodies were produced by plasma cells. These antibodies then bound to mast cells. A further dose of penicillin caused cross-linkage between the IgE antibodies. This acted as a signal for the rapid **degranulation** of the mast cells, with the release of potent chemicals into the bloodstream.

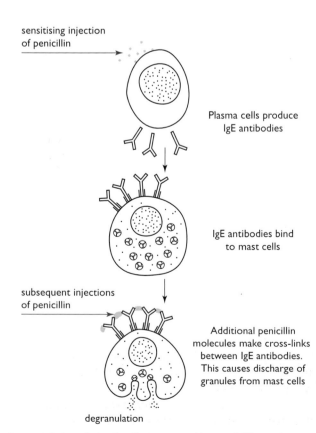

sensitising injection of penicillin

Plasma cells produce IgE antibodies

IgE antibodies bind to mast cells

subsequent injections of penicillin

Additional penicillin molecules make cross-links between IgE antibodies. This causes discharge of granules from mast cells

degranulation

Figure 6.5 Anaphylactic allergy caused by penicillin

Among the effects resulting from this event are oedema (swelling of tissues caused by leakage of plasma from the capillaries), acute inflammation, asthma (caused by smooth muscle contraction in the airways leading to and from the lungs), rapid changes in blood pressure and tissue damage. Extremely severe reactions occasionally caused sudden death.

6.1.6 Types of Immunity

Humans have **natural immunity** to most diseases in animals, such as fowl pest of chickens and foot-and-mouth disease of cattle. **Natural acquired immunity** occurs when individuals produce their own antibodies in response to an infection. Antibodies produced in response to an attack of mumps or measles generally give long-term protection against these diseases, often for life. During pregnancy, mothers pass some of their antibodies to the foetus via the placenta. After birth, infants obtain additional antibodies from their mother's milk. These antibodies are absorbed intact from the infant's small intestine without being broken down by digestive enzymes. This is **natural passive immunity**, the acquisition of antibodies from another individual of the same species. **Acquired immunity** results from vaccination (**immunisation**). **Passive acquired immunity** occurs when antibodies made in another species, such as a horse, are given to humans to combat diseases such as diphtheria and tetanus. **Active acquired immunity** occurs when individuals make their own antibodies, following vaccination with a weakened or attenuated form of an antigen.

6.2 Assisting the Immune System

There are a number of ways in which biotechnologists can assist the immune system in its battle against pathogenic micro-organisms. As prevention is always better than cure, vaccines offer a means of remaining healthy by preventing infectious diseases from attacking those who have been vaccinated. For those who have suffered infectious diseases, antibiotics and monoclonal antibodies can help to overcome infections, while steroids can reduce inflammation caused by severe immune reactions.

6.2.1 Vaccines and Vaccination

Edward Jenner (1748–1823), an English doctor, established the principles of vaccination in the late 18th century. At a time when smallpox, an acute infection, took many lives, Jenner was keen to find a

Clinical & forensic medicine

treatment that might give some protection against this lethal disease. A milkmaid told him that as she had contracted cowpox (vaccinia) while milking cows, she was unlikely to catch smallpox (variola). Cowpox was a common and widespread condition that affected the hands of milkers, producing watery pustules on their fingers.

Jenner experimented. He took some of the watery fluid from these cowpox pustules and introduced it into shallow scratches he had made on the skin of children who had not had smallpox. A strong reaction often followed. The site of the vaccination became red and raised. These children, however, acquired an immunity to smallpox as a result of this procedure. What Jenner didn't know, of course, was that the cowpox and smallpox viruses were closely related. Inoculation with cowpox antigens gave protection against smallpox antigens because both were of a similar form, eliciting the production of almost identical antibodies.

Today, vaccination against a wide range of infectious diseases is routine. Among the most widely recommended vaccines for children are DTP (diphtheria, tetanus and pertussis (whooping cough)), polio, MMR (measles, mumps, rubella), influenza and hepatitis B.

All vaccines are prepared from antigens. Most, but not all, come from the surfaces of pathogens. Some of these pathogens, killed by treatment with heat, formaldehyde or phenol, retain their antigens, but in an altered form which makes them much less likely to cause disease. **Dead cells** can be used as vaccines, but there is always a risk that the antigens will revert to a virulent form, and that other parts of the cell will trigger allergic reactions. **Attenuated cells** can be used as an alternative to dead cells. These have lost their virulence as a result of being kept in laboratory cultures for many years, without passing through their normal host. Measles and mumps vaccines, for example, are composed of attenuated viruses. These strains have lost their virulence but have retained their immunising antigens. Finally, some vaccines are prepared from chemically-altered exotoxins. Such substances are known as **toxoids**, which can be used to immunise safely against diphtheria and tetanus and can be given in fairly high doses.

With the development of biotechnology, a new generation of vaccines is being produced. These vaccines are prepared from those regions of antigens known as antigen determinants. As a result, purer vaccines are being manufactured, which will be more likely to promote antibody production, yet less likely to cause allergy or other side effects.

Hepatitis B

Hepatitis B is a viral disease of humans, causing malfunctions of the liver, and, in some cases, cancer of the liver. It was discovered that the blood serum from infected persons carried a surface antigen from the virus (HBsAg). The DNA which coded for this surface antigen was cloned in yeast cells. Large quantities of the surface antigen were subsequently produced by the yeasts. After purification, this antigen was found to be effective as a vaccine, raising antibodies that gave protection against the hepatitis B virus. If a vaccine is prepared from a surface antigen, rather than an attenuated virus, there is no possibility that vaccination will ever cause disease. This occasionally happened when attenuated strains of a virus, such as the poliomyelitis virus, recovered their virulence after injection into the bloodstream.

Cowpox

Cowpox or **vaccinia virus** is of considerable interest because it is one of the largest viruses and will accept large amounts of extra DNA. By a complex procedure involving bacterial plasmids and *E. coli*, the virus has been engineered to incorporate and express foreign DNA from HIV (the AIDS virus), influenza, herpes and the malarial parasite. The protein products of this foreign DNA are expressed at the surface of the vaccinia virus. It is hoped that these surface antigens can be used as vaccines, to raise antibodies against those organisms from which the foreign DNA was taken.

With the introduction of unstirred airlift fermenters (p.73), large scale tissue culture has become available for medical and veterinary virus vaccine production. Bacterial cultures for use in vaccine production are grown in relatively small stainless steel fermenters, of 1000 dm^3 or less. The internal pressure within these fermenters is kept below atmospheric pressure, to reduce the risk of pathogenic bacteria being blown out into the atmosphere. Furthermore, the exhaust gases pass through a sterilising filter, or incinerator, or both, so that there is effective containment.

The aim of vaccination is to build up a high titre of specific antibodies in the blood. This is rarely achieved by a single vaccination. A more common practice is to give two or more inoculations, with a suitable time interval between. The initial injection of antigen stimulates B cells to transform into memory cells and antibody-producing plasma cells. A few days after this injection, the antibody titre begins to rise. Soon it reaches a peak and then begins to fall. This is the **primary response**. At this stage, the antibody titre consists almost entirely of IgM immunoglobulins. If a second injection of antibody is

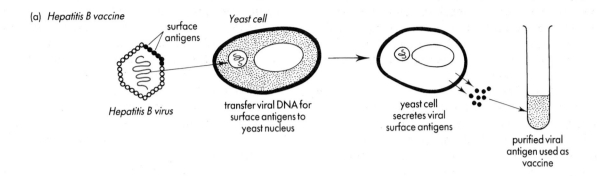

(a) *Hepatitis B vaccine*

surface antigens

Yeast cell

Hepatitis B virus

transfer viral DNA for surface antigens to yeast nucleus

yeast cell secretes viral surface antigens

purified viral antigen used as vaccine

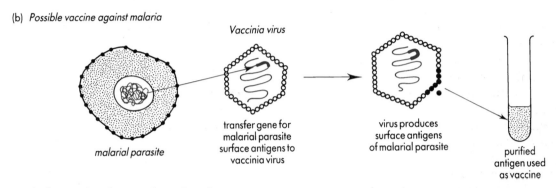

(b) *Possible vaccine against malaria*

Vaccinia virus

malarial parasite

transfer gene for malarial parasite surface antigens to vaccinia virus

virus produces surface antigens of malarial parasite

purified antigen used as vaccine

Figure 6.6 Producing vaccines by genetic engineering

given soon after the peak has been reached, the antibody titre rises to a much higher level and remains high for a much longer period of time. The higher titre level of antibodies is boosted by the production of IgG immunoglobulins, which are longer lived and give better protection. This is the **secondary response**, which gives effective immunisation lasting anything from a few years to a lifetime.

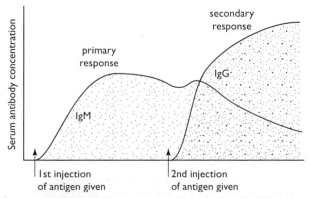

Figure 6.7 The effect of primary and secondary vaccination on serum antibody concentration

6.2.2 *Monoclonal Antibodies*

In the early 1970s, research into antibody function was thwarted by the problem that antibody-producing cells could not be maintained in culture for more than a few days. A solution came in 1975, following from the work of G. Kohler and C. Milstein. Their approach was to fuse the short-lived antibody-producing cells with cancer cells that live indefinitely. They injected mice with sheep red blood cells, which are highly antigenic. B lymphocytes were then harvested from the spleens of the mice and fused with myeloma cells from bone marrow to form hybrids, or **hybridoma** cells. After selection on appropriate semi-solid media, some clones of these cells specifically recognised sheep red blood cells. As all the members of the same clone produced the same antibody they were called **monoclonal antibodies.** The relatively simple production technique allowed specific monoclonal antibodies to be produced in response to any known antigen. As the role of an antibody is to seek out and tag a specific antigen, monoclonal antibodies hold the promise of acting like 'magic bullets', with the ability to find and bind any foreign material in the tissues, from a pathogen to a cancer cell.

Clinical & forensic medicine

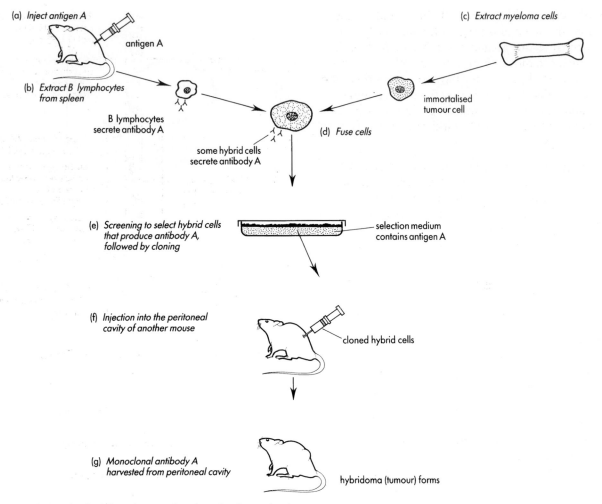

(a) *Inject antigen A*

antigen A

(c) *Extract myeloma cells*

(b) *Extract B lymphocytes from spleen*

B lymphocytes secrete antibody A

some hybrid cells secrete antibody A

immortalised tumour cell

(d) *Fuse cells*

(e) *Screening to select hybrid cells that produce antibody A, followed by cloning*

selection medium contains antigen A

(f) *Injection into the peritoneal cavity of another mouse*

cloned hybrid cells

(g) *Monoclonal antibody A harvested from peritoneal cavity*

hybridoma (tumour) forms

Figure 6.8 General principles of monoclonal antibody production

Clearly, specific or monoclonal antibodies have many uses, both in current clinical medicine and in medical research. Some of their more important applications are listed below:

(i) The ability to tag specific proteins with a marked antibody is an invaluable tool in biomedical research, because it enables researchers to follow the movements of a protein and find out exactly what it does.

(ii) Monoclonal antibodies, labelled with a fluorescent dye or radioactive isotope, are used to identify the distribution of antigens, such as those of pathogens or cancer cells, in tissue sections.

(iii) Before organ transplantation is undertaken, tissues of the donor and recipient are tissue-typed. The better the match between cell surface proteins, the better the chances of success, with less tissue rejection. Monoclonal antibodies, raised in response to these cell surface proteins, have allowed more accurate tissue-typing to be undertaken.

(iv) Patients who have undergone kidney transplants are currently treated with a monoclonal antibody called 'Orthoclone OKT-3'. This specifically reacts with the OKT-3 antigen on the surface of T lymphocytes, the cells that mount an attack on the 'foreign' kidney. It is claimed that this treatment has saved the kidneys of 90% of the patients whose bodies would have rejected them.

(v) Dipsticks, such as those used for pregnancy-testing, are impregnated with antibodies, some attached to coloured latex particles. The urine of pregnant women contains an additional component, namely human chorionic gonadotrophin (hCG), a product of the placenta. This hormone binds to coloured mobile antibodies at the base of the dipstick. As urine diffuses upwards, the antibody–hormone complexes travel with it, but are stopped about one-third of the way up by a row of immobilised antibodies that also bind hCG. The accumulation of coloured antibody–hormone complexes at this level results in the formation of a coloured band (usually blue), indicating that the woman is pregnant. Conversely, if the woman is not pregnant and has no hCG in her urine, the mobile antibodies travel further up the dipstick, until they bind to a second band of immobilised antibodies, capable of forming complexes with the mobile antibody. A blue band at this higher level indicates a negative result.

(vi) Drugs such as cocaine, amphetamines, opiates, steroids and barbiturates are excreted in the urine. Monoclonal antibodies are used in specific ELISA tests for each of these drugs, and for chemical derivatives of cannabis. A liquid reagent is mixed with a urine sample. If a specific drug is present, the liquid changes colour. The more intense the colour, the higher the drug concentration. One component of the reagent is a monoclonal antibody prepared using the drug as the antigen. The other major component is a derivative of the drug chemically combined with the enzyme glucose-6-phosphate dehydrogenase and the substrate of this enzyme, glucose-6-phosphate. The drug, if present, competes with the glucose-6-phosphate-drug derivative for monoclonal antibody. This sets enzyme free to act on its substrate. Drug concentration is directly related to enzyme concentration in the urine/reagent mixture, and the final colour of this mixture after a specified period of time.

Malignant tumours, viral, bacterial and other pathogens, all carry unique antigens on their surfaces. Monoclonal antibodies, prepared against each of these antigens, bind specifically to them and therefore have the ability to distinguish diseased cells from healthy ones.

(i) Combined with a powerful toxin, such as ricin, monoclonal antibodies could be targeted to bind to the surfaces of cancer cells, or pathogens such as viruses or bacteria. This site-specific release of toxins offers hope of destroying the foreign material without destroying surrounding healthy tissue.

(ii) Antibodies produced in response to drugs could be used to treat people who have taken an overdose. Blood of the overdosed person would be circulated outside the body, through a device containing monoclonal antibodies, which would remove the drug from the bloodstream.

(iii) Medically-important substances, such as interferon, could be purified by using monoclonal antibodies to remove organic contaminants.

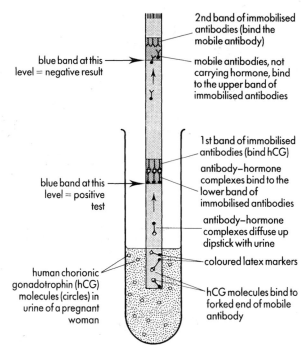

Figure 6.9 Antibody-based dipstick for pregnancy

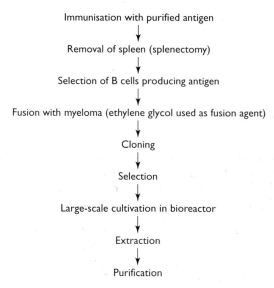

Immunisation with purified antigen
↓
Removal of spleen (splenectomy)
↓
Selection of B cells producing antigen
↓
Fusion with myeloma (ethylene glycol used as fusion agent)
↓
Cloning
↓
Selection
↓
Large-scale cultivation in bioreactor
↓
Extraction
↓
Purification

Figure 6.10 Stages in the commercial production of monoclonal antibodies

(iv) During heart attacks, one protein component of heart muscle, myosin, is exposed. A myosin-specific monoclonal antibody would therefore be useful for diagnosing the extent of heart damage following a heart attack.

6.2.3 Transgenic Animals

The production of medical products in transgenic animals – those that have had their genome altered by recombinant DNA technology (see section 8.1) – is an alternative to production by cell culture in fermenters.

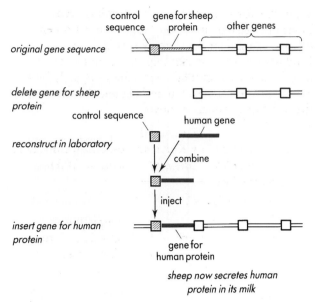

control sequence · gene for sheep protein · other genes

original gene sequence

delete gene for sheep protein

control sequence · human gene

reconstruct in laboratory

combine

inject

insert gene for human protein

gene for human protein

sheep now secretes human protein in its milk

Figure 6.11 Stages in the replacement of a gene for sheep protein, secreted into milk, with a gene for human protein

Transgenic sheep and cattle have already been used to produce products of medical importance, such as interferon, blood-clotting factors and enzymes that dissolve blood clots. The biotechnology involved consists of transforming an animal by adding a gene for protein synthesis upstream of the gene that codes for milk production (Figure 6.11). Successful integration of the new gene results in secretion of the required protein in the animal's milk. Collecting the milk, and separating out the required protein, is a relatively simple process. An alternative approach is to harvest the required protein from the eggs of transgenic chickens. The chicken has a gene that codes for the production of large amounts of egg albumen. Replacing this gene with one that codes for a human protein could soon provide large amounts of novel proteins from eggs.

The use of transgenic animals to produce drugs has a number of distinct advantages over the use of micro-organisms. These are:

(i)   It is infinitely more cost-effective, as expensive culture-vessels for large-scale production, continuous monitoring of equipment, and maintenance are not required.

(ii) Cells of animals such as sheep and cattle can add sugar residues to proteins. This makes them more effective and versatile synthesisers of desirable products than most micro-organisms.

(iii) Future demand for any product can be met by interbreeding transformed animals. The ability to secrete a required protein is passed from one generation to the next in accordance with Mendelian principles.

At the present time, however, there are problems in keeping transgenic animals alive. This means that the optimistic scenarios set out above are still some way off.

6.2.4   Antibiotics

Antibiotics are antimicrobial compounds produced by living micro-organisms, mostly actinomycetes and mould fungi. They are among the **secondary metabolites** of these micro-organisms, synthesised late in the growth cycle (Figure 6.12). Today, therapeutically-active antibiotics are widely used in clinical medicine and have saved many thousands of lives. Penicillin and streptomycin, that will destroy only a few species of bacteria, are known as **narrow spectrum antibiotics**. Conversely, tetracycline and chloramphenicol, effective against a wide range of organisms, are **broad spectrum antibiotics**. Elsewhere, outside medicine, antibiotics have many uses in the food industry, agriculture and research.

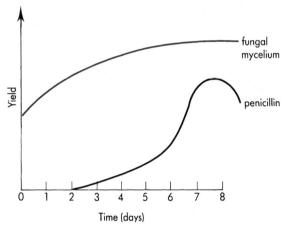

Figure 6.12 Penicillin production during a batch culture

Penicillin

Penicillin was discovered by Alexander Fleming at St Mary's Hospital, London in 1928–29. He noted that gram-positive bacteria, such as *Streptococcus sp.*, were killed by the diffusate from a colony of the mould fungus *Penicillium notatum*, an accidental contaminant of the culture plate. He called the active compound 'penicillin'. The subsequent extraction, purification and increase in the yield that made commercial production possible took almost another 20 years. Pioneer work was carried out by Howard Florey and Ernst Chain, based in Oxford, while in the USA, techniques for large scale production were developed. 'Cornsteep liquor', a by-product of starch manufacture from maize, was used as a nutrient.

By the early 1950s, penicillin yields of about 60 mg/dm^3 fungus-nutrient mixture were being obtained. At about this time *P. notatum* was replaced by *Penicillium chrysogenum*, a species that

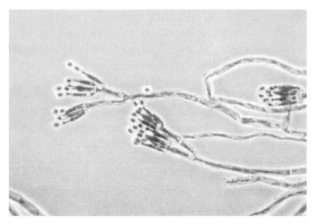

Penicillium notatum ×225

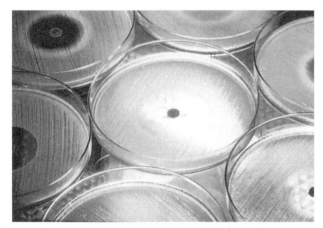

The inhibition of unidentified bacteria by antibiotic pellets at the centre of each dish

produced more penicillin and was more suited to culture in large-scale fermenters. As a result of mutation (induced by UV light and X rays), genetic manipulation, recombination and selection, geneticists had engineered a strain of the fungus that, by the 1980s, was producing yields of about 20 g/dm³ fungus-nutrient mixture.

In response to the enormous demand for penicillin, modern production is carried out in fermenters (p.72) with a capacity of up to 200 000 dm³.

The fungus is grown in liquid culture, fed with nutrient solution and aerated. Batch culture is preferred, because contamination by any other micro-organisms or toxins is extremely difficult to remove from the mixture, and can severely depress the yield. Optimal yields of penicillin are obtained after each batch has been cultured for 6–8 days (Figure 6.12). Separating out the penicillin involves filtration, continuous **counter-current extraction,** concentration and the addition of potassium compounds to precipitate crystals. The end product is benzyl penicillin, a relatively safe antibiotic with few serious side effects on those who take it. Even

so, in this form the drug can be administered internally only by injection, because it is broken down and made ineffective by stomach acid. Producing a form of the drug that could be taken orally, such as **ampicillin**, was achieved partly by a combination of microbial and chemical syntheses, as the following sequence shows:

Benzyl penicillin (degraded by digestive enzymes) — Fermented by *Kluyvera citrophila* → 6-aminopenicillanic acid (6-APA)

6-APA — Fermented by *Pseudomonas melanogenum* + DL–phenylglycine → Ampicillin (absorbed into blood stream via intestine)

Thousands of different antibiotics are currently in use as drugs. Many, like penicillin, are used to treat acute bacterial infections. Others, as Table 6.1 shows, are used to combat fungal infections or slow the rate of tumour growth. Those antibiotics that kill bacteria by inhibiting cell wall synthesis are relatively safe drugs, because human cells are not usually damaged by them. Many of the others, though, that work by inhibiting protein synthesis or damaging cell

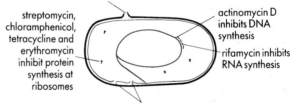

penicillin, cephalosporin and cycloserine inhibit cell wall synthesis

streptomycin, chloramphenicol, tetracycline and erythromycin inhibit protein synthesis at ribosomes

actinomycin D inhibits DNA synthesis

rifamycin inhibits RNA synthesis

polymixin B, amphotericin B and nystatin damage the cell membrane

Figure 6.13 Some effects of antibiotic drugs on bacteria

Table 6.1 Some therapeutic antibiotics

Antibiotic	Source	Action spectrum
Penicillin G	*Penicillium notatum*	antibacterial
Bacitracin	*Bacillus subtilis*	antibacterial
Polymixin	*Bacillus polymyxa*	antibacterial
Chloramphenicol	*Streptomyces venezuelae*	antibacterial
Amphotericin B	*Streptomyces nodosus*	antifungal
Actinomycin D	*Streptomyces parvullus*	antitumour

Clinical & forensic medicine

membranes, can also damage human cells. As bacteria and tumour cells multiply faster than healthy human cells, they are most vulnerable to this group of antibiotics. The human cells survive longer because they have slower rates of transcription and translation, and, in some cases, are less permeable to the antibiotics.

6.2.5 Steroids

Steroid-like substances from plants are converted into steroid hormone analogues by the action of micro-organisms. These laboratory made molecules, which resemble natural steroid hormones, are in considerable demand. They may be used as the principal ingredients of contraceptive pills, or for hormone replacement therapy. An almost equal demand exists for anti-inflammatory agents, used to treat autoimmune diseases, or to suppress the immune response after organ transplantation. Stigmasterol, from soya beans, can be used as the raw material for the synthesis of **prednisone** and **prednisolone**, anti-inflammatory drugs. Cell cultures from roots of the Mexican barbasco plant (*Dioscorea deltoidea*) are the source of a steroid called diosgenin. This is the raw material used to produce both **oestrogen** and **progesterone**. Typically, during fermentation, micro-organisms add a hydroxyl group to one of the 17 carbon atoms in the core of a steroid molecule, as in each of the following reaction steps:

Fermented by
Cunninghamella
Corticosterone *blakesleeana*
$\longrightarrow$

Fermented by
Mycobacterium
globiforme
hydrocortisone $\longrightarrow$ prednisolone

6.2.6 Disinfectants and Antiseptics

Disinfectants are chemical compounds, either organic or inorganic, that are used to kill micro-organisms on inanimate objects, such as floors, bench surfaces and toilets. Examples of disinfectants include ozone gas, a powerful oxidising agent, which is added to supplies of drinking water; copper sulphate, used as an algicide in swimming pools; and phenolic compounds, added to domestic and toilet products used to sterilise surfaces. Most disinfectants are toxic and corrosive, and are likely to cause burns if applied to the skin, or damage the digestive system if swallowed.

Antiseptics, on the other hand, are relatively mild anti-microbial agents, effective in inhibiting the growth of micro-organisms, and sufficiently non-toxic and non-corrosive to be applied to living tissues. **Iodine** and **alcohol** are antiseptics used for skin sterilisation before surgery. These compounds rapidly kill bacteria on the skin surface. Iodine iodinates tyrosine residues, whereas alcohol denatures proteins. Dentists apply **hydrogen peroxide** solution to drilled teeth in order to kill residual bacteria. The pink mouthwash, used after dental treatment, contains **potassium permanganate**. Both hydrogen peroxide and potassium permanganate are oxidising agents and kill bacteria by the rapid release of oxygen. Domestic antiseptics used as floor and toilet cleaners often contain a detergent, in addition to an essential oil such as pine. The detergent molecules remove grease, along with bacteria that stick to it. This type of antiseptic may contain **hypochlorites**, **phenols** or **cetrimide** which are all effective anti-bacterial agents.

The effectiveness of disinfectants and antiseptics is expressed by comparison with phenol, and is given a numerical value. Phenol and the antiseptic are both diluted with distilled water in the ratio 1:10 – 1:500. A fixed volume of a bacterial broth culture is then added to a fixed volume of each diluted antiseptic. At intervals of 2.5, 5.0, 7.5 and 10.0 minutes, a loopful of each mixture is transferred to a test-tube containing sterile nutrient broth. The tubes are then incubated at 37°C for 48 hours.

The operator looks for dilutions of the antiseptic and phenol that kill bacteria after 7.5 and 10.0 minutes, but not after 2.5 or 5.0 minutes. Then,

$$\text{Phenol coefficient} = \frac{\text{dilution factor of antiseptic}}{\text{dilution factor of phenol}}$$

e.g. if dilution factor of antiseptic = 1:100 and dilution factor of phenol = 1:50, the phenol

$$\text{coefficient} = \frac{100}{50} = 2.0.$$

The higher the phenol coefficient the more powerful the antiseptic.

6.3 Diagnosis and Identification

Monoclonal antibodies, as we have seen, have therapeutic and diagnostic applications. The remaining procedures described in this chapter are used mainly for diagnostic purposes and for identifying individuals by means of their unique and specific genetic make-up. **Gene therapy**, a possible future remedy for single gene disorders, is also outlined in this section.

6.3.1 Gene Probes

Recombinant DNA technology has revolutionised the study of human single-gene disorders, such as sickle cell anaemia. The use of **gene probes**, which are short lengths of single-stranded DNA (or RNA) capable of binding to complementary single-stranded DNA segments, has allowed researchers to pinpoint the regions on chromosomes where the defective genes are located. Furthermore, gene probes have provided a specific test for single-gene disorders, applicable to embryos in the womb and to young children.

Sickle cell anaemia is caused by a **point mutation** in the region of DNA that codes for the protein part of a haemoglobin molecule, the red pigment in blood. In the sickle celled condition, one of the bases in the DNA molecule, thymine, is replaced by adenine. That, in turn, leads to an amino acid sequence in which glutamate is replaced by valine. The resulting haemoglobin molecule (HbS) has a sticky patch on its surface and tends to form chains with other haemoglobin molecules. These distortions affect the shape of the red blood cells, which may become sickled, thereby losing some of their oxygen-carrying capacity, as well as becoming less efficient at releasing oxygen to the tissues. Affected individuals

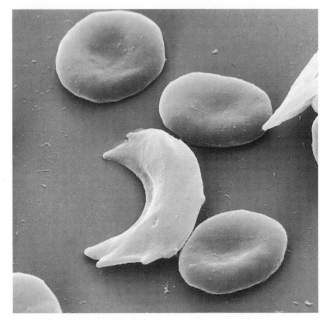

C4 A blood smear from someone with sickle cell anaemia. Note the sickled appearance of some red blood cells (*see Colour Section on inside cover*)

experience symptoms caused by the permanent destruction of their red blood cells, notably blocked vessels, anaemia and organ damage.

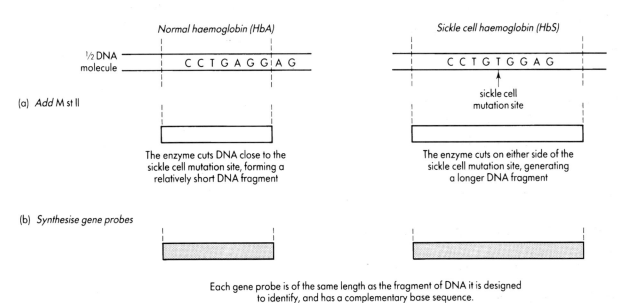

Figure 6.14 Stages in the cutting of DNA and the preparation of gene probes for the identification of sufferers and carriers of sickle cell anaemia

To identify a sickle cell carrier or sufferer, a purified DNA sample, usually extracted from white blood cells, is treated with the **restriction endonuclease *M st II*** (Figure 6.14). This enzyme cleaves the gene for normal haemoglobin (HbA) across the base sequence CCTGAGGAG. Cleavage takes place between the seventh (G) and eighth (A) bases in this sequence, generating a relatively short DNA fragment. The change of A → T in the gene for sickle cell haemoglobin (HbS) destroys the recognition site, or point at which the DNA is normally cut, thereby causing the enzyme to ignore the site. This means that the enzyme cuts the DNA of people with normal haemoglobin (HbA) and sickle cell haemoglobin (HbS) into fragments of different lengths. As Figure 6.14 indicates, the fragments from people with the sickle cell gene are slightly longer.

Figure 6.15 shows all the procedures leading up to the identification of gene fragments with gene probes. The fragments are transferred to a well in a flat plate of agarose gel, contained in a box. Separation of the fragments by **electrophoresis** takes place when the apparatus is switched on. The fragments move through the gel at different rates, depending on their length. Small fragments travel faster than large ones. After several hours the fragments become arranged in parallel bands, each band containing many DNA fragments of uniform

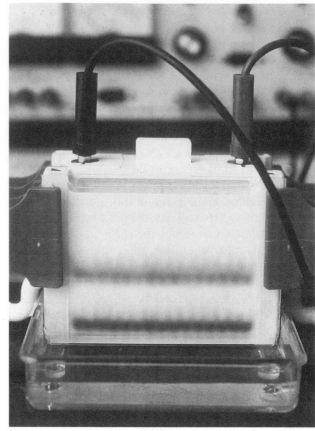

C5 A gel electrophoresis cell in use (*see Colour Section on inside cover*)

(a) *Extraction of DNA*

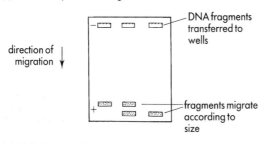

(b) *Cutting with restriction endonuclease M st II*

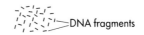
DNA fragments

(c) *Gel electrophoresis on agarose*

DNA fragments transferred to wells

direction of migration

fragments migrate according to size

(d) *Transfer to nitrocellulose filter*

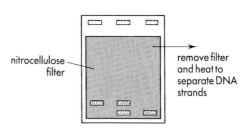

nitrocellulose filter

remove filter and heat to separate DNA strands

(e) *Hybridisation with radiolabelled DNA*

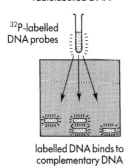

^{32}P-labelled DNA probes

labelled DNA binds to complementary DNA

(f) *Preparation of autoradiograph*

X-ray film

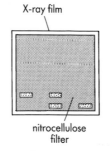

nitrocellulose filter

(g) *Development of X-ray film*

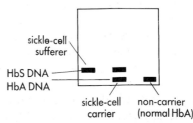

sickle-cell sufferer

HbS DNA
HbA DNA

sickle-cell carrier

non-carrier (normal HbA)

Figure 6.15 Stages in the detection of the sickle cell anaemia gene

length. The pattern is then blotted onto a nitrocellulose filter. Heating binds the DNA to the filter and also separates each DNA fragment into its two single strands of DNA that contain complementary base sequences. Such binding is detected by placing an X-ray film over the nitrocellulose filter (**autoradiography**). When the film is developed, a radioactive region shows up as a dark band.

Gene probes are also used to detect the presence of DNA from pathogens, as in the diagnosis of AIDS and other viral conditions. In the future, DNA probes may become available for the diagnosis of cancer. Cells become cancerous only after certain genes, called **oncogenes**, have been altered. Once altered, some cancerous cells produce a specific type of mRNA, not found in healthy cells. It should soon be possible to detect this mRNA by using a probe.

Other inherited diseases that can be diagnosed by the use of gene probes include cystic fibrosis, Huntingdon's disease and muscular dystrophy. Testing, to find carriers of these diseases or sufferers who may not yet be showing symptoms, is called **screening**. The essence of screening is to identify differences in DNA base sequences in the genes of sufferers and normals. Take, for example, the gene for cystic fibrosis. If present, this gene is located at a specific point on a chromosome. DNA taken from this point in a normal person, and cut with restriction endonucleases, produces a number of DNA fragments, each of a recognisable length. Conversely, DNA taken from the same point in someone with cystic fibrosis and cut with the same restriction endonucleases, produces DNA fragments of different lengths. These differences in the lengths of DNA fragments, between sufferers and normals, is known as **restriction fragment length polymorphism (RFLP)**. Such differences can be used to make an accurate diagnosis.

6.3.2 Gene Therapy

A possible cure for single-gene disorders, such as sickle cell anaemia, lies in gene therapy. **Gene enhancement therapy** is an attempt to boost the effect of a gene that is generally thought to be desirable. Height, intelligence and athleticism are traits resulting from complex gene interactions. Once the individual genes that contribute to these attributes have been identified, attempts could be made to add additional copies to the genome. **Somatic gene replacement therapy** is an attempt to replace defective genes with normal ones. The technique, when it is developed, should be applicable to single-gene disorders in which homozygous recessive (*aa*) individuals show symptoms of the disease. Therapy would consist of adding normal genes to the genome, so that the recipient gains a normal gene, while retaining the defective ones (e.g. *A* + *aa*).

In an attempt to cure sickle cell anaemia, for example, at the first stage in the laboratory process, some of these bone marrow cells would undergo genetic engineering. A single copy of the normal (HbA) gene would be inserted. Transformed cells would then be transferred to a suitable growth medium and allowed to multiply. At the appropriate time, the donor would receive radiation and drug treatment to destroy his or her own bone marrow cells. These would be replaced by an injection of the donor's own genetically-engineered bone marrow cells. Further treatment would ensure that the engineered cells continued to grow and multiply. At a point where the transplanted cells produced enough haemoglobin (HbA) to meet the individual's needs, a 'cure' would have been effected.

Two points should be noted in connection with gene replacement therapy. The first is that treated individuals continue to pass on defective genes in their sperm and eggs. In this case it is only the bone marrow cells, not other somatic cells or gametes, that contain the normal gene. The second point is that treated individuals carry three genes controlling

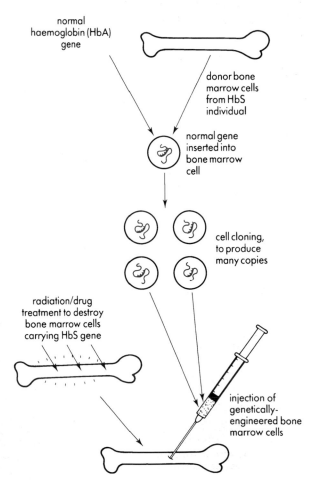

Figure 6.16 Possible gene therapy for sickle cell anaemia

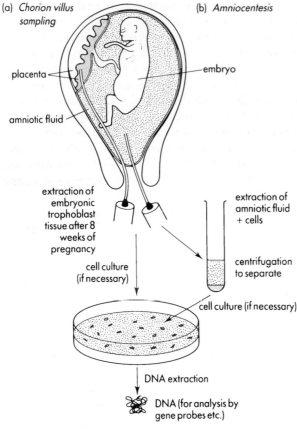

(a) *Chorion villus sampling*

placenta

amniotic fluid

(b) *Amniocentesis*

embryo

extraction of embryonic trophoblast tissue after 8 weeks of pregnancy

cell culture (if necessary)

extraction of amniotic fluid + cells

centrifugation to separate

cell culture (if necessary)

DNA extraction

DNA (for analysis by gene probes etc.)

Figure 6.17 Methods of prenatal diagnosis for single gene disorders in human embryos

globin synthesis (*A + aa*). Any harmful effects of this combination may take several years before they begin to show up.

A more distant aim of gene therapy is to effect a permanent cure for single-gene disorders by inserting normal genes into sperm and eggs. This is **germ-line gene replacement therapy (eugenic gene therapy)**, a technique that would enable a cure to be passed to the offspring of the treated individuals. At the present time, however, techniques are too imprecise to guarantee a predictable outcome.

6.3.3 *Genetic Fingerprinting*

As we have seen, restriction endonucleases chop up DNA into fragments of different lengths. Careful analysis of the lengths of these fragments, following gel electrophoresis and other methods of separation, have shown that when restriction endonucleases act on a person's DNA, they chop it up into a unique collection of differently-sized fragments, from which the individual can be identified.

Throughout the human genome there are regions, called **hypervariable regions**, which show considerable variation in length from individual to individual. Further analysis of these hypervariable regions shows that they contain short sequences of DNA (e.g. GGAGGTGGGCAGGAG), sometimes

called **minisatellites**, that are repeated many times over. The number of times these repetitive sequences occur at a single site on a particular chromosome is called the **variable number of tandem repeats (VNTR)**. When the DNA from two chromosomes with a different number of repeats at this particular locus is digested, the restriction fragments containing this DNA differ in size. Separating and identifying these VNTR fragments is the basis of genetic fingerprinting.

Stages in genetic fingerprinting are listed in Figure 6.18. In the step known as **Southern blotting** (named after Ed Southern), the agarose gel is placed over a filter paper wick which draws up the blotting buffer. A nylon sheet is placed over the gel. Numerous sheets of blotting or filter paper are then laid on top of the nylon before pressure is applied to draw DNA out of the gel and into the nylon sheet.

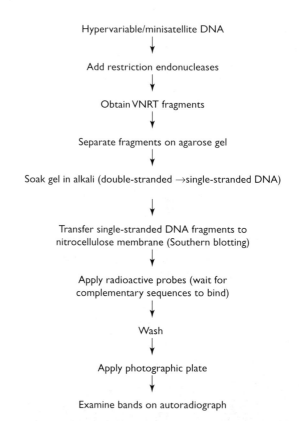

Hypervariable/minisatellite DNA

↓

Add restriction endonucleases

↓

Obtain VNRT fragments

↓

Separate fragments on agarose gel

↓

Soak gel in alkali (double-stranded →single-stranded DNA)

↓

Transfer single-stranded DNA fragments to nitrocellulose membrane (Southern blotting)

↓

Apply radioactive probes (wait for complementary sequences to bind)

↓

Wash

↓

Apply photographic plate

↓

Examine bands on autoradiograph

Figure 6.18 Stages in genetic fingerprinting

A completed fingerprint (Figure 6.19), consisting of many parallel bars (rather like the bar code on groceries), was found to be unique to each individual. Moreover, when the genetic fingerprint of a child was compared with those of its parents, each band of the child's print was seen to derive directly from either its father or its mother. This provided a method of establishing true blood relationships in cases of disputed parentage.

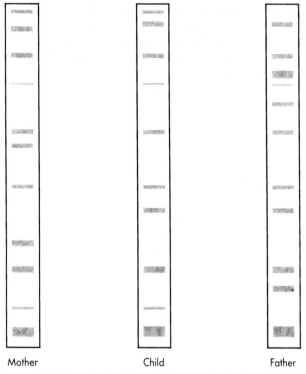

Mother | Child | Father

Figure 6.19 Hypothetical 'genetic fingerprints' of a child and its parents. Note that each individual has a unique print and that the child's print is derived from its mother and its father

The DNA fingerprinting technique, discovered in 1984, was used to determine the father of the above litter of Siberian huskies in order to register them with proof of pedigree

Genetic fingerprinting provides a powerful tool for identifying individuals. It is, in most cases, superior to ordinary fingerprinting, but is not infallible. The technique has proved of great value in forensic science. Blood, semen or hair, left at the scene of a crime, can be used as a source of DNA, from which a genetic fingerprint can be produced. This can then be compared with the genetic fingerprints of suspects. Genetic fingerprinting evidence is accepted in court, although there are one or two cases where anomalous results were obtained as a result of DNA samples being contaminated, and almost identical results were obtained from individuals who were not related. Genetic fingerprinting is also used by animal breeders, to establish the pedigree of their animals, and to settle ownership disputes. In some animal groups the accuracy and specificity of the test is less than it is in humans.

6.3.4 Polymerase Chain Reaction

In many instances, there is insufficient DNA available for a genetic fingerprinting test. This problem is overcome by using the polymerase chain reaction to make multiple copies of whatever DNA is available. **DNA polymerases** are enzymes that make double-stranded DNA from single strands. Stages in the process, carried out in a PCR machine, are illustrated in Figure 6.20.

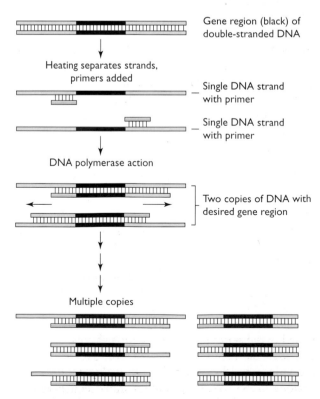

Gene region (black) of double-stranded DNA

Heating separates strands, primers added

Single DNA strand with primer

Single DNA strand with primer

DNA polymerase action

Two copies of DNA with desired gene region

Multiple copies

Figure 6.20 Polymerase chain reaction

Clinical & forensic medicine

The machine works at high temperatures, close to boiling point, and uses DNA polymerases from bacteria that live in hot springs. DNA primers are added to single DNA strands. After attaching to one end of the DNA strand, a new complementary DNA strand is built on each template.

QUESTIONS

6 Draw and label an antibody.

7 In the preparation of monoclonal antibodies from mice, a) what organ is used as a source of B cells, and b) what type of cell is fused with these B cells to form a hybridoma?

8 State three applications of monoclonal antibodies.

9 Name three diseases, caused by gene defects, which can be diagnosed by DNA analysis.

10 In genetic fingerprinting, what name is given to the regions of DNA that are separated by gel electrophoresis?

Clinical & forensic medicine

CHAPTER 6 SUMMARY

Protection against pathogenic micro-organisms is provided by the body's immune system. This consists of a number of different types of cell, which act against intruders. Some ingest them, while others produce a range of chemical compounds that either kill them or render them ineffective.

Pathogenic micro-organisms carry foreign macromolecules, known as antigens, on their surfaces. B cells of the immune system respond to specific antigens by producing antigen-specific complementary proteins called antibodies.

There are probably more than a million different types of B cells in the immune system, each type producing a different antibody. This property has been exploited by biotechnologists. By fusing specific B cells with myeloma cells, which live indefinitely, large quantities of antigen-specific, or monoclonal, antibodies have

been produced. These monoclonal antibodies are being used in an ever increasing number of diagnostic and therapeutic applications.

One of the earliest and most important antibiotics to be produced was penicillin, a secondary metabolite of a mould fungus. Mass cell culture techniques, pioneered in penicillin production, are being used to produce a wide range of antibiotics, together with other useful drugs, such as steroids.

A powerful tool for establishing individual differences consists of cutting DNA into fragments with restriction endonucleases, separating them by gel electrophoresis, and comparing the banding patterns obtained. Single gene defects, such as cystic fibrosis, can be diagnosed by this technique. Individual identity can be established by a closely-related technique known as genetic fingerprinting.

CHAPTER 6 QUESTIONS

1 The diagram opposite shows the effects of four different antibiotics on the bacterium *Bacillus subtilis*.

a) Suggest names for the four antibiotics, each indicated by their first and second letters.

b) List the antibiotics in order of their potency.

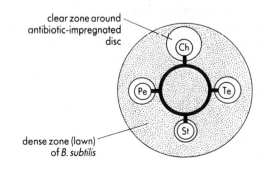

clear zone around antibiotic-impregnated disc

dense zone (lawn) of *B. subtilis*

c) Use the formula πr^2 to find the area of the clear zone around each disc ($\pi = 3.14$). By what numerical factor is

  (i)   Ch more potent than Pe, and
  (ii) Te more potent than St?

d) Comment on the accuracy of the results.

2 The diagram below shows an agarose gel used in electrophoresis to separate fragments of DNA. Copy the diagram.

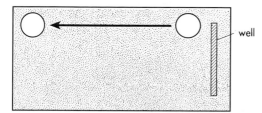

  well

a) Add an arrow to one side of your diagram to indicate the direction of electrophoresis.

b) On the opposite side of your diagram indicate the position of the anode (+) and cathode (−).

c) Three double-stranded fragments of DNA are separated by gel electrophoresis. Indicate on your diagram the relative positions of these strands after electrophoresis.

  (i) TTAGC   (ii) ATCGGGC   (iii) AACCGTATTCG
       AATCG   TAGCCCG   TTGGCATAAGC

d) How is the double-stranded DNA fixed and separated?

e) Write out the base sequences of DNA probes that would bind to the longest DNA fragment.

f) How may binding between a DNA probe and its complementary DNA fragment be detected?

3 Distinguish between narrow- and broad-spectrum antibiotics.

  Give an account of the discovery and subsequent large-scale production of an antibiotic such as penicillin.

  Explain how penicillin and other antibiotics kill bacteria.

4 What is a vaccine?

  Describe the effects of vaccination in terms of changes within the immune system. What new approaches to vaccine production are offered by biotechnology?

5 Describe the production, and therapeutic applications of:

  a) monoclonal antibodies,

  b) steroids,

  c) interferon,

  d) human insulin or growth hormone.

6 Describe a gene probe and discuss how gene probes have been used in forensic medicine.

  How would you use a gene probe to diagnose a disease such as sickle cell anaemia?

7 What is gene therapy?

  Outline ways in which single gene defects might be treated by gene therapists.

  Discuss the ethics of manipulating the human genome.

8 Write an essay on 'cells of the immune system, their actions and interactions'.

9 Discuss the production and economic importance of monoclonal antibodies.

Clinical & forensic medicine

BIBLIOGRAPHY

Clinical & Forensic Medicine
Brock, TD (1989) *Microbes and Infectious Diseases* Scientific American Books, New York

Brown, CM and Duffas, JH (1984) Health impact of biotechnology *Swiss Biotechnology* (2) 7–32

Chang, TMS ed (1977) *Biomedical Application of Immobilised Enzymes and Proteins* (vol 1 and 2) Plenum Press, New York

Cherfas, J (1995) *Antibiotics Explained* Biotechnology and Biological Sciences Review Council

Hartley, BS, Atkinson, T and Lilley, MD eds (1983) *Industrial and Diagnostic Enzymes* The Royal Society, London

Lowrie, P and Wells, S (1991) *Microorganisms, Biotechnology and Disease* Cambridge University Press

Roitt, IM (1994) *Essential Immunology* 8th Edn Blackwell Scientific, Oxford

Rosazza, JP (1982) *Microbial Transformations of Bioactive Compounds* CRC Press, Florida

Tizard, IR (1995) *Immunology: An Introduction* 4th Edn Saunders College Publishing, New York

CHAPTER 7

Industrial chemicals

Many commercially useful chemical compounds are produced by micro-organisms. The range is almost limitless. Those that are most widely manufactured, or used in industrial processes, fall within the broad categories of proteins, polysaccharides, fuels, solvents and organic acids. Micro-organisms are also widely used in oil and metal extraction. They serve either to enhance oil recovery or to increase the amount of metals, notably iron, copper and uranium, that can be recovered from ores.

7.1 Proteins

Enzymes are the most important group of commercial proteins, with a wide range of uses as therapeutic and catalytic agents. A large market also exists for three hormones: insulin, human growth hormone (HGH) and bovine growth hormone (BGH). Other human proteins with therapeutic potential that are also in demand include those used to treat thrombosis (e.g. urokinase), respiratory disorders (e.g. lung surfactant protein) and tumours (e.g. interferon and interleukin–2).

7.1.1 Enzymes

The majority of enzymes used commercially are obtained from microbial sources. Relatively few come from plants or animals. **Extracellular enzymes**, secreted by bacteria and fungi into their surroundings, are harvested by filtration and then concentrated. **Intracellular enzymes**, retained within cells, are released by breaking down cell walls and membranes with detergents, alkalis or lysozyme. After centrifuging and filtering off the debris, the enzymes can be 'salted out' by adding high concentrations of very soluble salts such as ammonium sulphate, sodium sulphate and

phosphate buffers. The solubility of many enzymes at high salt concentrations decreases logarithmically as the salt concentration increases. Further purification involves precipitation in organic solvents such as methanol, ethanol and acetone. Large-scale purification can be achieved by various chromatographic techniques. In **affinity chromatography**, for example, antibodies are raised against an enzyme by injecting it into an animal such as a rabbit. These antibodies are harvested, purified and attached to an appropriate chromatographic matrix. The required enzyme binds selectively to the antibody. Subsequent desorption, by changing the pH or adding a dissociating agent such as urea, releases the enzyme from its antibody.

Enzymes are in many ways ideal catalysts for industrial processes because they occupy little space, react with only one component in a given mixture, and have a high rate of activity. They are, on the

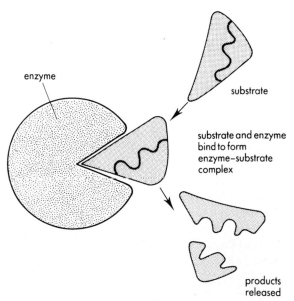

enzyme

substrate

substrate and enzyme bind to form enzyme–substrate complex

products released

Figure 7.1 The role of an enzyme in a catabolic reaction

other hand, expensive to purify and often unstable in the purified state. Furthermore, optimal activity can be only achieved within fairly narrow limits of temperature and pH.

Figure 7.1 shows how a catabolic (breaking down) enzyme is believed to operate. The essential role of the enzyme is to provide an active site where large molecules bind to a template of complementary shape. Here, as they bind and break away in rapid succession, each molecule is cleaved into two smaller fragments.

7.1.2 Uses of Enzymes

The commercial applications of enzymes, already numerous, are increasing year by year. Table 7.1 lists some of these industrial, medical, analytical and manipulative applications. Some of the other applications are more complex, requiring an explanation.

Urea, for example, is a toxic compound that accumulates in the blood as a result of kidney failure. By using **microcapsules** containing urease, glutamate dehydrogenase and glucose dehydrogenase, possibly mixed with charcoal to

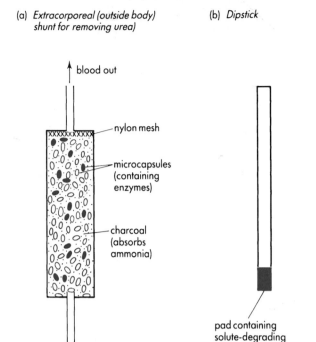

(a) *Extracorporeal (outside body) shunt for removing urea)*

(b) *Dipstick*

blood out

nylon mesh

microcapsules (containing enzymes)

charcoal (absorbs ammonia)

blood in

pad containing solute-degrading enzyme, peroxidase and redox dye

Figure 7.2 Two medical applications of enzymes

Table 7.1 Some commercial applications of enzymes

Enzyme	Reaction	Application
Industrial		
Amylase	starch → glucose	glucose syrup for food industry 'biological' washing powders
Glucose isomerase	glucose → fructose	fructose syrup for food industry
Papain	proteins → peptones	tenderising meat
Proteases	proteins → peptones + amino acids	removal of 'haze' from beer (brewing) breakdown of gluten in flour (baking) coagulation of milk (cheese-making) removal of hair from hides (leather-making)
Pectinesterases	pectin → polygalacturonate + methanol	removal of 'haze' from beer
Medical		
L-asparaginase	breakdown of L-asparagine	cancer chemotherapy (L-asparagine is needed for tumour growth)
Cholesterol oxidase	oxidation of cholesterol	estimation of cholesterol in blood
Glucose oxidase + peroxidase	oxidation of glucose	estimation of glucose in blood
Urokinase	plasminogen activation	removal of fibrin clots (after heart attacks)
Analytical		
Carbonic anhydrase	inactivation by some insecticides	detection of insecticides in drinking water
Cholinesterase	inactivation by some insecticides	detection of insecticides in drinking water
Urease	Urea → CO_2 + NH_3	estimation of urea in urine and blood
Manipulative		
Lysozyme	peptide hydrolysis	disrupts bacterial and yeast cell walls

absorb some of the ammonia, it may in future be possible to remove urea from the blood of a patient with kidney failure by use of enzymes (Figure 7.2a).

Enzymes are also a component of dipsticks (Figure 7.2b) used by doctors for the rapid estimation of glucose, urea, ketones, cholesterol etc. in blood and urine. A small chemically-treated paper pad at one end of the stick changes colour if glucose or cholesterol, say, is present. The intensity of the colour indicates the approximate concentration of the solute. The pad usually contains an enzyme, which is specific for the substrate of interest, and peroxidase with a redox dye that changes colour when oxidised. The reaction takes place in two steps:

(i) D-glucose + H_2O + O_2
$\downarrow$ glucose oxidase
H_2O_2 + D-glucuronolactone
OR
Cholesterol + H_2O + O_2
$\downarrow$ cholesterol oxidase
H_2O_2 + cholest–4–en–3–one

(ii) H_2O_2 + reduced dye (coloured or colourless)
$\downarrow$ peroxidase
oxidised dye (coloured or differently coloured) + H_2O + $\frac{1}{2}O_2$

In both medicine and the food industry there is an increasing demand for **amino acids**. Twenty amino acids are required to make human proteins, and nine are essential constituents of the diet, because we cannot make them ourselves. Many micro-organisms, however, can synthesise these essential amino acids. To date, enzymes from microbial sources have been used to produce lysine, an essential amino acid that is deficient in cereals. This product may provide a valuable food supplement for people living largely on vegetables, enabling them to utilise more of the other amino acids present in their food.

7.1.3 Immobilisation of Enzymes

Until quite recently, many enzyme-catalysed reactions were operated on a commercial scale by using enzyme/substrate/water mixtures. This system led to enzymes being wasted. It was often difficult to remove enzymes from the end-products, and even more difficult to purify the recovered enzyme, so that it could be used again. An increasing demand for pure enzymes and their products led to **enzyme immobilisation**. This is a technique whereby an enzyme is bound immovably to a surface, and not allowed to mix with a solution of its substrate. Binding the enzyme to a solid support means that it cannot contaminate the end-products of a reaction,

(a) *Adsorption*

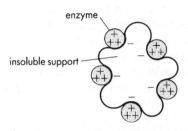

The enzyme is held in position by interactions between oppositely charged particles

(b) *Entrapment*

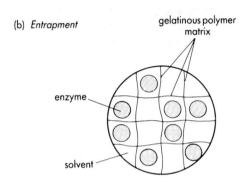

The enzyme is entrapped in a gelatinous matrix

(c) *Covalent bonding*

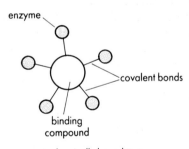

The enzyme is chemically bound to a supporting material

Figure 7.3 Methods of enzyme immobilisation

and also that the same enzyme can be used over and over again. Furthermore, immobilisation enables some enzymes to retain their activity in high concentrations of organic solvents, including alcohol (ethanol). This is important in fuel alcohol production.

Enzyme immobilisation may be used to bind either the enzymes themselves, or cells capable of producing them. Three principal methods of immobilisation are currently in use.

(i) **Adsorption**, or physical binding to a support such as glass beads, dextran microbeads or DEAE–cellulose. This process stems from physical rather than chemical reactions. Charge effects and hydrophobic interactions may be involved.

(ii) **Entrapment** within a gelatinous or fibrous polymer matrix of sodium alginate, polyacrylamide or collagen. The enzyme is trapped in a droplet of solvent, within a gelatinous polymer matrix.

(iii) **Covalent bonding** to carboxymethylcellulose. The enzyme is tightly bound to its supporting system.

Immobilisation may affect the shape and properties of enzyme molecules. The enzyme substrate, for example, may not be bound so effectively, which causes the rate of reaction to fall. This disadvantage, however, may be offset by the fact that immobilisation may increase the temperature and pH range over which an enzyme remains active.

7.1.4 *Enzyme-based biosensors*

At present there is a lot of commercial interest in rapid biochemical analysis. Biosensors, for analysing biologically-active compounds in solution, could simplify the work of doctors, the police and analytical chemists. If doctors obtained rapid estimates of glucose, urea and hormones in blood samples, they could make more rapid diagnoses, saving time on procedures that are currently carried out in hospital laboratories. Self-testing by the public for, say, glucose levels in urine, or blood pressure, could have important implications for preventative medicine. Biosensors would also be of value to the police. They could obtain rapid estimates of blood alcohol (ethanol) levels in drink-drive suspects, or rapidly identify a drug from blood samples of those who had overdosed. The work of analytical chemists would also be simplified if they could read off levels of nitrates, herbicides and phenols in water supplies.

Three main types of enzyme-based biosensors are currently in use or under development: enzyme transducer sensors, enzyme thermistors and biochips. A simple **enzyme transducer sensor** or **enzyme electrode**, for measuring the amount of urea in blood or urine, is shown in Figure 7.4. Immobilised urease, surrounded by a membrane that is permeable to urea, is packed around the tip of an ammonium ion probe. When the probe is dipped into a solution containing urea, molecules of the solute diffuse through the membrane and are broken down into carbon dioxide and ammonium ions by the immobilised enzyme:

$$\text{Urea} + H_2O \rightarrow CO_2 + NH_4^+$$

The volume of ammonium ions released in a given time is proportional to the concentration of urea in the solution. An appropriate transducer converts levels of the ammonium ions into an electrical signal. This signal, after amplification, is

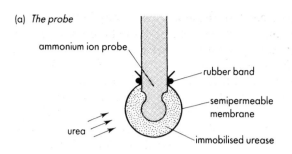

(a) *The probe*

ammonium ion probe
rubber band
semipermeable membrane
urea
immobilised urease

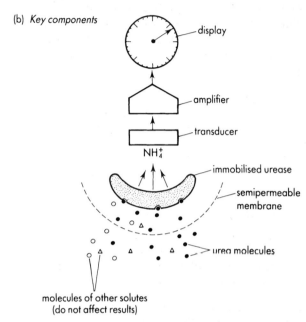

(b) *Key components*

display
amplifier
transducer
NH_4^+
immobilised urease
semipermeable membrane
urea molecules
molecules of other solutes (do not affect results)

Figure 7.4 An enzyme electrode

displayed. The strength of the electric current is proportional to the concentration of urea.

An **enzyme thermistor** is a biosensor that measures minute changes in temperature during exothermic reactions. Such devices are sensitive to temperature changes between 0.004°C and 1.0°C, the amount of heat generated during a reaction being directly proportional to the concentration of the reactants. In these biosensors, the thermistor is mounted at the centre of a well-insulated, immobilised enzyme column.

The miniaturisation of biosensors has led to the production of a **biochip**. In a biochip used to detect glucose, for example, a key element is immobilised glucose oxidase, which catalyses the reaction:

$$\text{Glucose} + O_2 + H_2O \rightarrow \text{Gluconic acid} + H_2O_2$$

This reaction generates acids, or more specifically positive charges (H^+) which collect in the immobilised enzyme at the upper surface of the insulating layer. Negatively-charged electrons (e^-) from the silicon support are attracted to the positive charges. The flow of electrons, through the silicon terminals, generates a current which is proportional to the amount of glucose in solution.

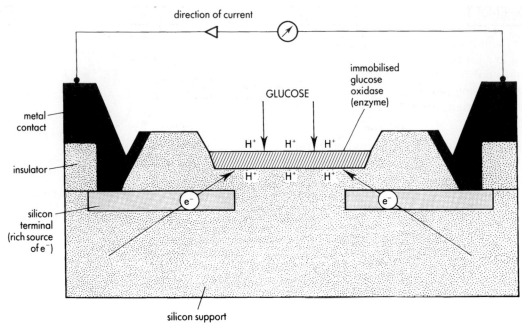

Figure 7.5 A glucose-sensitive biochip (sectional view). H$^+$ ions, generated by the reaction between glucose and glucose oxidase, attract electrons (e$^-$), thus creating a current

7.2 Polysaccharides

Some bacteria have a polysaccharide layer outside their cell wall. Aqueous suspensions of these **exopolysaccharides** have high viscosity. This viscosity falls as stress (pressure) is applied. Xanthan gum, synthesised by *Xanthomas campestris*, is used in the extraction of oil from wells. This compound, mixed with water, a surfactant and hydrocarbons, is pumped into the ground via an injection well. As it passes through rock pores this highly viscous polymer flushes out oil droplets. A water-gum-oil mixture collects at the bottom of the production well. After pumping this mixture to the surface, oil separates out as a surface layer.

Emulsan, a polysaccharide from *Acinetobacter calcoaceticus*, mixed with a surfactant, is used to break up oilspills. The gum ensures that the surfactant remains in contact with the oil. Gelatinous dextrans, produced by *Leuconostoc mesenteroides*, are used as adsorbants and blood expanders. *Pseudomonas* is the source of gellan, a food gelatinising agent.

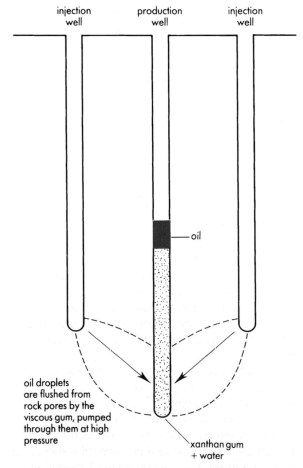

Figure 7.6 Oil extraction. Xanthan gum, driven down the injection wells, increases oil flow into the production well

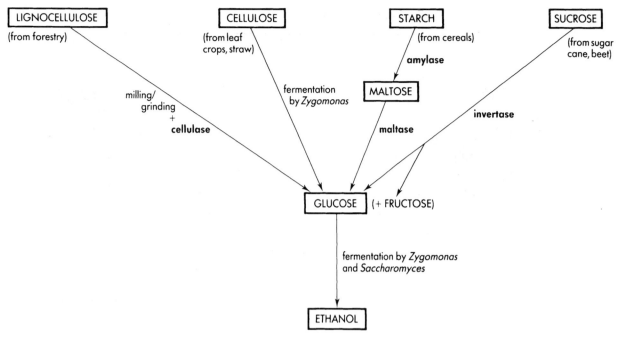

LIGNOCELLULOSE	CELLULOSE	STARCH	SUCROSE
(from forestry)	(from leaf crops, straw)	(from cereals)	(from sugar cane, beet)

amylase

MALTOSE

milling/
grinding
+
cellulase

fermentation
by *Zygomonas*

maltase

invertase

GLUCOSE (+ FRUCTOSE)

fermentation by *Zygomonas*
and *Saccharomyces*

ETHANOL

Figure 7.7 Possible routes to ethanol production from different substances

QUESTIONS

1 Name two enzymes that are used a) in the food industry, b) as therapeutic agents in medicine and c) for detecting environmental pollutants.

2 What do you understand by the 'active site' of an enzyme?

3 Name three different methods of enzyme immobilisation.

4 What are a) a biochip and b) an enzyme thermistor?

5 a) What is an exopolysaccharide?

   b) State three commercial uses of exopolysaccharides.

7.3 Fuels and Solvents

Using micro-organisms to produce fuels has many advantages. Cell fermentations operate at temperatures between 30–50°C, whereas coal- or oil-based fuel production processes require much higher temperatures, driven by the burning of fossil fuels. In addition to generating smoke, coal- and oil-based processes operate under conditions that may be extremely acid or alkaline. Furthermore, they may depend on expensive catalysts such as platinum. Biological processes don't pollute the atmosphere, they operate at moderate pH, and are driven by enzymes.

Ethanol (alcohol) is a solvent, an intermediate in the production of many chemical compounds and a fuel. As combustion engines can be driven on petroleum, ethanol, or a mixture of both, there is considerable interest in ethanol production in those countries that do not have their own oil reserves. As Figure 7.7 shows, it is possible to use lignocellulose, cellulose, starch and sugar as raw materials for

Ethanol – containing petrol

ethanol production, but these must first be converted into glucose and fructose before they can be fermented by yeasts (*Saccharomyces sp.*). Bacteria of the genus *Zygomonas*, however, can make direct use of cellulose as a substrate in a sequence of reactions that also results in ethanol production. For this reason, and because *Zygomonas* can tolerate higher

Industrial chemicals

117

ethanol concentrations before its activity is inhibited, it is the most widely used organism in biological ethanol production.

During World War I there was considerable demand for **glycerol**, used as an ingredient in explosives. It was produced by adding bisulphite to the fermentation broth, when glucose was fermented by *Saccharomyces cerevisiae*. Dihydroxyacetone phosphate, and not acetaldehyde, was formed as an intermediate, with the consequent generation of glycerol in place of ethanol. Today, glycerol and some of its derivatives are used as anti-freeze agents. In some countries, glycerol is being produced by the unicellular green alga *Dunaliella salina*, a holophyte, which converts solar energy directly into glycerol. The normal function of glycerol in this organism is to counteract the high osmotic pressure created by high salinity in its natural environment.

Acetone, produced by the fermentation of starch by the aerobic bacterium *Clostridium acetobutylicum*, is important in the manufacture of explosives used to propel heavy artillery shells. **Butanol**, a second product of the same fermentation process, is used in the manufacture of brake fluid, resins and plasticisers. A third product of the reaction is **hydrogen**. Interest in this product is increasing, mainly as a result of its use as rocket fuel, and in the production of electricity. It seems very probable that photosynthetic bacteria will be utilised as the future producers of this gas.

7.4 Organic Acids

Acetic (ethanoic) acid is the most commercially important organic acid, used in the manufacture of rubber, plastics, fibres and insecticides. Strains of *Acetobacterium* and *Clostridium* are capable of converting cellulose into acetic acid.

Lactic acid is used in the food processing industry, in tanning and for making plastics. It is produced from starchy material, treated with amylases, then fermented by *Lactobacillus bulgaricus* and closely-related species.

Citric acid is used in the manufacture of soft drinks, confectionery and foods, where it acts both as a flavouring and an antioxidant, preventing the breakdown of vitamin C. The acid is also used as a cleaning and descaling agent. Sodium citrate replaces phosphates in some detergents. Zinc citrate is added to toothpaste, where it prevents the formation of dental plaque. The mould fungus *Aspergillus niger* is used in the manufacture of citric acid. Molasses is the usual substrate. The fungus is grown either in open trays, or in a fermenter. Slaked lime is added to the end-product to precipitate citric acid as calcium citrate. The acid is freed by adding sulphuric acid, then purified using activated carbon and ion exchange resins.

Several other organic acids, including malic, tartaric, salicylic, succinic and pyruvic, can be made by biological processes. At the present time their industrial uses are somewhat limited but are likely to increase in the future.

7.5 Plastics

Plastics produced from oil-based products are not biodegradable. The only way in which they can be destroyed is by burning. Many bacteria, including *Alcaligenes eutrophus*, *Azotobacter beijerinckii* and *Bacillus megaterium*, store a thermoplastic polyester called poly–B–hydroxybutyrate (PHB), as granules, in their cytoplasm. This material, after extraction with chloroform and methanol, yields a plastic which is biodegradable under anaerobic conditions. After scientists have found ways of producing this plastic in large quantities it will, no doubt, find many applications.

7.6 Metal Extraction

Micro-organisms are used in the extraction of iron, copper, zinc and uranium from their ores. The technique is to make a massive pile of mineral-bearing ore, sometimes as high as 300 metres. These so-called **leach dumps** are sprayed with a dilute solution of sulphuric acid at pH 1.5–3.0, which creates a favourable environment for bacteria, which are found in natural association with the ore, to leach out valuable mineral salts. One of the most important of these bacteria is *Thiobacillus ferrooxidans*, a chemoautotrophic species that obtains its energy from the oxidation of ferrous iron (Fe^{2+}) to ferric iron (Fe^{3+}) and from the oxidation of reduced forms of sulphur to sulphuric acid. This bacterium causes either the direct oxidation of sulphides to sulphates, or produces sulphates by a less direct route:

(i) $MS + 2O_2 \rightarrow MSO_4$ (general equation, in which M = metal)
(ii) $4FeS_2 + 15O_2 + 2H_2O \rightarrow 2Fe_2(SO_4)_3 + 2H_2SO_4$
(iii) $2CuS + 2Fe_2(SO_4)_3 \rightarrow 2CuSO_4 + 4FeSO_4 + 2S$

When copper is mined, leach solutions emerging from the bottom of the leach dumps are retained in leach basins. Iron is then added to precipitate copper as given by the reaction

$$CuSO_4 + Fe \rightarrow Cu + FeSO_4$$

The copper is further purified by smelting. Attempts are currently under way to produce genetically-engineered strains of *T. ferrooxidans* that show faster reaction rates, greater tolerance to acid and saline conditions, and increased tolerance to toxic metal ions.

In the future, bacteria and fungi may be used to recover metals from solution. Negatively-charged molecules in the cell walls of these micro-organisms bind and retain positively-charged metal ions. This process, called **'biosorption'**, is readily reversed when acids are added. With further development, the process could be used to remove heavy metal ions (e.g. Hg, Pb, Cu, Cd, Zn) from toxic wastes, or to recover precious metals from their ores.

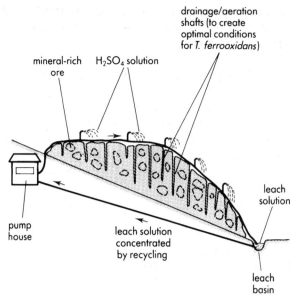

Figure 7.8 A mineral leaching operation

QUESTIONS

6 Name three waste materials that can be used to make fuel alcohol.

7 In the production of fuel alcohol, what is the advantage of using *Zygomonas* rather than *Saccharomyces*?

8 What micro-organisms are used to produce a) glycerol and b) acetone?

9 Name three organic acids that are produced by fermentation processes.

10 a) What bacterium is used in the extraction of copper from its ore?

b) Write an equation to represent the chemical changes brought about by this bacterium.

CHAPTER 7 SUMMARY

Micro-organisms are used in a number of industrial processes, most notably the production of enzymes, fuels, solvents and organic acids. In addition, bacteria are used directly or indirectly in the extraction of oil and metals.

Enzymes have industrial, medical and diagnostic applications. By immobilising enzymes, manufacturers can set up processes that are cost-effective, requiring less labour. Furthermore, the enzymes can be recycled and don't need to be separated from the product.

Waste materials, such as wood shavings and straw, can be used in the manufacture of fuel alcohol. Micro-organisms convert cellulose residues into glucose, which is then fermented by organisms such as *Saccharomyces* and *Zygomonas*.

Xanthan gum, an exopolysaccharide produced by bacteria, is used to flush out oil droplets from rock pores during oil exploration.

When minerals are extracted from their mostly sulphide ores, bacteria are used to oxidise the sulphides to sulphates, from which metals are more readily recovered.

Industrial chemicals

INVESTIGATING ENZYME ACTIVITY

Biological washing products

Biological washing products contain mixtures of amylases, proteases and lipases. These remove stains from clothing by catalysing the following reactions.

Macromolecules	Enzymes	Water-soluble end product
	Amylase	
Starch	$\longrightarrow$	Maltose
	Proteases	
Proteins	$\longrightarrow$	Amino acids
	Lipases	
Lipids	$\longrightarrow$	Fatty acids + glycerol

a) *Comparing enzyme activity in two washing powders or liquids*

Make a comparison between the levels of enzyme activity in two washing powders, or two washing liquids. It is important to work with enzyme solutions of roughly comparable concentrations.

1 Take 1 g of each powder, or 1 cm³ of each liquid, and add distilled water to obtain a total volume of 100 cm³. Stir the mixtures with a glass rod until all of the powder has dissolved, or until the liquid is evenly dispersed.

2 Prepare the following agar gels in petri dishes, using the mixtures listed below.

To detect amylases:	**Starch agar**	
	Soluble starch	200 g
	Bacteriological agar powder	20 g
	Distilled water	1 dm³

To detect proteases:	**'Marvel' milk agar**	
	'Marvel' milk powder	20 g
	Bacteriological agar powder	20 g
	Distilled water	1 dm³

Note: Use only freshly opened 'Marvel' milk for the gels. Older milk powder is not cleared from gels by proteases.

To detect lipases:	**Tributyrin agar**	
	Tributyrin	20 cm³
	Bacteriological agar powder	20 g
	Distilled water	1 dm³

3 After the agars have cooled and hardened, take a 0.5–2.0 cm diameter cork borer, sterilise by dipping into 95% ethanol, and use to cut two wells in each agar plate, spaced roughly as shown in the figure above.

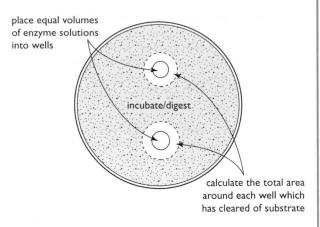

Comparing the relative strengths of washing products

Use a 1 cm³ plastic syringe to place equal volumes of the two enzyme solutions into each well. Replace the lids of the petri dishes and stand them in a warm place for 24–48 hours.

4 Overpour the starch agars with bench iodine solution, then wait for 1–2 minutes before washing off any excess iodine solution with distilled water or tap water. Measure and record the diameter of the clear zones that develop around the wells. Use the formula πr^2 to calculate the area of each clear zone. The concentration of enzymes in each product is directly proportional to the area cleared of enzyme substrate.

Juice extraction from fruits

The cell walls of fruits, such as tangerines, contain the insoluble compounds cellulose and pectin, which limit the amount of juice that can be extracted from these fruits by cutting or squeezing. The use of enzymes, such as pectinase and cellulase, to break down the cell walls of fruits increases the amount of juice that can be extracted from them.

b) *Extracting juice from tangerines*

Tangerines, which are readily available throughout the year, are useful for demonstrating the value of enzymes in juice extraction.

1 Peel 6–8 tangerines and remove the membranous coverings from each segment. Alternatively, open a can of mandarin oranges and use the peeled segments. Use a sharp knife to cut each peeled segment into 4–5 pieces.
Set up four 250 cm³ beakers, numbered from 1–4. Place 100 g of cut, peeled tangerine or mandarin orange segments into each beaker.

2 Make the following additions to each beaker.

- Beaker 1: add 200 cm³ distilled water

- Beaker 2: add 200 cm³ pectinase solution

- Beaker 3: add 200 cm³ cellulase solution

- Beaker 4: add 100 cm³ pectinase
  solution + 100 cm³ cellulase solution

Cover each beaker with 'clingfilm' and place all the beakers into an incubator at 35°C for 24–48 hours.

3 Set up four 250 cm³ measuring cylinders. Place a filter funnel, lined with filter paper, above each measuring cylinder.
Filter the contents of each beaker and record the volume of each filtrate.

Immobilised enzymes

In a number of industrial processes, enzymes are immobilised by binding them to solid surfaces, or entrapping them within a gel. This allows the enzyme to be used over and over again and eliminates the problem of removing enzymes from end-products. Immobilising enzymes is therefore cost-effective, both in terms of saving on raw materials and because a reduced work force is required to supervise manufacturing processes.

c) To immobilise an enzyme

Entrapment is the simplest method for immobilising enzymes. Enzymes are entrapped in an agarose gel, similar to the agars used for growing micro-organisms. The addition of calcium ions to sodium alginate results in the formation of a rigid, clear gel.

1 Add enzyme powder or liquid to a 3%$^{w/v}$ suspension of sodium alginate in distilled water. Stir with a glass rod to obtain an homogenous mixture.

2 Draw some of the enzyme/sodium alginate mixture into a 10 cm³ plastic syringe. Pipette this mixture, drop by drop, into a 3%$^{w/v}$ solution of calcium chloride, contained in a beaker.

As the drops of sodium alginate gel fall into the calcium chloride solution, semi-solid beads of calcium alginate will form. These should be washed in distilled water and kept in a moist place until required.

d) Using immobilised enzymes to catalyse chain reactions

Some reactions, such as the conversion of starch to glucose, are linear, proceeding by two or more steps.

$$\text{Starch} \xrightarrow{\text{Amylase}} \text{Maltose} \xrightarrow{\text{Maltase}} \text{Glucose}$$

Immobilised enzymes can be used to carry out each stage of this reaction in an appropriate sequence, so that starch can be fed into one end of a reactor and glucose obtained from the other end of it.

A simple piece of apparatus, which demonstrates some principles of immobilised enzyme use, is illustrated in the figure below. This apparatus can be prepared from a large plastic drinks bottle, a glass jam-jar, some cotton wool, a plastic freezer bag and some washed silver sand.

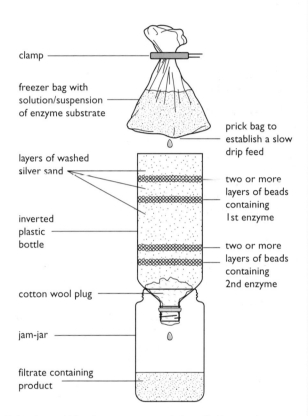

Using immobilised enzymes to catalyse chain reactions

1 Prepare agarose beads containing amylase and maltase, using the method outlined in c).

2 Use scissors to remove the bottom of the plastic bottle. Invert the bottle and plug the neck with cotton wool. Support the inverted neck of the bottle in the jam-jar.
Place a layer of washed silver sand immediately above the cotton wool, then place a layer of agarose beads containing maltase on this sand layer. Cover the beads with a layer of silver sand

and then place a second layer of maltase-containing beads on top. Near the top of the inverted plastic bottle, place alternate layers of washed silver sand and agarose beads containing amylase. Ensure that the top layer consists of washed silver sand.

3 Place 200–250 cm³ of a solution or suspension of enzyme substrate (e.g. soluble starch) into the freezer bag. Set up the bag, supported from a clamp, above the open, inverted end of the plastic bottle. Prick the bag with a pin to establish a slow drip-feed through the apparatus.

4 Test the filtrate for the presence of glucose. Use semiquantitative tests, such as 'Clinitest' or 'Clinistix'. Use the apparatus to determine the effects of i) the number of layers of beads and ii) the distance between layers of beads in determining the concentration of glucose in the filtrate.

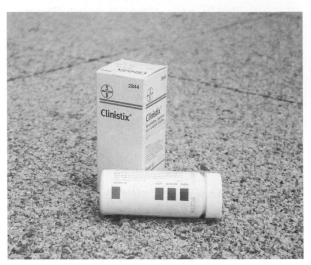

 A Clinistix reagent container showing the colours used in semiquantitative tests (*see Colour Section on inside cover*)

CHAPTER 7 QUESTIONS

1 The graph below shows the relationship between temperature and the activity of two proteolytic enzymes, trypsin and papain.

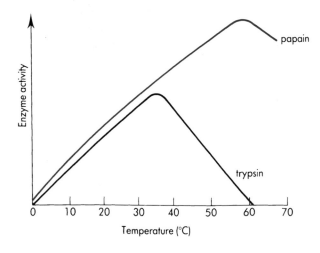

a) Name suitable sources of (i) trypsin and (ii) papain.

b) By reference to the graph explain why the activity of trypsin

   (i)   increases over the temperature range 0–35°C, and

   (ii)   falls over the temperature range 40–60°C.

c) What is the optimal temperature for the activity of (i) trypsin and (ii) papain?

d) In what way does the activity of papain differ from that of trypsin?

e) How do you account for this difference?

f) Explain why papain is of particular interest to biotechnologists.

g) Give a brief account of two commercial applications of papain.

2 Each of the following terms may be used in descriptive accounts of enzymes. What do you understand by each term?

a) Catalysis

b) Active site

c) Allosteric site

d) Turnover number

e) Denaturation

f) Specificity

g) Immobilisation

h) Oxidoreductase

3 Name four commercial sources of enzymes. How are raw enzymes **a)** extracted and **b)** purified?

Describe how enzymes are being used in **a)** medicine, **b)** the food industry and **c)** agriculture.

Industrial chemicals

4   The development of enzyme immobilisation techniques since the 1950s has led to a boom in the industrial uses of enzymes.

Describe techniques for immobilising enzymes, and the industrial uses of enzymes in an immobilised form.

5   What are biosensors and how do they work?

Describe and discuss ways in which biosensors are being used in medicine, industry and agriculture.

6   Natural fuel resources will eventually run out. Discuss the use of micro-organisms as producers of fuel for the future.

What advantages and disadvantages do you foresee in microbial fuel production?

Outline biochemical pathways by which starch, cellulose and hemicellulose might be converted into ethanol (alcohol).

7   Write notes on each of the following:

a)   Microbial proteins and polysaccharides

b)   Microbes and oil extraction

c)   Microbes and metal extraction

BIBLIOGRAPHY

Industrial Chemicals

Bickerstaff, GF (1987) *Enzymes in Industry and Medicine* (New Studies in Biology) Hodder and Stoughton

Birch, GG, Blakebrough, N and Parker, KJ eds (1981) *Enzymes and Food Processing* Applied Science Publishers, London

Carr, PW and Bowers, LD (1980) *Immobilized Enzymes in Analytical and Clinical Chemistry* John Wiley and Sons, New York and London

Gacesa, P and Hubble, J (1987) *Enzyme Technology* Open University Press, Milton Keynes

Godfrey, T and West, S eds (1996) *Industrial Enzymology: The Application of Enzymes in Industry* 2nd Edn Stockton, New York

Goldstein, IS (1981) *Organic Chemicals from Biomass* CRC Press, Florida

Hacking, AJ (1986) *Economic Aspects of Biotechnology* Cambridge University Press, Cambridge

Rothman, H, Greenshields, RN and Calle, FR (1983) *The Alcohol Economy: Fuel Ethanol and the Brazilian Experience* Frances Pinter, London

Trevan, MD (1980) *Immobilised Enzymes* John Wiley and Sons, New York and London

Wynn, CH (1985) *The Structure and Function of Enzymes* 2nd Edn (Studies in Biology, No. 42) Edward Arnold, London

Industrial chemicals

CHAPTER 8

Agriculture & horticulture

In the past, conventional breeding techniques have been used to improve farm animals, crops and ornamental plants. By selecting individuals with desirable traits, and crossing them so that there is sexual exchange and reshuffling of genes, breeders have produced offspring in which desirable traits have been combined. This method has been very successful in producing new varieties, but is often laborious and time consuming. In addition, recombination does not always separate tightly linked genes, so that undesirable traits may appear alongside the desirable ones.

Biotechnology offers techniques that can break through the rules which limit variations achieved by sexual crossing. Genetic engineers can now transfer useful genes into farm stock, to improve their growth rates, milk or meat production. Although genetic engineering in plants has lagged behind, there are now several different techniques for improving yields from crop plants, and other procedures that increase plant variation. Micropropagation, widely used by horticulturists, provides a rapid method for obtaining large numbers of genetically-identical plants.

8.1 Transgenic Farm Animals

A transgenic animal is an individual in which a gene (or genes) from another individual has been artificially inserted. In most of these animals the new genetic information forms a permanent part of the genome, and is passed on to their offspring according to the normal rules of Mendelian inheritance. So far, transgenic cattle, sheep, pigs, rabbits and chickens have been produced.

Figure 8.1 shows stages in the development of a mammalian embryo during its first six days of life.

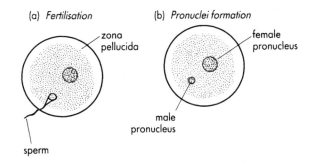

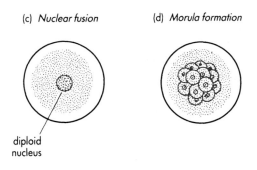

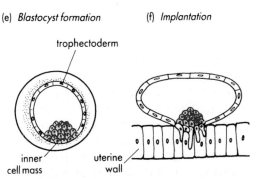

Figure 8.1 Stages in the early development of a mammalian embryo

Immediately after a sperm has penetrated an egg, genes from the male and female gametes are present in two small structures known as pronuclei. After the pronuclei have fused, the cell starts dividing.

Successive mitotic divisions cleave the cell into 2-, 4-, 8-, 16- and 32-celled stages, transforming it into a solid ball of cells called a morula. This morula is surrounded by a clear gelatinous outer covering, the zona pellucida. By the end of the fifth day, further cell divisions and cell movements, have transformed the developing embryo into a hollow, fluid-filled ball, called a blastocyst. The blastocyst's outer flattened layer of cells is its trophectoderm, from which the placenta forms. Its inner cell mass will go on to form the embryo proper. Implantation begins when the blastocyst sticks to the uterine wall and produces villi that anchor it into position (Figure 8.1).

Working with these early mammalian embryos, genetic engineers have used three different methods for introducing foreign genes:

(i) **Injection of genes – sequences of DNA – into a pronucleus.**
This is called microinjection. A fertilised egg is held, by suction, in a pipette. Several hundred copies of the foreign gene are injected into one of the pronuclei via a micropipette. This method is the most widely used and has, to date, proved the most successful. Even so, 30% of treated embryos degenerate and die within a few hours.

(ii) **The use of retroviruses as vectors to carry foreign DNA into morulas.**
After removing the zona pellucida, which viruses cannot penetrate, a morula is placed on a culture of fibroblasts infected with retroviruses. The retroviruses, genetically engineered to carry foreign DNA, infect cells of the morula as they are shed from the fibroblasts. This technique, however, often creates 'mosaic' offspring, where some cells contain the foreign gene, while others do not. The method also has limitations because the modified virus cannot leave the transgenic species. Under certain conditions it could mutate, regaining its ability to cause disease in the tissues where it occurs.

(iii) **Retroviral infection of stem cells, which are then injected into the cavity of another blastocyst.**
Stem cells, from the inner cell mass of an embryo, are infected with genetically-engineered retroviruses, then injected into the central cavity of a different blastocyst. The injected cells colonise the new embryo and participate in the formation of all the tissues, including the ovaries and testes from which cells are formed. So far, researchers have successfully used this technique for producing transgenic mice and hamsters. In the future they hope to develop the technique so that it can be used with farm animals.

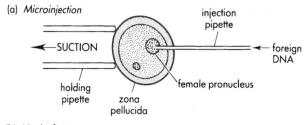

(a) *Microinjection*

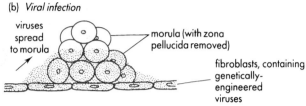

(b) *Viral infection*

(c) *Injection of stem cells*

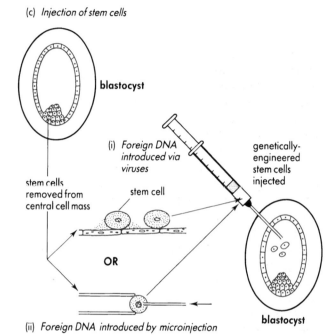

(i) *Foreign DNA introduced via viruses*

(ii) *Foreign DNA introduced by microinjection*

Figure 8.2 Methods used to introduce foreign DNA into a mammalian embryo

Early research into the production of transgenic animals revealed a simple method for producing hybrids, called **chimeras**, between closely-related species. Sheep–goat chimeras were produced by mixing four-celled sheep embryos with eight-celled goat embryos. After removing the zona pellucida from each egg, pressing the eggs together and incubating at 37°C, the cells reorganised and went on to form hybrid blastocysts. These blastocysts were then transferred to sheep foster mothers, where they continued their growth and development until the sheep gave birth. Each hybrid offspring contained both sheep and goat cells in all its tissues. As a result, the coats of these animals resembled a patchwork, made up from small irregular patches of sheep and goat fur. Although the chimeras proved to be of considerable academic and popular interest, combining features of the two species, they have, to date, had little economic significance.

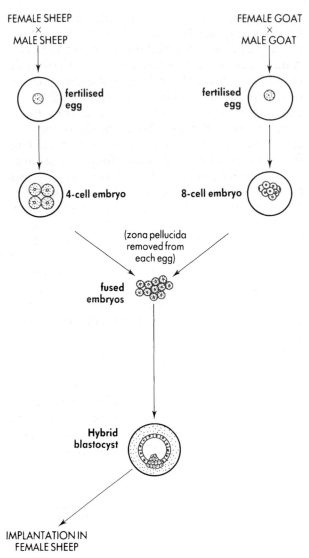

Figure 8.3 Stages in the production of a sheep–goat chimera

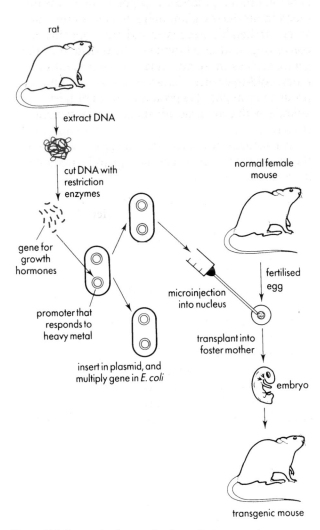

Figure 8.4 Stages in the production of a transgenic mouse

The first transgenic animals produced were mice, into which a gene cloning for rat growth hormone was inserted by microinjection. Interestingly, the gene for growth hormone was linked to the promoter from a gene which responded to the presence of heavy metals. This acted as an unusual control mechanism, allowing the gene to be turned on by exogenous compounds, such as zinc. After extracting the appropriate DNA segment from a rat, it was cloned in a plasmid and grown up in a standard laboratory culture of *E. coli* (Figure 8.4). The plasmids were then extracted, purified and converted to a linear form by adding the appropriate restriction endonucleases. Two techniques were used to introduce the new gene into the mouse genome:

(i) As many as 10 000 copies of the rat gene were injected into a pronucleus of a fertilised mouse egg, using a microneedle.

(ii) After treatment with calcium chloride, to make them more permeable, the rat DNA was applied to the outside of a 2–8-celled mouse embryo in culture.

The treated eggs, or embryos, were then transplanted into foster mothers, where they continued their development. Embryos which had taken up the new gene were identified by DNA hybridisation with small samples of DNA from white blood cells or skin cells.

Transformed adult mice mainly produced the growth hormone in their livers, rather than in its normal site of synthesis, the pituitary. When fully grown, the body mass of these animals was about twice that of normal mice. They grew faster than the normal mice and converted their food more efficiently into body mass. Furthermore, their growth rate could be carefully controlled by altering the zinc

Agriculture & horticulture

content of their diet, a neat and simple method of control. From a practical viewpoint, interest is not so much in producing giant animals as in strains that reach marketable size faster and are more efficient in converting food into **biomass**. The transfer of other genes, such as those affecting the properties of hair, hides, cold-tolerance, disease-resistance and milk production might also produce strains of farm animals with economic advantages over existing stocks.

An account of the role of transgenic animals in the production of pharmaceutical products is given in section 6.2.3.

8.2 New Breeding Techniques

In the future, the quality of farm animals may be improved by two laboratory-based breeding techniques, notably embryo manipulation and embryo cloning.

Embryo manipulation has made it possible for farmers to increase their farmstock by novel methods. Female sheep and cattle produce, on average, one offspring per pregnancy. Twins are rare. The relatively simple technique of bisecting the fertilised egg at the two-celled stage, and transplanting each half into different regions of the uterus, has almost doubled the reproductive rate. Among treated animals **twin births** become the rule, not the exception. The technique of **embryo surgery**, used to produce twin births, is currently being extended to help conserve rare breeds. After their eggs are fertilised in the laboratory, the young embryos of rare animals are dissected into anything from 2–8 cells. Each cell, successfully transplanted into a **surrogate mother** of a common breed, grows to produce a new individual of the rare type. Another variation of the technique allows surrogate mothers to carry embryos of a different species. Horses, for example, can give birth to zebras, from zebra embryos implanted at the blastocyst stage. The horse is tricked into accepting the zebra embryo by exchanging its own outer layer of trophectoderm for that of a zebra embryo. This exchange doesn't affect development of the inner cell mass, the true embryo-forming region.

Embryo cloning is a technique that allows many genetically-identical copies of an animal to be produced. Imagine that a mutation occurred in a cow making her an exceptional milk producer, significantly better than other members of her strain. Cross-breeding her with a bull would reshuffle her genes, and result in the loss of her unique

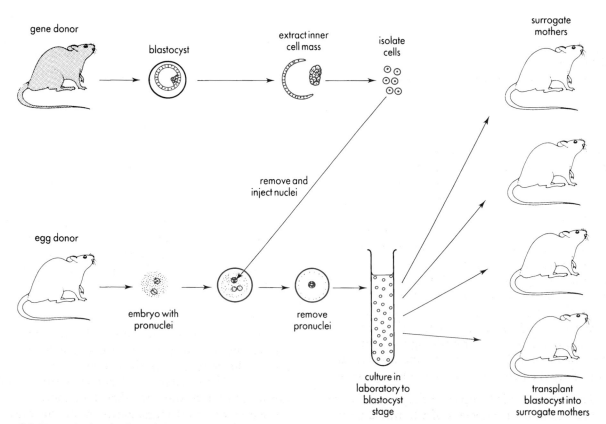

Figure 8.5 Stages in the cloning of the grey mouse

characteristics. **Cloning**, to produce identical copies of the cow, is the only technique that will conserve her unique features for future generations.

Although it may be some years before the cloning of cattle becomes a common practice, success with mice shows the feasibility of techniques that are currently being used. An egg from the donor is grown in the laboratory to the blastocyst stage, then dissected to remove the inner cell mass. The mass is separated out into individual cells. A nucleus from each of these cells is injected into a one-celled embryo containing two pronuclei. After removing the pronuclei, the embryos are cultured in the laboratory until they reach the blastocyst stage. They are then transplanted into surrogate mothers.

8.3 More Milk with BST

Bovine somatotrophin (BST), also called growth hormone, is a natural protein hormone produced by a cow's pituitary gland. The hormone has three different physiological effects:

(i)   it stimulates growth;

(ii) it affects the balance between fat and carbohydrate metabolism;

(iii) it increases milk production, partly by boosting food intake, but also by diverting a larger proportion of the cow's food into milk production.

During the 1970s, genetic engineers inserted the gene for BST into bacteria. As a result, large amounts of BST became available. When injected into cows, it was found to increase milk production by anything from 25–40 per cent. The meat from treated cattle was leaner, making it more attractive to the consumer.

Table 8.1 Some advantages and disadvantages of using bovine somatotrophin (BST)

Advantages	Disadvantages
Increased milk yields	cows eat more
	cows lose fertility
Higher profits for farmers	greater risk of mastitis and other bovine diseases
	milk overproduction
	fall in milk prices
	possible adverse effects on human health
	possibly a cruel and inhumane practice

By contrast, treated cows often became infertile, failing to respond to artificial insemination, or losing their embryos through spontaneous abortion. Widespread use of the product, and its subsequent appearance in milk and meat, led to public concern about its possible long-term effects on human health. Although research showed that BST was broken down in the human gut, and was physiologically active only in cattle, many people continued to have reservations about its use, not least because it seemed a somewhat cruel way of extracting milk from cows.

8.4 Transgenic Plants

Transgenic plants, like their animal counterparts, are genetically-engineered varieties containing one or more artificially-inserted genes. The broad aim of carrying out such transformations is to improve crop yields, increase variety, and give cultivated plants

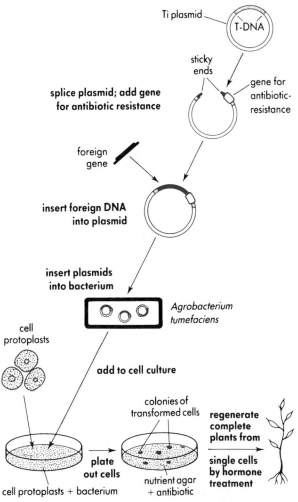

Figure 8.6 Using *Agrobacterium tumefaciens* to produce transgenic plants

Agriculture & horticulture

more protection against pests, parasites and harsh environmental conditions. Biologists first created transgenic plants by exploiting the bacterium *Agrobacterium tumefaciens*. This bacterium, the cause of crown gall disease, carries tumour-inducing (Ti) plasmids. One region of the plasmid, the so-called T–DNA region, integrates into any one of the plant's chromosomes. From its position on the chromosome, one part of the T–DNA codes for enzymes that synthesise the plant growth hormones auxin and cytokinin. Additional amounts of these hormones cause rapid cell division, resulting in the formation of a tumour.

Genetic engineers have exploited the discovery that any piece of foreign DNA, inserted between the left and right borders of the plasmid's T–DNA region, is transferred to one of the plant's chromosomes, where it becomes integrated. Since it was first discovered, this natural system for DNA transfer into plants has been improved in a number of ways. The genes that made the cells produce more hormones were deleted. As a result, transformed cells no longer grew into tumours, but retained their natural characteristics. Next, a gene for antibiotic resistance was added between the borders of the T–DNA region. Thirdly, sticky-ends were attached, so that the foreign DNA could be inserted.

After inserting the desired gene into a Ti plasmid, the remaining stages in producing a transgenic plant are fairly straightforward. Naked plant cells, or protoplasts, from which the cell walls have been removed, are placed into a petri dish and covered by a nutrient solution. A culture of *A. tumefaciens*, containing genetically-engineered plasmids, is added. The mixture is incubated at 25–30°C for several days. Cells are then plated out on to nutrient agar, to which the appropriate antibiotic has been added. Only those plant cells that have taken up the gene for antibiotic-resistance – and with it the foreign DNA – will grow on this medium. After allowing several days for growth, living cells are harvested. Each cell may then be grown to produce a complete plant by cultivation on nutrient media containing different mixtures of plant hormones.

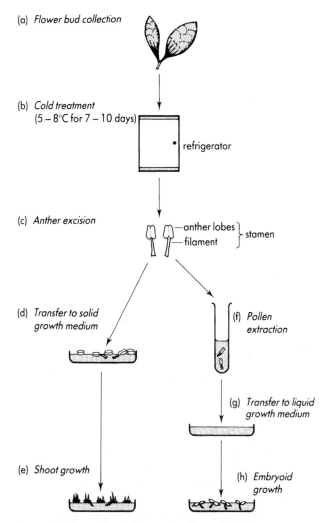

Figure 8.7 Stages in anther and pollen cultivation

(a) *Flower bud collection*

(b) *Cold treatment*
(5 – 8°C for 7 – 10 days) — refrigerator

(c) *Anther excision* — anther lobes, filament } stamen

(d) *Transfer to solid growth medium*

(e) *Shoot growth*

(f) *Pollen extraction*

(g) *Transfer to liquid growth medium*

(h) *Embryoid growth*

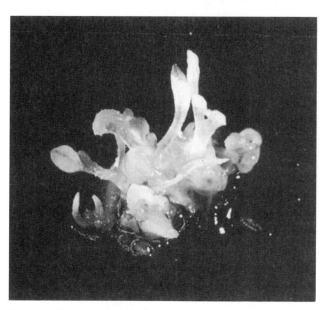

Anther **callus** with shoots

Genetic variation in flowering plants can also be increased by methods that do not involve bacterial vectors. The flowering plants are all diploid (2n). In the majority of cases, sexual reproduction is species-specific and follows fertilisation of a haploid egg, or ovum, (n) by a haploid male gamete (n), formed in a germinating pollen grain. Haploid plants (n) can sometimes be formed by allowing pollen grains or anthers to grow on solid or in liquid cultures, to which an appropriate mixture of nutrients and growth hormones has been added. The plantlets produced by pollen and anther culture are haploid,

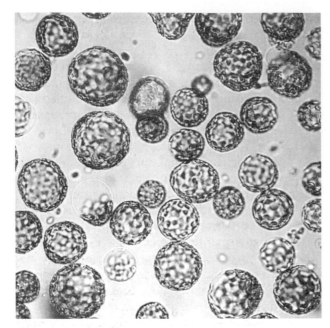

Leaf cell protoplasts

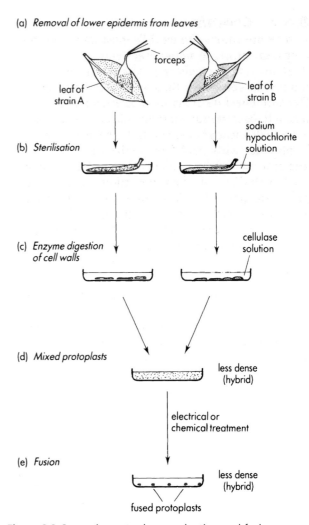

Figure 8.8 Stages in protoplast production and fusion

with only one copy of each gene. They often resemble their diploid parents, but may also show significant variation. By using colchicine, a **mutagen** which causes chromosome numbers to double during cell division, polyploid plants can be obtained with entirely new homozygous characteristics. This technique has been used to produce pure-breeding lines in less than half the time taken by conventional cross-breeding methods.

Protoplast fusion provides an additional technique for inducing variation in plant crops. The protoplast is the living part of a plant cell, surrounded by the cell membrane, from which the cell wall has been removed. By fusing protoplasts from different strains of species, it is possible to transfer genes from one strain to another. The protoplasts are prepared by immersing sterilised plant material in a solution of the enzyme cellulase, either from fungi or the alimentary canal of snails.

Protoplast fusion between varieties of a species, or closely-related species, is achieved by adding ethylene glycol, or by applying an electric field (see section 8.4.1 on Cereals). The technique has been successful in transferring genes for resistance to late blight fungus from one variety of potato to others. Only limited success, however, is reported in attempts to transfer genes for salt tolerance and disease-resistance from wild rice into cultivated varieties. Effective transfer occurred, but hybrids were difficult to identify and to grow on into mature plants. Research into protoplast fusion is continuing, with a view to finding new approaches to overcome these difficulties, enabling this technique to become a powerful tool in generating novel variations in plants.

QUESTIONS

1 How does a chimera differ from a clone?

2 List **a)** two advantages and **b)** two disadvantages of boosting milk production with BST.

3 **a)** Name the bacterium that causes crown gall disease.

   b) What is it about this bacterium that makes it useful for introducing new genes into some crop plants?

4 **a)** What are protoplasts?

   b) How are protoplasts obtained?

   c) Why are protoplasts of interest to genetic engineers?

5 What are the advantages of genetic engineering over selective breeding?

Agriculture & horticulture

130

8.4.1 Cereals

Cereals are among the world's most important food crops. In nature, *A. tumefaciens* (see section 3.3.2) does not attack cereals and so cannot be used to modify the genome of these plants. If, however, the DNA of wheat dwarf virus is inserted into a Ti plasmid, bacteria carrying this plasmid will attack wounded wheat plants. Similarly, bacteria carrying Ti plasmids with DNA from maize streak virus will attack wounded maize plants. The technique, first used in 1987, is called **agroinfection**. Mature cereal plants are infected with plasmid-carrying bacteria. Transformed cells develop symptoms of the viral disease, and do not therefore need to be identified by selection. The infection spreads from cell to cell until all the cells of the cereal plant have been transformed. Researchers hope they will soon be able to use this technique for introducing foreign DNA into cereals.

Several other novel methods of gene transfer have been applied to cereals, all relying on the direct uptake of DNA without the use of a bacterial vector.

In a technique called **electroporation**, plant protoplasts are mixed with foreign DNA and given an electric shock. The electric pulse causes pores to open up in the cell membranes, increasing the amount of exogenous DNA that enters. After the current is switched off, the pores reseal. A small amount of the foreign DNA becomes incorporated into the chromosomes, causing some of the protoplasts to undergo transformation. So far, however, this technique has only been used successfully with maize and rice protoplasts. Similar results have been obtained by treating protoplasts with the chemical ethylene glycol, which makes them more permeable to exogenous DNA.

Attempts to transfer foreign DNA into wheat have mostly focused on young embryos. Results obtained from the direct **microinjection** of foreign DNA into young embryos have been mixed, with some transformations reported. Another similar method, **macroinjection**, involves the use of a syringe to inject foreign DNA into the space surrounding a young inflorescence. Success for this approach has

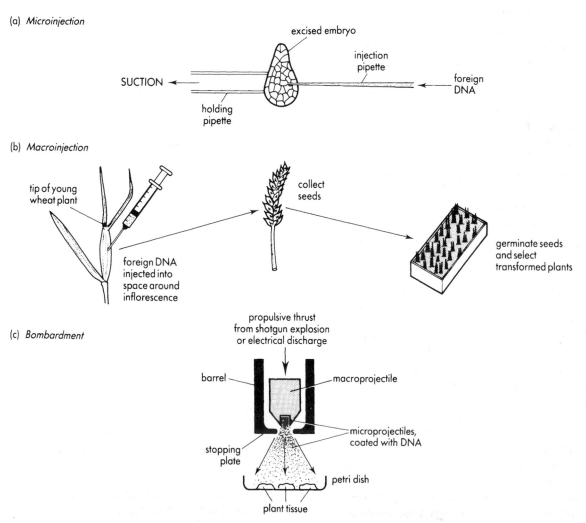

Figure 8.9 Methods used to introduce foreign DNA into cereals

been claimed in the transfer of a gene for resistance to the antibiotic kanamycin. Alternative approaches have included surrounding pollen grains, young carpels and mature seeds with exogenous DNA in the hope that they will take it up and undergo transformations. A different, novel and more promising approach involves the **bombardment** of intact plant cells with very small (1–4 μm in diameter) DNA-coated spheres of tungsten or gold. These microprojectiles are shot from a macroprojectile, resembling a bullet with an open tip, which is itself held by a stopping plate. The propulsive force which gives the microprojectiles sufficient acceleration comes either from a shotgun 'explosion' or an electrical discharge. Already successfully used in transforming soya beans, this approach could open a new chapter in the transformation of cereals.

Clearly the number of transformations that could be made in cereals is legion. Transferring **nif-genes** from legumes, so that cereals could fix atmospheric nitrogen, ranks high on the list of priorities. If cereals became self-sufficient in obtaining all their nitrogen, this would reduce the need for artificial fertilisers, and ease the problem of river pollution by nitrates. Rice growers might gain similar financial benefits if genes for salt-tolerance could be transferred into rice from one of the salt marsh grasses, or some other halophyte. Other transformations that might usefully be applied to cereals are equally applicable to other crops. Most consist of giving the crop plant better protection against its pests and parasites, while making it more resistant to harsh environmental conditions.

8.5 Crop Protection

Herbivorous insects are the greatest scourge of food crops, causing damage estimated at about £1.5 billion a year worldwide. One approach is to introduce micro-organisms into an area plagued by insects. *Baculovirus*, for example, is used to control spruce sawfly in coniferous forests. The fungus *Beauvaria bassiana* is effective in controlling aphids and the Colorado beetle on potatoes. *Bacillus thuringiensis*, a bacterium, is parasitic in the larvae of certain butterflies and moths. When the bacterium sporulates it produces a crystalline protein that kills the caterpillars. Sprayed over crops as a mixture of the bacterium and its crystalline toxin, this preparation has been effective in the control of inchworms and gypsy moth caterpillars. The toxin is commercially attractive as a means of pest control because it has no harmful effects on humans or other vertebrates.

An alternative approach has been to transfer the gene for this toxin directly into plants. Transgenic tobacco and tomato plants, which carried the gene, gained effective protection from insect damage. Red kidney beans are rarely eaten by insects because they carry a gene that makes a protease inhibitor. If an insect ingests the inhibitor, trypsin, one of its protein-digesting enzymes, is broken down. Introduced into tobacco plants, this gene gave better protection against a wide range of grazing insects. By making their own insecticides, transgenic plants allow biologists to direct a specific attack against insect pests. The beneficial insects, such as pollinators and nectar-feeders, are not generally affected.

After insects, viral and fungal parasites probably take the heaviest toll of crop plants. Resistance to a number of viral parasites has been achieved by transferring genes that make proteins of the viral coat. The presence of large amounts of these proteins acts as an inhibitor of further production, interfering with the early stages of viral replication. Through the use of 'antisense' RNA, researchers have successfully blocked the replication of several parasitic micro-organisms that attack potatoes. Success for the technique is claimed against viral, bacterial and fungal parasites.

Weeds are the major plant pests of cultivated crops. Genetic engineers have transformed wheat and maize with genes that increase their resistance to herbicides such as chlorsulfuron and glyphosate. Proteins produced by the gene degrade or detoxify the herbicide. As a result, farmers can achieve better weed control by growing crops that are herbicide-resistant.

Late frosts in April and May frequently damage potato crops. A bacterium called *Pseudomonas syringae*, almost always present on the surface of leaves, feeds on frost-damaged plants. This bacterium helps to cause frost damage because it carries an 'ice-nucleation' gene. This gene produces a protein around which ice crystals form at temperatures between 0 and $-7°C$. If such bacteria are not present on a plant, ice crystals do not form until temperatures drop below $-7°C$.

Genetic engineers have produced so-called ice-nucleation inactive (INA−) strains of *P. syringae*, by removing the gene for ice-nucleation. Sprayed over potatoes and other crops, this strain competes favourably with those that are positive for ice-nucleation, and soon replaces them. As a result, the ice crystals do not form on treated plants unless the temperature falls below $-7°C$. This treatment has been used to lengthen the growing season in several frost-tender plants, including potatoes, strawberries (in which the flowers are subject to frost-damage), runner beans and dwarf beans.

8.6 Micropropagation

Micropropagation, sometimes called test-tube plant culture, is an extremely cost-effective method of producing large numbers of genetically-identical, herbaceous perennials, shrubs and trees. These genetically-identical plants, the product of vegetative propagation, are clones of a single parent. As an example of the advantages of micropropagation, a raspberry bush might produce from 5–20 plants from each parent in a year. Micropropagation could produce 50 000 new plants in the same time. Moreover, there would be considerable saving in terms of the space required for bedding, and in labour costs.

Micropropagation gives plant breeders a number of economic advantages. It allows them to perpetuate particular unique genotypes. Houseplants, for example, with unusual flower colours or leaf patterns, can be mass-produced from a single parent plant. In large-scale hybrid seed production, micropropagation gives breeders the large numbers of genetically-uniform parent plants that they require. Plant breeders who need to store large numbers of plants, or transport them to other parts of the country, find in micropropagation a technique that saves space and cuts the cost of heating and lighting.

Four steps are generally followed in the micropropagation of plants. These are:

(i) Selection of a suitable explant, such as a stem segment or bud, from a choice parent plant, and its **sterilisation** in sodium hypochlorite solution ($1–2\%^{w/v}$), or some other disinfectant, followed by washing in distilled water.

(ii) Transfer of the sterilised material to a **nutrient (basal) medium**, generally solidified with agar ($0.7–1.0\%^{w/v}$). This medium contains salts of nitrogen, other mineral salts, sucrose, amino acids and vitamins, but generally no growth regulators. Stem explants survive for several

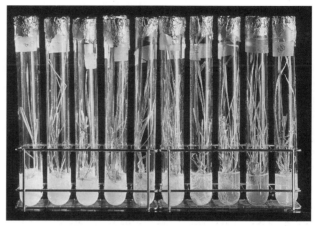

C7 Cereal plants being grown by micropropagation (see *Colour Section on inside cover*)

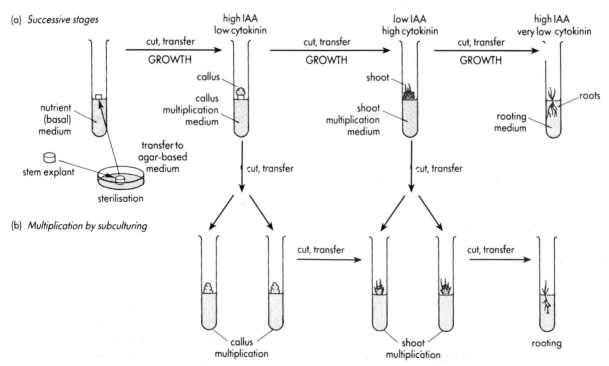

Figure 8.10 Plant micropropagation

A micropropagated orchid plant before transplantation from agar

called a callus (Figure 8.10). Higher cytokinin concentrations stimulate the formation of shoots. Both the callus and the young shoots are multiplied every 4–6 weeks by subculturing on the appropriate growth media. It is this subculturing that greatly increases the number of plantlets in the clone.

(iv) Transfer to **rooting (storage) medium**. This medium contains a relatively high concentration of IAA, indole–3–butyric acid (IBA), naphthaleneacetic acid (NAA) or 2,4–dichlorophenoxyacetic acid (2,4–D), to induce root development. After the roots have developed, the plantlets may again be subdivided, to produce many more plantlets for further subculture on the same medium. When these plants have reached a suitable size, they are removed and potted up in potting compost.

Micropropagation has also proved an invaluable method of removing viruses from infected plants. This possibility exists because the apical meristems, or growing points of shoots, are virus-free. By removing the apical bud from a virus-infected plant, and in some cases applying heat treatment, micropropagation can be used to regenerate virus-free stock. The technique has been used to good effect on potatoes, tomatoes, raspberries, strawberries and many other crop plants.

Although the advantages of micropropagation greatly outweigh the disadvantages, there are two major problems associated with the technique. The first is that micropropagation requires aseptic conditions. Failure to meet this requirement causes bacterial or fungal contamination of the culture medium, with subsequent loss of the plants that are being cultured. A second problem is an increased rate of mutation in medium-grown cells. This leads to abnormalities in the plantlets, a feature that can spread rapidly unless the technologist makes regular inspections and removes any defective individuals.

months on this medium. Some buds elongate, forming a single short shoot with strong apical dominance; that is, preferential growth of the terminal bud, while the growth of the lateral buds is suppressed.

(iii) Transfer to a **multiplication medium**, containing indole acetic acid (IAA), to promote cell elongation, and a cytokinin such as 9–benzylaminopurine (BAP) or 6–furfurylaminopurine (kinetin), which are growth regulators that stimulate mitosis. A low cytokinin concentration stimulates the formation of an undifferentiated mass of cells

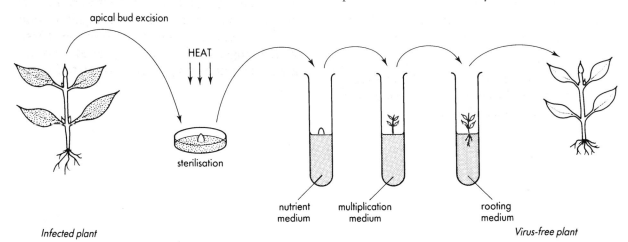

Infected plant

apical bud excision

HEAT

sterilisation

nutrient medium

multiplication medium

rooting medium

Virus-free plant

Figure 8.11 Stages in the removal of a virus from an infected plant

8.7 Flavr-savr Tomatoes

The Calgene Corporation of America has successfully engineered a tomato with a longer shelf-life and improved flavour. These *flavr-savr* tomatoes do not become soft and mushy, like normal over-ripe tomatoes, and can be left on the vine until a much later stage of maturity, thereby acquiring a full flavour. Normal tomatoes produce an enzyme, **polygalacturonase**, after ripening, which breaks down pectin in the cell walls. As a result, the soft parts of the fruit beneath the skin liquefy, spoiling the flavour and causing the fruit to shrink and wrinkle. Polygalacturonase is the produce of a single structural gene, which produces an mRNA molecule. In *flavr-savr* tomatoes this mRNA molecule is blocked by a complementary **anti-sense mRNA** molecule, the product of an added *flavr-savr* gene (see section 3.5). Binding between the two mRNA molecules prevents translation of the polygalacturonase gene into the sequence of amino acids required to form the enzyme. In the absence of this enzyme, fruits remain firmer for longer, and can be left on the vine to develop their full, red colour and tangy flavour.

In the production of this tomato, plasmids are used with genes for resistance to two antibiotics, kanamycin and neomycin. As these antibiotics are not used to treat human diseases, the tomatoes are generally considered safe for human consumption. Environmentalists, however, express some concerns about the possibility of antibiotic-resistant genes being released into soils when the tomatoes decompose.

QUESTIONS

6 What methods can be used to introduce new genes into crop plants?

7 If *nif*-genes from legumes could be transferred into cereals, how might farmers benefit?

8 List two ways in which micro-organisms are being used to protect crops.

9 How can a virus be removed from a plant?

10 List a) three advantages and b) two disadvantages of micropropagation.

CHAPTER 8 SUMMARY

Recombinant DNA technology offers a distinct advantage over cross-breeding in the production of valuable new genetic variations, both in farm animals and in crop plants. Single gene traits, added to the existing genome of these organisms, increase their value and usefulness.

New breeding techniques have been developed for producing transgenic farm animals. Among the potential advantages of these techniques are more cost-effective meat production, and the extraction of therapeutic substances from milk.

Transgenic plants with improved environmental resistance, faster growth rates and improved yields, can be produced by a variety of different techniques, namely agroinfection, electroporation, microinjection and bombardment with DNA-coated projectiles.

Three different techniques, developed by biotechnologists, have brought financial rewards to farmers and market gardeners. Genetically-engineered bovine somatotrophin (BST), produced in bacteria, has been injected into cows to increase their milk yields. Micropropagation is a cost-effective method of producing large numbers of genetically-identical plants, shrubs and trees. *Flavr-savr* tomatoes, with a longer shelf-life and improved flavour, are an example of a genetically-modified crop plant.

Agriculture & horticulture

1 Imagine you have a number of shoot cuttings from a choice potted plant. Someone asks you to micropropagate it, using each of the stages listed below:

Select
explant
↓
Sterilisation
↓
Basal
nutrient
medium
↓
Shoot
multiplication
medium
↓
Shoot-tip
rooting
medium

a) From which part of the shoot would you select the explants?

b) What solution would you use for sterilisation?

c) For how long would you leave the explants in this solution?

d) Explain the reason for a final washing in distilled water.

e) Give the names of three different nutrients in the basal medium.

f) At what point would you transfer explants from the basal to the shoot multiplication medium?

g) Give the name of a plant hormone contained in shoot multiplication medium, and its principal effect on the explants.

h) What treatment would you give to the explants after they had developed axillary branches?

i) Give the name of the plant hormone contained in shoot-tip rooting medium.

j) Outline any further treatment of the rooted cuttings.

2 Farmers can produce 'instant grass' by growing seeds in trays for 8 days, under artificial illumination.

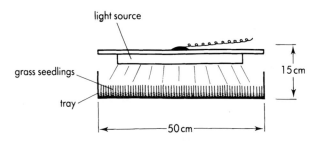

light source

grass seedlings

tray

15 cm

50 cm

Grass seedlings are watered with a solution of mineral salts, then removed and fed to cattle. A single production unit is shown in the diagram. Each of the seed trays is 50 × 50 × 10 cm.

A farmer buys a sealed metal trailer, with rear doors opening outwards, for towing behind a lorry. The trailer is 4 m high, 3 m wide and 10 m long. You are asked to convert the trailer into an 'instant grass' production unit.

a) Draw a plan and elevation of your design, to accommodate the maximum number of production units. (Remember that you need a central gangway, wide enough for an attendant.)

b) What is the total area of 'instant grass' your unit produces every 8 days?

c) List the items you would need to set up the venture. Attempt to estimate your total costs in setting up the unit.

d) List your running costs.

e) Under what climatic condition is the unit most likely to be cost-effective?

3 What do you understand by the term 'transgenic animals'?

How may transgenic animals be produced?

Discuss the current and potential uses of transgenic animals in **a)** agriculture and **b)** the production of compounds with medical (therapeutic) applications.

4 Describe, and evaluate from a scientific and economic viewpoint,

a) the use of new breeding techniques to raise farm animals, and

b) the use of micropropagation to mass produce plants for the home and garden.

5 Write a brief account of each of the following, emphasising their economic importance:

a) Bovine somatotrophin (BST)

b) Anther and pollen culture

c) Plant protoplast production

d) *Bacillus thuringiensis*

e) *Pseudomonas syringae*

6 The bacterium *Agrobacterium tumefaciens* causes crown gall disease in a number of dicotyledons. How have biologists exploited this bacterium in the production of transgenic plants?

As cereals are not normally attacked by this bacterium, how have biologists introduced foreign DNA into this group of plants?

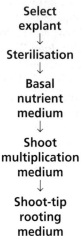

Agriculture & horticulture

Agriculture & Horticulture

Agricultural and Food Research Council (1987) *Biotechnology in Agriculture*

Biotol Project *Biotechnological Innovations in Crop Improvement* (1991) Butterworth-Heinemann, London

Freeland, P (1991) *Micro-organisms in Action (Practical Guide)* Hodder and Stoughton, London

Hayes, S, Madden, D and Schollar, J (1990) *Dairy Biotechnology* National Dairy Council, London

Hussey, G (1978) The application of tissue culture to the vegetative propagation of plants *Science Progress* (65), 258, 185–208

Lee, B (1989) Cereal transformation *Plants Today* (1), 9–11

Storr, A (1985) *Plant Tissue Culture* Association for Science Education, Hatfield

Straughan, R and Reiss, M (1996) *Ethics, Morality and Crop Biotechnology* Biotechnology and Biological Sciences Review Council

Wilkins, CP and Dodds, JH (1983) The application of tissue culture techniques to plant genetic conservation *Science Progress* (68), 270, 259–284

Wymer, P (1990) *Biotechnology in Practice* Hobson's Publishing Co.

CHAPTER

9

Water treatment & waste disposal

Water treatment and waste disposal are the principal services provided by biotechnology. Humans use water for drinking, washing and flushing away excreta. As water is a natural resource, sometimes in short supply, it is important that the waste water from households is recycled. This is made possible by the efficiency of modern sewage works, where organic matter, micro-organisms and chemical wastes are removed from the water before it is returned to domestic consumers. The efficiency of modern sewage plants often contrasts markedly with the conditions found on farms, where excreta from pigs and cattle may drain, via open ditches, into rivers. In the future, animal excreta may be more widely processed, either to break it down into biogas, or to produce a safe organic fertiliser.

Cleaning up environmental pollution caused by oil spillages, industrial effluents or agricultural chemicals is another area of waste disposal in which biotechnologists are prominent. The use of genetically-engineered bacteria to break down crude oil is one example of this type of service.

9.1 Water Purification

Before it reaches the tap, water has usually received the following treatments:

Sedimentation → flocculation → sand filtration → chlorination

Rain water, collected in streams and rivers, is stored in reservoirs, where large particles separate out under gravity to form a sediment. Smaller particles of suspended organic matter are broken down by micro-organisms. From the reservoir, water is pumped to a **mixing tank**. The addition of aluminium potassium sulphate (alum) forms a floc, consisting of fine mud particles and micro-organisms, which is removed in a flocculation tank.

The water is then filtered through a deep bed of sand. Like water that has filtered naturally through rocks, water that has passed through a **sand filter** is chemically and biologically purer than before filtration. Purification is assisted by a mass of bacteria, algae and protozoa that builds up in the upper layers of the sand bed. Biological oxidations and reductions occur in this layer.

Testing the purity of drinking water in the Sudan, East Africa

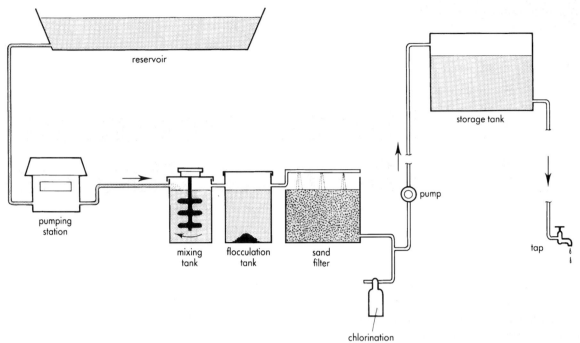

Figure 9.1 Stages in the treatment of the domestic water supply

Predatory protozoans feed on bacteria. After it has passed through a sand bed, about 99 per cent of all the bacteria and viruses in the water have been removed.

The final treatment is chlorination. Chlorine kills all the remaining bacteria, but is less effective against viruses and protozoa. The chlorine is added in sufficient amounts to provide continued protection in the water system, although there is currently some concern about these levels, based on the possibility that they might pose a long-term threat to human health. Ozone, generated electrically, could provide an alternative treatment, but does not give lasting protection from pathogenic micro-organisms. Following chlorination, the disinfected water is pumped to storage tanks, situated on high ground.

Aerial view of a sewage treatment plant

9.2 Sewage Disposal

Household sewage consists mainly of toilet wastes, bath water, handwashings and dishwashings. Sewage that enters a municipal drainage system passes to a sewage works, where it receives primary, secondary and tertiary treatments. **Primary treatment** begins at a coarse filter, where paper and other suspended or floating material is removed. In the primary settling tank, which receives raw sewage, a sewage effluent forms an upper layer above a solid sewage sludge.

Secondary treatment of sewage effluent is carried out either in an activated sludge system or in trickling filters. The **activated sludge system** has an aeration tank, where pure oxygen or air is bubbled

through the primary effluent. In this tank, aerobic bacteria oxidise dissolved organic matter, and dissolved mineral salts. The principal reactions are:

$$\text{Carbon compounds} \rightarrow CO_2$$
$$NH_4^+ \rightarrow NO_3^-$$
$$H_2S \rightarrow SO_4^{2+}$$

A settling tank, next to the aeration tank, collects a sludge formed mostly from living and dead micro-organisms. This material, or floc, absorbs some soluble organic matter from the overlying effluent. Pipes beneath the sedimentation tank carry the sludge away for further processing.

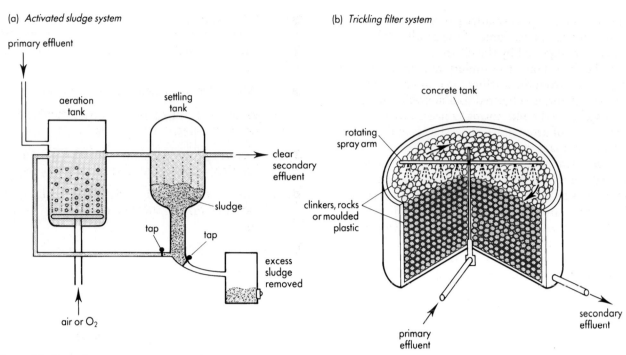

Figure 9.2 Secondary sewage treatment

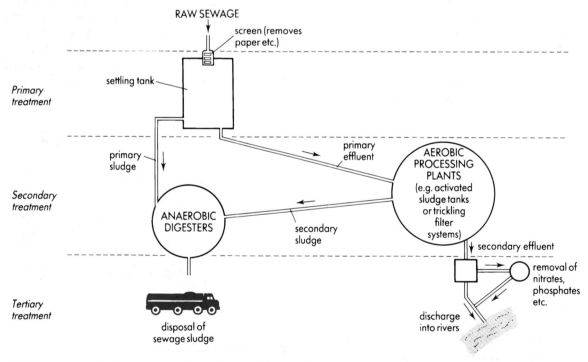

Figure 9.3 General layout of a sewage works, which would normally have several aerobic processing plants and anaerobic digesters arranged in series

In a **trickling filter system,** primary effluent is sprayed from four or more rotating horizontal arms over beds of clinkers, rocks or moulded plastic, contained in a circular concrete tank. As the effluent percolates through the beds, aerobic micro-organisms on the surface of the solid material oxidise most of the organic matter. The concrete tank retains any solid matter. Drainage pipes carry away this

secondary sludge for further treatment. Bacteria belonging to *Bacillus, Proteus* and *Pseudomonas* species occur in aerobic treatment plants, together with an extremely important floc-forming species, *Zoogloea ramigera.* Ciliate protozoa also abound, notably *Vorticella,* whose numbers provide a useful indication of the course of microbial oxidation in activated sludge systems. The bacteria break down

Water treatment & waste disposal

organic materials into smaller particles and water-soluble end products. Some of the small solid particles are digested by the ciliates.

In the final stage of secondary treatment, sewage sludge, both from the settling tank and aerobic treatment plant, is subjected to **anaerobic digestion** in a large, closed tank, normally heated to a temperature of around 30–40°C. Here, in the presence of anaerobic bacteria such as *Methanobacterium*, the volume of solids is greatly reduced, mainly by the conversion of organic compounds into gaseous end products, such as CO_2, CH_4 and H_2, along with water and mineral salts.

The tertiary treatment of sewage involves further purification of the effluent and disposal of the sludge. **Tertiary effluent treatment** removes any remaining organic matter, nitrates and phosphates. Small particles of solid material and some dissolved chemicals are removed by filtration through beds of fine sand and activated charcoal. Nitrates are converted by micro-organisms to ammonia and evaporated from stripping towers into the air. Phosphates are precipitated out by combining them with chemicals such as lime, alum or ferric chloride. Chlorine may also be added to inhibit the growth of any remaining micro-organisms, and oxidise any persistent odour-producing substances. Any water that has passed through this series of treatments is normally clean enough to be pumped into rivers. **Sewage sludge**, the solid product of sewage treatment, is of little commercial value. In many parts of the country it is emptied into the sea or incinerated. Elsewhere, after drying, it may be used for landfill or as a soil conditioner.

From time to time raw sewage, or sewage that has not completed its processing, seeps into rivers. The presence of coliform bacteria, from the human intestine, and the eggs of invertebrate gut parasites in this effluent may pose a health risk. More often, however, it poses a threat to the animal and plant life of the river. The sudden influx of a nutrient-rich solution results in increased numbers of bacteria, whose demand for oxygen is so enormous that larger organisms may become starved of oxygen. An indication of bacterial activity, and hence of the extent of sewage pollution, can be made by determining the **Biochemical Oxygen Demand (BOD)** of the water. A BOD test measures the amount of oxygen absorbed by a water sample over a 5-day period at 20°C. Results bear a direct relationship to the amount of organic matter in the water. The higher the figure for oxygen consumption, the more organic matter the water sample contains.

QUESTIONS

1 List four stages in the purification of drinking water.

2 a) Why is chlorine added to drinking water?

   b) What are the objections to adding chlorine to drinking water?

3 What occurs during the a) primary treatment and b) secondary treatment of sewage?

4 Name a) three gases and b) two solid or liquid products that result from the breakdown of sewage.

5 State three possible fates of sewage sludge.

9.2.1 Animal Egesta/Excreta

In isolated parts of the UK, where there is no municipal sewage disposal, farmers may use septic tanks or biogas generators to break down animal excreta. The solid matter that drains into a **septic tank** settles out under gravity, then undergoes partial decomposition to form a sludge. Liquid effluent flows from an outlet pipe in a clinker or rock-based 'soakaway', before entering the surrounding soil.

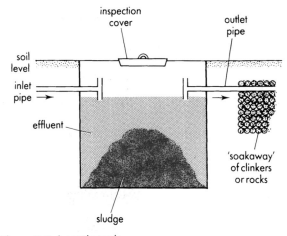

Figure 9.4 A septic tank

Micro-organisms in the soil decompose any solid material in the effluent (Figure 9.4). Septic tanks require careful management and may constitute a health hazard. The sludge, for example, must be dug or pumped periodically from the holding tank. Heavy rain may cause the sewage effluent to rise, flooding the soil surface, contaminating streams, and emitting an offensive odour. There is also a risk that pathogenic coliform bacteria, present in the soil surrounding a septic tank, may contaminate farm

Water treatment & waste disposal

Methane driven power generator

crops. The anaerobic digestion of excreta results in the production of methane, a high-energy, clean gaseous fuel. **Biogas generators** are anaerobic digesters that produce methane from a number of organic wastes, including excreta and the leafy remains of vegetable crops. Methane production occurs in two stages:

(i) Carbohydrates, fats and proteins are broken down by anaerobic pathways into a mixture of alcohols and fatty acids, together with CO_2 and H_2.

(ii) Methanogenic bacteria (methanogens), belonging to the genera *Methanococcus*, *Methanobacterium* and *Methanosprillum*, produce methane by reducing CO_2 with H_2:

$$CO_2 + 4H_2 \rightarrow CH_4 + 2H_2O$$

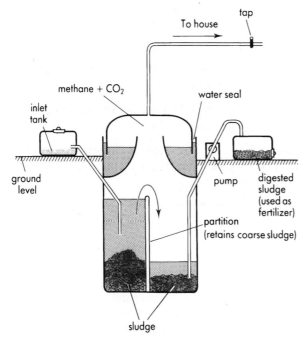

Figure 9.5 A domestic biogas generator

At the same time acetate, a lower fatty acid, is split to yield methane and carbon dioxide:

$$CH_3COOH \rightarrow CH_4 + CO_2$$

The gas that collects above the fermentation tank is mostly methane and carbon dioxide. It can be used as a domestic fuel, or compressed into cylinders for use in cars and tractors. Throughout China there are more than 7 million small, family scale biogas generators, making a significant contribution to the energy budget of that country. These decompose human sewage as well as the excreta from animals kept on smallholdings.

It has been known for many years that decomposing sludge soon becomes colonised by large populations of earthworms, mostly *Eisenia fetida*. The deliberate cultivation of earthworms for economic purposes is called **vermiculture**, a small and profitable branch of biotechnology. Earthworms are decomposers. They speed up the rate at which sludge and other waste materials such as straw are broken down. Any pathogenic bacteria in the sludge are destroyed as they pass through an earthworm's alimentary canal. The worms' faeces build up to form a brown-black mineral-rich organic compost, marketed through garden centres. There is also a substantial market for the worms themselves. They may be sold to improve the fertility of agricultural land, reclaim waterlogged soil, as bait for fishes or as food for a number of aquatic and terrestrial animals.

Biotechnologists have attempted to speed up the rate at which earthworms break down organic wastes. Yeasts, bacteria, energy sources (e.g. sucrose) and nitrogen sources (e.g. urea) are among additions that have been made to the raw materials. *Lumbricus rubellus*, a surface-feeding red earthworm, *Allelobophora chlorotica*, a green, shallow burrower, and *Lumbricus terrestris*, a red-brown deep burrower, have been used in combination to ensure that decomposition takes place at all levels in a heap of organic waste material.

9.3 Biodegradable Pollutants

Most pollutants are biodegradable and are harmful for only a short period before they are broken down by saprophytes. Sewage, for example, discharged into the sea is eventually rendered harmless by saprophytic bacteria and other organisms. Some pollutants, however, retain their harmful characteristics for a long time. **Crude oil** spilt from tankers, clings to the pebbles and rocks of beaches and devastates shore-dwelling communities, before it is eventually broken down and dispersed. The slow natural degradation of crude oil is brought about by

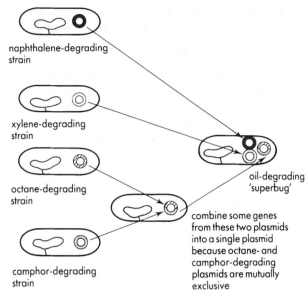

naphthalene-degrading strain

xylene-degrading strain

octane-degrading strain

camphor-degrading strain

oil-degrading 'superbug'

 combine some genes from these two plasmids into a single plasmid because octane- and camphor-degrading plasmids are mutually exclusive

Figure 9.6 Stages in the creation of an oil-degrading 'superbug'

C8 A dead cormorant washed ashore on a beach following the Shetland oil spill in 1993 (*see Colour Section on inside cover*)

several species of fungi, including yeasts, and bacteria belonging mainly to the genera *Pseudomonas desulphovibrio.*

The bacterium *Pseudomonas aeruginosa* carries several different genes on its plasmids, each capable of degrading a different hydrocarbon. Distinct naphthalene-, xylene-, octane- and camphor-degrading genes have been identified. Genetic engineers have attempted to create an oil-degrading 'superbug' containing all of these genes. This task is complicated by the fact that plasmids carrying octane- and camphor-degrading genes cannot co-exist in the same individual. By combining these two genes into a single plasmid (Figure 9.6), the problem has been resolved. Oil-degrading 'superbugs' are useful in dispersing small oil slicks, especially if used together with detergents, which break the oil into small droplets. Even so, the dispersal of large oil slicks still presents a major ecological problem.

Other pollutants, including lead, mercury and insecticides, persist in the environment, and accumulate in organisms through natural food chains. Bacteria that accumulate heavy metals may one day be used to remove these toxic compounds from industrial effluents. Genetically-engineered plasmids, combining genes for the degradation of various aromatic compounds, should eventually extend the range of biodegradable pollutants to insecticides, herbicides and other chlorinated hydrocarbons.

QUESTIONS

6 Suggest a reason for each of the following.

   a) Most biogas generators are found in China.

   b) Biogas generators are often placed underground.

   c) Amount of biogas produced by UK generators shows seasonal variations.

7 What are the flammable components of biogas?

8 How may the production of compost from fallen leaves be speeded up?

9 Name four different hydrocarbons that can be broken down by bacteria.

10 Apart from breaking down hydrocarbons, in what other ways can bacteria be used to clean up the environment?

Water treatment & waste disposal

CHAPTER 9 SUMMARY

The principal services provided by biotechnologists are water purification, sewage disposal and the removal of environmental pollutants.

Water purification involves stages by which bacteria and viruses are removed from water, so that it becomes fit for drinking. The first step in this process involves the use of predatory protoctistans to feed on the bacteria, while the second is a chemical step, involving the addition of chlorine or ozone to destroy any remaining pathogens.

Sewage disposal is a two-stage process. During primary treatment, coarse suspended material is filtered out. In secondary treatments, bacteria and protoctistans are used, via a series of aerobic and anaerobic stages, to break down organic material into gases, water and mineral salts.

Some end products of sewage breakdown are useful. Biogas, generated by decomposers, is used as a source of fuel for heating and lighting. Sewage sludge is sold as a soil conditioner and for landfill.

Several species of bacteria have contributed to environmental clean-up operations, following oil spillages and pollution from toxic metals, insecticides and herbicides. Biotechnologists have produced oil-degrading 'superbugs', with plasmid-borne genes capable of breaking down a number of hydrocarbons.

CHAPTER 9   QUESTIONS

1 The diagram below shows a sectional view of a water filter bed. Copy the diagram.

   a) Name the materials labelled A and B.

   b) State the functions of each of these materials.

   c) Label, with the letter C, the layer in which most biological activity takes place.

   d) What is the chemical nature of most of this biological activity?

   e) Give the names of three types of micro-organism that might be found in layer C.

   f) Explain the reason for periodic backflushing through layer C.

   g) After water has passed through the filter bed, what further treatment is necessary before it enters the domestic supply?

   h) Name two water pollutants that may pass through the filter bed to enter the domestic water supply.

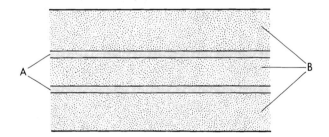

2 The diagram below is a sectional view of a sewage treatment plant. Copy the diagram

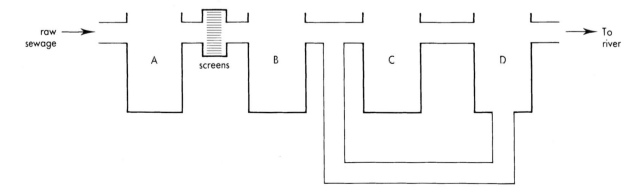

Water treatment & waste disposal

a) Add the appropriate title above each tank: settling tank 1, settling tank 2, activated sludge tank, road grit separation.

b) Explain the function of the screens.

c) In which tank are the reactions mainly (i) aerobic and (ii) anaerobic?

d) What is the main gaseous by-product of the aerobic tank?

e) Name two additional gases that are by-products from the anaerobic tank.

f) What flows (i) from tank D into the river and (ii) from tank D into tank C?

g) State three possible fates of sewage sludge.

3 What treatments are given to water before it reaches the tap? Explain the role of micro-organisms in water purification.

4 Describe the primary, secondary and tertiary processing of municipal sewage. Discuss the role of **a)** aerobic and **b)** anaerobic micro-organisms in sewage disposal. What methods are available for the disposal of sewage sludge?

5 Write notes on each of the following:

a) earthworms and waste disposal

b) septic tanks

c) biogas generators

d) oil-degradation by micro-organisms.

BIBLIOGRAPHY

Water Treatment & Waste Disposal
Bitton, G (1994) *Wastewater Microbiology* Wiley-Liss, New York

Henderson-Sellers, B and Markland, HR (1987) *Decaying Lakes: The Origins and Control of Cultural Eutrophication* John Wiley and Sons

Magruder, GC and Gaddy, JL (1981) Production of farm energy from biomass In *Advances in Biotechnology* 2, 269–274

Mason, CF (1981) *Biology of Freshwater Pollution* Longman

Salter, JH and Bull, AT (1982) Environmental Biotechnology: biodegradation *Philosophical Transactions of the Royal Society* B297, 575–595

Water treatment & waste disposal

Glossary

Active immunity: resistance to infectious diseases achieved by self-production of antibodies

Aerobe: an organism that grows in the presence of oxygen

Algae: aquatic, often unicellular or filamentous, photosynthetic protoctistans, without multicellular sex organs, leaves, stems or roots

Allergy: a harmful immune reaction, causing damage to cells and tissues

Anaerobe: an organism that grows in the absence of oxygen

Antibiotic: an organic compound, produced by one micro-organism, that kills or inhibits the growth of another micro-organism

Antibody: a protein (immunoglobulin) produced by lymphocytes in response to a foreign substance, or antigen

Anticodon: a sequence of three nucleotides in a transfer RNA molecule that is complementary to the amino acid-specifying codon in messenger RNA

Antigen: a foreign protein, polysaccharide or lipid which stimulates antibody production

Antiseptic: a chemical compound that kills or inhibits the growth of micro-organisms, but is non-toxic to cells

Attenuation: the selection of non-virulent strains of pathogens which retain their antigenic properties

Autoradiography: a method of detecting radioactively-labelled DNA (and other molecules) through exposure to an X-ray sensitive photographic film

B cells: lymphocytes that have matured in bone marrow and which develop into antibody-secreting plasma cells in response to a specific antigen

Bacteria: small, typically one-celled micro-organisms belonging to the kingdom Prokaryotae, characterised by the absence of a nucleus or membrane-bound organelles

Bacteriophage (phage): a viral parasite of bacteria, used as a cloning vector

Basophil: a type of granulocyte, which stains with basic dyes

Batch culture: a closed-system culture of micro-organisms in which the volume is fixed

Biomass: dry mass of organisms from any trophic (feeding) level in an ecosystem

Biosynthesis: the production of complex molecules from simple ones in any living organism

Biotechnology: the commercial exploitation of living organisms, chiefly to manufacture useful products or degrade harmful substances

Callus: an undifferentiated mass of plant tissue

Cell-mediated response: an immune response involving the activities of non-antibody producing cells, such as T lymphocytes

Chemoautotroph: a bacterium that uses chemical energy released by specific inorganic reactions to power its life processes

Chemostat: a stirred vessel for the continuous culture of micro-organisms and cells

Chimera: an artificial hybrid, containing recombinant DNA (also used to describe organisms composed of cells from different species)

Clone: a population of genetically-identical cells or organisms

Codon: a sequence of three nucleotides in a messenger RNA molecule that specifies one amino acid

Counter-current extraction: extraction at the interface of two liquids, flowing in opposite directions

Cytokine: a chemical compound, usually produced by phagocytes, that acts as a modulator within the immune system

Disinfectant: a chemical compound that kills micro-organisms, but which may also be toxic to cells and tissues

Distillation: collecting the vapours obtained from heating liquids, a method of increasing the ethanol (alcohol) content of some wines and all spirits

DNA: deoxyribonucleic acid, the genetic material of all organisms

DNA ligase: an enzyme that joins molecules of DNA together

DNA polymerase: an enzyme that synthesises a new strand of DNA in the 5'–3' direction, using an existing strand of DNA as a template

DNA probe: a radioactively-labelled single-stranded DNA molecule, with at least some of its base sequence complementary to the base sequence of a gene

Downstream processing: separating useful products from solvents etc. at the end of fermentation and other processes involving the use of micro-organisms

Endotoxin: an intracellular toxin, produced by bacteria and other pathogens

Enzyme: a protein that acts as a catalyst in reactions between organic compounds

Enzyme immobilisation: binding an enzyme immovably to a surface, so that it cannot mix with reactants or contaminate the end products

Eukaryote: a cell with membrane-bound organelles, most notably a nucleus

Exons: the coding sequence of a split gene, retained in the second mRNA transcript of eukaryotes

Exotoxin: an extracellular toxin, secreted by bacteria and other pathogens

Fermentation: anaerobic respiration, especially the degradation to sugars to produce ethanol (alcohol)

Fermenter: the vessel (also called a bioreactor), usually made of stainless steel, used for the large-scale culture of cells or fungal hyphae

Fungi: eukaryotic organisms, without chlorophyll, that feed as saprophytes or parasites and reproduce by spores

Gel electrophoresis: the separation of molecules, according to size, in an electric field, by diffusion through a gelatinous matrix

Gene: the biological unit of genetic information, self-reproducing and located in a definite position in a DNA molecule

Gene expression: a change in an organism resulting from the operation of a gene

Gene mapping: plotting the relative positions of genes on a DNA molecule

Gene probe: a short length of single-stranded DNA (or RNA) capable of binding to a complementary single-stranded DNA segment

Gene therapy: an attempt to cure genetic disorders by replacing defective genes with normal ones

Genetic engineering: changing an organism's genome by adding or deleting genes

Genome: all the genes present in an organism

Grana: chlorophyll-containing regions of a chloroplast, where light is trapped and ATP is made

Granulocytes: white cells, with granules containing inflammatory mediators, such as histamine, heparin, serotonin, bradykinin etc.

Humoral response: an immune response involving antibody production by plasma cells

Hybridoma: fusion product of an immortal cell (e.g. myeloma) with a lymphocyte to produce an immortal lymphocyte

Immunisation: induction of immunity by injection of antigens, antibodies or immune cells

Immunity: the ability of an organism to resist infectious diseases

Inflammation: tissue redness, swelling, heat and pain caused by an antigen or noxious stimulus

Interferon: a protein produced by cells in response to viral infections, which slows the rate of viral infection in neighbouring cells

Intron: the non-coding sequence of a split gene, discarded in the second mRNA transcript of eukaryotes

Macrophage: a large, non-circulating phagocytic cell

Mast cell: a type of granulocyte, active in tissues surrounding blood vessels

Micropropagation: rapid, test-tube vegetative propagation of plants from small pieces of tissue called explants

Monoclonal antibodies: antibodies of a single type, typically produced by the fusion product of a cancer cell and a lymphocyte

Monocyte: a circulating phagocyte, that can differentiate into a macrophage

Mutagen: a chemical or physical factor capable of causing a mutation on organisms

Mutation: an inheritable change in the DNA base sequence or chromosome number of an individual

Mycorrhiza: fungal hyphae which form a symbiotic association with plant roots

Mycosis: a disease caused by a fungus

Natural killer (NK) cell: a specialised lymphocyte that recognises and destroys foreign cells or infected host cells in a non-specific manner

Neutrophil: a circulating white cell, with a lobed nucleus

Glossary

nif-genes: a cluster of genes responsible for nitrogen fixation in certain micro-organisms

Operator gene: a specific region of DNA, at the initial end of a gene cluster, producing a repressor protein that blocks mRNA synthesis

Operon: a cluster of genes controlled by a single operator

Parasite: an organism that feeds on another living organism belonging to different species, causing it harm

Passive immunity: immunity acquired by the transfer of antibodies from an immune individual to a non-immune individual

Pathogen: a disease-causing organism

Phagocyte: a cell which ingests, and then digests, foreign particles, bacteria etc.

Photoautotroph: a bacterium that uses light energy to power its life processes

Plasma cell: a large, fully-differentiated B cell, which produces antibodies

Plasmid: a double-stranded circular piece of DNA, which acts independently of the chromosome, and is widely used as a cloning vector to introduce foreign DNA into bacterial and yeast cells

Point mutation: a mutation resulting from a change in the DNA sequence of bases

Polymerase chain reaction (PCR): a method used to amplify small amounts of DNA, using the enzyme DNA polymerase

Prokaryote: a cell without a nucleus or other membrane-bound organelles

Promoter: a short nucleotide sequence, upstream of a gene, signalling the point at which transcription starts

Protozoa: heterotrophic, mostly unicellular, members of the phylum Protoctista

Recombinant DNA: an artificial DNA molecule, created in the laboratory by piecing together nucleotide sequences

Restriction endonucleases: enzymes used to cut DNA into shorter segments

RNA: ribonucleic acid, an intermediate in converting the genetic code of DNA into the amino acid sequence of a polypeptide

Saprophyte: an organism, notably a bacterium or fungus, that feeds on dead organic matter

Sewage sludge: the solid organic sediment that remains after raw sewage has been degraded by aerobic and anaerobic micro-organisms

Single cell protein (SCP): protein-rich, dried cellular products obtained from the large scale culture of micro-organisms

Southern blotting: a method of fusing single-stranded DNA, or RNA, to DNA fragments immobilised on a filter (procedure named after E. Southern)

Sparger: perforated metal disc in an aerobic fermenter through which air or pure oxygen enters

Symbiosis: a physiological relationship between two organisms of different species, mutually beneficial to both participants

Synthesis: the combination of one or more molecules into one or more compounds of greater complexity

T cells: lymphocytes that have matured by passing through the thymus gland, where they have acquired the ability to respond to a specific antigen

Taxonomy: the classification of organisms

Terminator: a short nucleotide sequence, downstream of a gene, signalling the point at which transcription stops

Transcription: the process in which genetic information is transferred from DNA to messenger RNA

Transgenic organism: a plant or animal into which one or more foreign genes has been artificially inserted

Translation: the process by which genetic information contained in messenger RNA is converted into a sequence of amino acids in a polypeptide

Vaccine: commercially produced antigens, usually injected in amounts sufficient to stimulate antibody production, without causing symptoms of a disease

Vector: a gene carrier, such as a bacteriophage or plasmid, used to introduce foreign DNA into cells

Virus: a minute intracellular parasite, with a nucleic acid core and a protein coat

Glossary

Search engines

Search engines are programmes that note the words you type, look for documents that contain them, and provide a list of web sites that are most likely to meet your requirements. The following search engines probably carry a lot of information about biotechnology and related topics. It should be noted that this material may be catalogued under different headings, including science, biology, health, medicine, disease etc.

http://altavista.digital.com
http://www.infoseek.com
http://www.hotbot.com
http://www.mckinley.com
http://www.webcrawler.com
http://www.yahoo.com

Boolian operators

When searching the Internet for information, the words AND, OR and NOT help to speed up a search by eliminating irrelevant material.

For example, immune system AND complement, initiates a search for the role of complement in the immune system.

Immune system OR blood cells, broadens a search for the role of cells with an immune function, that may be listed under either heading.

Immune system NOT phagocytes, excludes aspects of the immune system that are mediated by phagocytes.

In *AltaVista*, and some other search engines, the menu allows searches to be refined. A search for information about the immune system may, for example, be refined by selecting pharmacological or biological aspects of the topic.

Useful web sites

The following, very limited, list of web sites illustrates some different aspects of biotechnology that can be perused via the Internet. The addresses given are correct at the time of publication, but may be subject to change.

General information on biotechnology

http://www.reading.ac.uk/NCBE
http://www.bbsrc.ac.uk
http://www.biotech.chem.indiana.edu/
http://www.gene.com/ae/AB/index.html (includes information on the Human Genome Project)

General microbiology

http://www.ch.ic.ac.uk/medbact/.index.html

AIDS/HIV

http://www.roche-hiv.com
http://www.avert.org/statindx.htm

Brewing

http://www.breworld.com

Agriculture/horticulture

http://www.hri.ac.uk/frames/news.htm
http://www.nal.usda.gov/bic/

Immobilised enzymes/cells

http://144.124.112.75/ienzymes.htm
http://144.124.112.75/icells.htm

Biotechnology companies

http://www.glaxowellcome.co.uk
http://www.bio.com/news/

Books on biotechnology

http://www.blackwell.co.uk/bookshops/
http://www.dillons.co.uk/

Careers in biotechnology

http://www.ukplus.co.uk (click on work and then type in: biotechnology)

Internet resources

1 BDH Chemicals Ltd
Poole
Dorset
BM12 4NN

Resources: biochemicals and TLC plates

2 Blades Biological
Cowden
Edenbridge
Kent
TN8 7DX

Resources: bacteria, fungi, agars

3 Difco Laboratories
East Molesey
Surrey
KT8 0SE

Resources: agars

4 Griffin and George Ltd
Gerrard House
Worthing Road
East Preston
West Sussex
BN16 1AS

Resources: biochemicals, bacteria, fungi, materials for plant micropropagation

5 Chris Hansen Laboratories Ltd
476 Basingstoke Road
Reading
Berks
RG2 0QL

Resources: cheese and yoghurt-starter cultures

6 Philip Harris Biological Ltd
Oldmixon
Weston-super-Mare
Avon
BS24 9BJ

Resources: biochemicals, bacteria, fungi, materials for plant micropropagation

7 Hughes and Hughes (Enzymes) Ltd
Elms Industrial Estate
Church Road
Harold Wood
Romford
Essex
RM2 0HR

Resources: enzymes, glass-marking pens

8 The National Centre for Biotechnology
University of Reading
Whiteknights
P.O. Box 228
Reading
RG6 6AJ

Resources: DNA, enzymes, gel electrophoresis kit

9 National Centre for School Biotechnology
Department of Microbiology
University of Reading
London Road
Reading
Berks
RG1 5AQ

Resources: enzymes

10 National Collection of Yeast Cultures
Food Research Institute
Colney Lane
Norwich
NR4 7UA

Resources: yeasts

11 Oxoid Ltd
Basingstoke
Hants
RT24 0PW

Resources: agars

12 Sigma Chemical Co Ltd
Fancy Road
Poole
Dorset
BH17 7NH

Resources: biochemicals, prepared media for plant micropropagation

Equipment Suppliers

Answers

Chapter 1 Answers
In-text questions, 1st set

1 Viruses replicate, but don't grow, feed, respire, excrete or respond to stimuli

2 a) Monera/prokaryotae, b) Bacteria

3 Small size, circular chromosome, plasmids, mesosome, glycocalyx, lipid/protein cell wall

4 Shape of individual cells, appearance of colony, colour of colony, reaction to Gram stain

   Bacteria: polypeptidan-based cell walls

   Archaea: protein/lipid-based cell walls

5 Large size, cell wall contains cellulose, organelles present, rod-like chromosomes, microtubules in cytoplasm

6 Transformation – uptake of naked DNA and expression by a bacterium
   Transduction – transmission of DNA, via a bacteriophage, from one bacterium to another
   Conjugation – exchange of DNA between two bacteria, via a conjugation tube

In-text questions, 2nd set

7 b) The bacteriophage could be a parasite of the bacterium

8 b) Unicellular, eukaryotic, hyphae, if present, without cross walls, autotrophic or heterotrophic

9 b) Eukaryotic, hyphae have cross walls, heterotrophic, digestive enzymes act externally

End-of-chapter questions

1 a) A – head, B – capsomeres, C – DNA, D – collar, E – shaft/tail, F – tail plate, G – tail fibre
   b) Bacteria
   c) DNA
   d) Complex
   e) Lysis – destruction of host cell by virus; lysogeny – incorporation of viral DNA into host DNA, with subsequent expression

2 a) Mesosome – chromosome attachment
   b) Cell membrane – selective permeability
   c) Mitochondrion – ATP synthesis
   d) Vacuole – stores water
   e) Golgi apparatus – cell wall synthesis
   f) Flagellum – motility
   g) Capsid – enclose DNA or RNA
   h) Nuclear envelope – encloses chromosomes
   i) Cell wall – maintains cell shape
   j) Pilus – adherence to other cells
   k) Glycogen granule – stores carbohydrate
   l) Nucleolus – ribosomal RNA synthesis
   m) Bacteriophage tail – transfer of genetic material

3 a) Economic importance – the way in which an organism can be exploited for financial gain, or causes financial loss

Chapter 2 Answers
In-text questions, 1st set

1 a) Autotrophs synthesise all their nutritional requirements
      Heterotrophs require complex organic molecules as essential nutrients
   b) Photoautotrophs use energy from sunlight to synthesise nutrients
      Chemoautotrophs use energy from chemical reactions to synthesise nutrients

2 Symbiosis (mutualism), saprophytes, parasites

3 a) carbon dioxide and water, b) ethanol, c) lactic acid/lactate

4 Colony area, cell density with a light meter, cell numbers with a haemocytometer

5 a) *Anabaena*, b) *Paramecium*, c) *Bacillus subtilis*

In-text questions, 2nd set

6 a) Nitrogen + hydrogen = ammonia,
   b) Ammonia → nitrite → nitrate
   c) Nitrite → oxides of nitrogen
   d) Proteins → ammonia

7 $2N_2 + 3H_2 \rightarrow 2NH_3$ (+ glutamate) → glutamine + other amino acids → proteins

8 a) Ammonia, b) Carbohydrate (e.g. glucose)

9 a) Virus, b) Bacteria, c) Protoctista, d) Fungus,
   e) Fungus

10 a) Sporozoite → liver cyst → merozoite → trophozoite
    b) Gametocytes → gametes → zygote → sporozoite

End-of-chapter questions

1 a) $10.0/0.5 \times 100 = 2000, 2000 - 100 = 1900$
   b) (i)   1.13 cm
      (ii)   2.54 cm
      (iii) $2.54 - 1.13 = 1.41$,
             $1.41/1.13 \times 100 = 124.7\%$

2 a) Acquired immune deficiency syndrome
   b) Human immunodeficiency virus
   c) Intercourse, shared use of needles, blood transfusions

d) America – homosexual transmission, Africa – heterosexual transmission

e) Destruction of T lymphocytes, lymphocytes and phagocytes not activated

f) Kaposi's sarcoma, pneumonia

g) Virus 'hides' in immune system; rapid mutation of surface antigens

h) Use a condom during sexual intercourse, remain with one sexual partner, do not share needles if a drug-user

3 a) A = nitrogen fixation, B = Nitrification, C = Denitrification, D = Ammonification

b) All of them

c) Amino acids, proteins, nucleic acids, ATP

d) *Rhizobium* bacteria contained within root nodules

Chapter 3 Answers
In-text questions, 1st set

1 Exon – coding sequence in a structural eukaryotic gene
Intron – non-coding sequence in a structural eukaryotic gene
Codon – triplet of bases that codes for one amino acid
Cistron – a structural gene
Operon – a cluster of genes controlled by a single operator

2 c)

3 a), b) and c)

4 a) 3' TAACCGTCGTC 5'
b) 3' UAACCGUCGUC 5'

5 Messenger RNA, transfer RNA, ribosomal RNA

In-text questions, 2nd set

6 Transcription – genetic code written in base sequence of mRNA
Translation – genetic code interpreted as sequence of amino acids in a polypeptide

7 a) Produce enzymes, b) binds RNA polymerase, c) stops producing repressor, d) switches on structural genes

8 a) An agent for transferring DNA from cell to cell
b) Bacteriophages, plasmids

9 R-plasmids, F-plasmids

10 a) Yes, b) No

End-of-chapter questions

1 a) A = adenine, T = thymine, G = guanine, C = cytosine

b) Purines = adenine, guanine
Pyrimidines = thymine, cytosine, uracil

c) UAGGCCAAUUGGGTUCAAUGCCUAAAUCGU

d) A triplet of bases; codes for one amino acid

e) 10

f) CTA

g) No introns; exons only

h) Adenine = 23%, thymine = 23%, guanine = 27%, cytosine = 27%

2 a) Resistance (R)-plasmids

b) To enable bacteria containing the plasmid to grow on foods containing antibiotic-producing fungi

c) Via a conjugation tube

d) Promoter, terminator

e) Starts/terminates mRNA transcription

f) Bacterial

g) It would be resistant to one or more antibiotics

h) Bacteria with plasmids containing the structural gene lose their ability to grow on media containing the antibiotic

i) Transfer to ampicillin agar (growth), then to kanamycin agar (growth inhibited)

3 a) The function of gene X would be destroyed. Compound X would not be broken down

b) *Bam H1* and *Sal 1*

c) (i) 2, (ii) 4, (iii) 4, (iv) 7

d) (i) 5.8 and 7.0, (ii) 1.0, 1.6, 2.3 and 7.9, (iii) 1.5, 2.1, 3.0, 6.2

e) −7.9, 2.3, 1.6, 1.0+

Chapter 4 Answers
In-text questions, 1st set

1 a) High fructose syrup, low alcohol beer, 'vegetarian' cheese, b) monoclonal antibodies, purer vaccines, magic bullets for treating cancer, c) micropropagation of food/ornamental crops, introduction of nitrogen-fixing bacteria into cereal crops

2 a) Membranes of fertilised hen's eggs, animal/plant cells, b) bacteria on an agar plate

3 Small piece of tissue capable of forming new cells

4 Lack of oxygen, high temperatures, low (acid) pH

5 Batch – closed vessel, in which process proceeds to conclusion without addition or removal
Continuous – open vessel, allowing nutrients etc. to be added and products removed, as required

In-text questions, 2nd set

6 a) Paddles – stir mixture, b) sparger – adds air bubbles, c) heat exchanger – cools mixture (fermentation is an exergonic process), d) air filter – excludes foreign micro-organisms

7 Temperature, pH, oxygen concentration, carbon dioxide concentration, foam

8 Flocculation, filtration, centrifugation, drying

9 a) Using heat to drive off a solvent in order to concentrate a product, b) whisky manufacture, penicillin production

End-of-chapter questions

1 a) A = motor, B = steam/nutrient inlet, C = water jacket, D = paddles, E = sparger, F = harvest pipe, G = waste gas pipe

b) B

c) To cool the fermenter. Fermentation is an exergonic process

d) As the mixture thickens following cell growth, a greater strain is placed on the motor
e) Cells do not stick to stainless steel – easy to clean. Steel resists internal gas pressure. Good conductor of heat
f) Draught-tube, airlift

2 a) Introducing N-fixing bacteria, improving resistance to grazing insects, b) low/high alcohol beer, higher barley yields, c) better tolerance of low light intensity and drought conditions, d) purer antigens, vaccines with fewer side effects, e) large scale production of natural plant pigments, some novel colours (e.g. blue), f) insulin, human growth hormone, g) treatment of cancer, pancreatitis, h) extraction of copper, iron, i) increased recovery from crude oil, more efficient oil mining, j) breakdown of oil slicks, treatment of birds with oil-contaminated feathers, k) alcohol from waste materials, biogas from farm wastes, l) detection of glucose, urea in blood

Chapter 5 Answers
In-text questions, 1st set

1 a) Supplies enzymes that ferment sugar and break down fibrous protein molecules in flour, b) source of carbon dioxide that causes bread to rise, c) maintains acid pH, enhances the raising of dough

2 a) Malt = soluble products that result from the digestion of stored materials in barley grains
b) Wort = a solution obtained by dissolving malt in boiling water

3 a) Ethanol → acetaldehyde → acetic acid
b) Oxygen present

4 a) *Leuconostoc cremoris*, *Leuconostoc lactis*, *Streptococcus cremoris*
b) *Penicillium camemberti*, *Penicillium roqueforti*

5 Cheese – *Leuconostoc* and *Streptococcus* bacteria added, together with rennet
Yoghurt – *Lactobacillus* and *Lactococcus* bacteria added. No rennet

In-text questions, 2nd set

6 a) Protein made by a fungus
b) High protein, high fibre, low fat, no known toxic effects

7 Denatures enzymes, kills micro-organisms

8 a) Preserves colour of meat, kills bacteria, b) may form nitrites, which combine with other compounds to form carcinogenic agents

9 *Salmonella, Campylobacter, Listeria*

10 a) Kills pathogenic micro-organisms and prevents sprouting in potatoes and onions, b) destroys vitamins and essential fatty acids

End-of-chapter questions

1 a) (i) $1000 \times 92/180 = 511.1$ cm^3
(ii) $22.4 \times 1000/180 = 124.4$ dm^3
(iii) $1000 \times 180/92 = 1956.5$ g. It is assumed that 1 cm^3 alcohol weighs one gram
b) Internal gas pressure could break thin glass
c) Sterilise beer-making utensils, use an air-lock to exclude foreign micro-organisms
d) (i) Breaks down haze, caused by cell wall components
(ii) Removes any remaining yeast cells

Chapter 6 Answers
In-text questions, 1st set

1 a) Penicillin, chloramphenicol
b) Bacitracin, polymixin

2 Prednisone, prednisolone

3 Promote a stronger antibody response; less likely to cause allergy/side effects

4 a) Monocytes, neutrophils, b) basophils, eosinophils, mast cells, c) B cells, T cells

5 T helper, T killer, T suppressor, T memory

In-text questions, 2nd test

7 a) Spleen, b) myeloma

8 Dip-sticks for pregnancy test; test for drugs in urine; magic bullets for diagnosing/treating cancer; protecting transplanted organs

9 Sickle cell anaemia, Huntingdon's disease, cystic fibrosis

10 Hypervariable regions/minisatellites/VNTRs

End-of-chapter questions

1 a) Pe = penicillin, Ch = chloramphenicol, Ta = tetracycline, St = streptomycin
b) Ch → Te → Pe → St
d) Depends on thickness/depth of gel; temperature, molecular size of diffusing molecules

2 a), b)

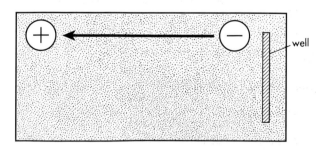

c) (i), (ii), (iii)
d) Fixed onto a nitrocellulose membrane; separated by heat/alkali
e) AACCGTATTCG. TTGGCATAAGC
f) Radioactivity on an autoradiograph

Chapter 7 Answers

In-text questions, 1st set

1 a) Glucose isomerase, amylase, papain,
b) L-asparaginase, cholesterol oxidase, c) carbonic anhydrase, cholinesterase

2 Region in which substrate molecules are bound to form an enzyme–substrate complex

3 Absorption, entrapment, covalent bonding

4 a) A miniaturised biosensor, b) a biosensor that measures temperature changes resulting from a chemical reaction

5 a) Gelatinous polysaccharide, forming surface layer in some bacteria, b) oil extraction, surfactant, blood expanders, gelatinising agent in food industry

In-text questions, 2nd set

6 Wood shavings, straw, leaves

7 Tolerant of higher alcohol concentrations

8 a) *Saccharomyces cerevisiae* and *Dunaliella salina*
b) *Clostridium acetobutylicum*

9 Acetic acid, lactic acid, citric acid

10 a) *Thiobacillus ferrooxidans*
b) $2CuS + 2Fe_2(SO_4)_3 \rightarrow 2CuSO_4 + 4FeSO_4 + 2S$

End-of-chapter questions

1 a) (i) Pancreas of calves, (ii) papaya fruit
b) (i) Shape of active site changes to accommodate more substrate molecules
(ii) Enzyme is denatured; its shape is changed so that it loses the ability to react with substrate
c) (i) 30–40°C, (ii) 60–70°C
d) Papain not denatured by temperatures in range 37–60°C
e) Structural configuration of papain not changed by higher temperatures; more heat-stable
f) Papain can be used to break down proteins at relatively high temperatures – faster
g) Meat tenderisation – injected before or shortly after death. Removal of hair from hides in leather-making

2 a) Catalysis – acts as a catalyst; speeds up the rate of a chemical reaction
b) Active site – that part of an enzyme molecule where substrate molecules are bound
c) Allosteric site – region of an enzyme molecule where an effector molecule binds
d) Turnover number – the number of molecules of substrate split/joined by an enzyme in a given period of time.
e) Denaturation – changes in the 3-D configuration of a protein/enzyme, which renders it ineffective. Denaturation may be caused by changes in temperature or pH
f) Specificity – the ability of an enzyme to bind a specific substrate. Most enzymes are substrate-specific

g) Immobilisation – an enzyme attached to a solid support over which substrate is passed and converted into product
h) Oxidoreductase – an enzyme that catalyses the removal of H atoms from a substrate, or the addition of O atoms to it

Chapter 8 Answers

In-text questions, 1st set

1 Chimera – hybrid, produced by fusing embryos from two different species
Clone – two or more cells/individuals descended from a common parent, and with an identical genotype

2 a) Increased milk yield, higher profits for farmers
b) Cows eat more food, possible adverse effects on human health

3 a) *Agrobacterium tumefaciens*
b) It carries Ti plasmids, which integrate DNA into one or more of the plant's chromosomes

4 a) Naked plant cells (no cell walls)
b) Cellulase enzymes used to digest away walls
c) Hybrids between species can be produced by fusing protoplasts

5 One gene only added to existing genome. Other genes not reshuffled, therefore none of the existing desirable traits lost

In-text questions, 2nd set

6 Agroinfection, electroporation, microinjection, bombardment

7 Less expenditure on fertilisers. River pollution/eutrophication less likely to occur

8 Protein from *B. thuringiensis* used to kill caterpillars. Ice-strain of *P. syringae* used to protect early crops from frost damage

9 Excise terminal bud, apply heat, grow new plants from heat-treated bud

10 a) Rapid production of new plants, preservation of desirable genotypes over successive generations, cost-effective, space-efficient, transport-efficient
b) Contamination with bacteria/fungi, increased rate of mutation

End-of-chapter questions

1 a) Apical bud, lateral bud, root tip
b) Sodium hypochlorite (bleach), alcohol
c) 20–30 minutes
d) The disinfectant may inhibit growth
e) Sucrose, amino acids, vitamins
f) After a callus has formed
g) Cytokinin; cell division
h) Either cut and transfer to more shoot multiplication medium, or transfer to rooting medium
i) Auxin
j) Transfer to soil or compost, keep moist/mist spray, gradually harden off plantlets

Chapter 9   Answers

In-text questions, 1st set

1 Sedimentation, flocculation, sand filtration, sedimentation

2 a) To destroy viruses and bacteria
   b) Gives treated water a 'chemical' taste. Possible long-term adverse effects on human health

3 a) Removal of large suspended particles
   b) Breakdown of organic components by micro-organisms, notably bacteria and protoctistans

4 a) Carbon dioxide, methane, hydrogen
   b) Water, mineral salts

5 Incinerated, compost maker/soil conditioner, landfill

In-text questions, 2nd set

6 a) Rural economy. Other forms of fuel not available
   b) Above-ground biogas generators are unsightly, risk of explosion, more uniform temperature
   c) Bacterial activity/breakdown of organic matter is affected by temperature

7 Methane, hydrogen

8 Add sewage sludge, yeasts, earthworms. Stack in piles, compress, moisten and cover to retain heat

9 Naphthalene, xylene, octane, camphor

10 Disperse oil slicks, remove heavy metals from industrial effluents, degrade insecticides, herbicides and chlorinated hydrocarbons

End-of-chapter questions

1 a) A = sand, B = gravel
   b) A – provides filtering system, B – forms substratum for protoctistans that feed on bacteria
   c) C = surface of uppermost layer of gravel
   d) Oxidation/reduction. Hydrolysis of organic compounds
   e) Bacteria, fungi, protoctistans
   f) Prevents channels in gravel from being blocked by the growth of micro-organisms
   g) Chlorination
   h) Insecticides, herbicides

Index

Index

Index